Alou

Alou

MY BASEBALL JOURNEY

FELIPE ALOU

with **PETER KERASOTIS** Foreword by **PEDRO MARTÍNEZ**

University of Nebraska Press · Lincoln & London

Library of Congress Control Number: 2017958106

Set in Garamond Premier Pro by E. Cuddy.

For Lucie, who has been a gift from God. And for the eleven children Jehovah God allowed me to have—Felipe, Maria, José, Moisés, Christia, Cheri, Jennifer, Felipe José, Luis, Valerie, and Felipe Jr.

Felipe Alou

For Shelley, my treasure from heaven.

Peter Kerasotis

The rain that is going to fall doesn't wet you.
—Dominican proverb

CONTENTS

FOREWORD

I love Felipe Alou.

Felipe is a treasure in my country, in the game of baseball, and, most important, in my heart.

When I was growing up in the Dominican Republic our history books instructed us on the story of the Alou brothers, especially Felipe. He was the first to go directly from our country to Major League Baseball (MLB). There were others who followed him from our soil—Juan Marichal, Julián Javier, Manny Mota, and, of course, two other Alou brothers, Matty and Jesús. But Felipe was the first. He paved the way. For those of us who followed him from our small island to the big leagues, Felipe was the light at the end of the tunnel.

Although the Alou brothers are in our country's history books, I didn't need those books to know about them. I grew up hearing about the Alous from my parents, my uncles, and other grownups, about how three Dominican brothers occupied the same outfield for a Major League team. I also heard the stories about how my father played against Felipe when they were both young amateurs. The Alous are baseball royalty in my country. It started with them, with Felipe. If you trace the genes of baseball in the Dominican Republic, you will arrive at the name Alou.

Imagine, then, what I was thinking when I first got to know Felipe. Sometimes you meet somebody you've heard about your whole life and looked up to from a distance, and you're disappointed. Felipe was different. Felipe exceeded my expectations. He still does.

I was a Minor League pitcher in the Los Angeles Dodgers organization when Felipe selected me to play for the Dominican Republic team he was managing in the 1992 Caribbean Series. It was an honor, and I was surprised because I didn't even know he was aware of me, this scrawny kid who was trying to prove he belonged. Not only was Felipe aware of me, but he also saw in me the potential that would eventually take me to the National Baseball Hall of Fame. We were playing a game in Hermosillo, Mexico, during that Caribbean Series. I was pitching when there was a rain delay. It wasn't too long, maybe forty-five minutes. When it stopped raining and I headed back to the mound to pitch, Felipe stopped me.

"No, no, no!" he shouted. "Wait a minute. I need to protect you. You're too young. I'm not going to have you waiting a long time and then have you go back out there. We need to protect you. You're a top prospect."

I was stunned. It's very rare when you find someone who cares about you without really exchanging a word with you. But that's Felipe. That's when I realized what kind of heart he has.

It was later when I learned what kind of head he has, when I had the privilege of playing for Felipe in the Major Leagues. It was a blessing I'll never forget. I did not anticipate that Felipe would come back into my life, but he did, and it was at a time early in my career when I was struggling with two things—getting people to believe me and getting people to believe *in* me.

I was twenty-two years old and had pitched two years for the Dodgers when they traded me to the Montreal Expos before the 1994 season. I felt at the time, and still do now, that the Dodgers gave up on me. I also know that Felipe, who was managing the Expos, had something to do with Montreal acquiring me. With the Dodgers I had yo-yoed back and forth between being a starting pitcher and a reliever, and it was difficult. I wanted to be a starter, but I didn't know what the Expos had in mind.

That first spring training, as soon as I got dressed in my uniform, I heard Felipe's voice. "Hey, Pedro, come into my office." Felipe was sitting at his desk, holding a baseball. "Hey, listen. You see this ball?" he said. "This ball is for you. You're my number-four starter. My number-four starter!"

It startled me for a moment. "Does this mean I'm going to be a starting pitcher?" I stammered.

"Yeah, you are my number four."

But he didn't stop there. Not Felipe. He's always explaining, expanding on what he's thinking.

"Nobody is going to take you away from there, either," he said. "This is my decision. If I go, you go. And I'm here to stay. They do what I say, and I say you are my number-four starter. And when I say number four, I say number four because there are people in front of you who have earned the respect to be named ahead of you. But in reality you are number one when your turn comes up. Because the number one, the number two, and the number three cannot pitch in your spot. So you are my number one that day. Never forget that. You are my number one whenever you take the ball."

I could almost feel my chest expanding. With those few words Felipe built my confidence in a way I'll never forget and I'll forever appreciate. At the same time he taught me a lesson that never went away. From that day forward, whenever I took the ball on the pitcher's mound, my mind-set was that I am the number-one starter.

There are so many other lessons, too. I found myself always trying to sit close to Felipe, listening, observing, trying to see what he saw, because Felipe saw so much more in the game of baseball than anyone else I've ever known. He's like an encyclopedia, an encyclopedia that is always open to you, always sharing.

When I got to the Expos I already had a reputation as a headhunter. I've never apologized for pitching in, for challenging hitters inside. And while some criticisms of me have some merit, so much of it was unfair. Felipe was wise enough to see the difference.

My second year in Montreal I was still learning to pitch, still trying to harness my talent. But it had gotten to the point where it seemed like every time I pitched inside, it was perceived to be with intent. Already, early that season, there were a few incidents where guys charged the mound or glared at me threateningly—as if I, weighing only 164 pounds, was looking for a fight.

It reached a head in a May 29, 1995, game in Montreal against

San Francisco. Darren Lewis was the Giants' leadoff batter. My first pitch was up and away, ball one; the second pitch was low and in, ball two; and the third pitch was in again, ball three. Three pitches in the top of the first inning, and all of a sudden umpire Bruce Froemming was ripping off his mask, taking a few steps toward me, and with a pointed finger giving me a warning.

Felipe stormed out of the dugout, furious. Pulling at his hair, he got in Froemming's face. "You see this gray hair?" he shouted. "I grew this gray hair in baseball! You're not going to tell me what's wrong and right! You guys are running to judgment early! Way too early! He's thrown three pitches in this game, and you're already chasing this kid! What's wrong with you?"

Froemming tried to say something, but Felipe wasn't done. "You should look at some of the positives this kid is doing instead of judging him!" he said. "He has Cy Young type of numbers! But you guys are not even noticing the positive things this kid is doing!" Once again, Felipe pulled at his hair. "I grew these gray hairs in this game! I know this game! And I'm telling you that what you are doing to this kid is not fair!"

It's hard to describe the feeling you have for a man—much less your manager—who has your back like that. But that was Felipe. He had my back, and I was never far from his side, learning lessons.

Felipe was always ahead of the game, always seeing things before anybody else did. When everyone else was on step one, he was already on steps three and four. Felipe didn't need sabermetrics. It was all in his head, beneath that gray hair.

I remember one time early in his son Moisés's career, when Moisés came to the plate with the bases loaded. Moisés was a great first-ball hitter, and at the time he was hitting better than .500 on the first pitch. But there was Felipe, signaling to the third base coach to signal to Moisés to take the first pitch. Moisés, however, refused to look. He was up there to hack, and he was going to hack at that first pitch no matter what. Well, the first pitch was a slow roundhouse curve, and Moisés swung so hard that he corkscrewed himself as his helmet toppled off his head.

Felipe started laughing. "Hey, Mo! Hey, Mo!" he shouted from the dugout with a big grin on his face. "What do you think this is? This is the big leagues. Everybody knows you're hitting five-something on the first pitch. What do you think they are going to do, throw you a cookie?"

By now, everybody was laughing.

"Shut up, Papá," Moisés muttered.

That was Felipe. He anticipated the game better than anybody I've ever been around. I would see him take out a left-hander and bring in a right-hander to pitch to Tony Gwynn—one of the greatest left-handed hitters of all time. It went against the book, and it would probably explode the heads of today's sabermetrics geeks, but Felipe would have a feeling based on how he could analyze and assimilate even the smallest details. And then he would explain why he was doing what he was doing—always teaching. Through all those types of decisions—going against the book, going with his gut—I rarely saw Felipe fail.

It's amazing how often I think about Felipe even now, as I work as a TV analyst. My way of watching baseball and looking at every detail comes from years of watching Felipe do his thing.

One of the things he used to tell me that I've never forgotten is this: "Follow the ball, and the ball should lead you. Don't take your eyes off the ball, and you will learn everything you have to learn about the game. The ball dictates everything. It shows you what the pitcher does, what the catcher does, what the hitter does. You see what the body does to throw the ball, to hit the ball, to field the ball. You see so many things. If you follow the ball, you'll learn a lot of things."

And then there is the bat. Felipe taught me to follow the bat, too. He would tell me to watch what hitters do when they first step into the batter's box, to take notice of the bat waggle, because he's telegraphing to you where he wants the ball. "Once you see that," Felipe instructed, "all you have to do is keep the ball away from where they want it." I took that tidbit of wisdom with me and applied it to the rest of my career.

But the one thing I couldn't take with me was Felipe. After I won my first Cy Young Award in 1997, and it was apparent that Montreal was not going to be able to afford to keep me, the Expos looked for trade partners. But I did not want to leave Felipe's side. I went to our general manager (GM), Jim Beattie, and told him I was willing to take a big discount to stay in Montreal, to stay with Felipe. But even with the discount I was willing to take, the Expos still couldn't afford me.

That's when I heard what Felipe was doing behind the scenes. "Please get Pedro to a place where he can win," he told ownership and the front office. "Pedro deserves to win. If we're going to trade him, let's trade him somewhere where he can get a chance to win."

Instead, the Expos traded me to the Boston Red Sox, who finished twenty games out of first place that year. As it turned out I was able to help Boston win a World Series title in 2004, while also capturing two more Cy Young Awards there.

I had Felipe for only four years in Montreal. It was like getting a college degree. I'm so glad I was able to pass through the school of Felipe Alou. I'm so thankful I've had him in my life in every aspect.

As I mentioned, I love Felipe Alou. I also owe him most of the success of my career and the wisdom I have about baseball. My only wish is that one day someone will have that kind of perspective, that kind of appreciation, that kind of respect for me that I have for Felipe Alou.

Pedro Martínez
Member of the National Baseball Hall of Fame

Alou

Introduction

My eyes are still strong for an eighty-two-year-old man. But I didn't realize they were this strong, able to reach back seventy-plus years and grab hold of myself as a boy, pulling me from my youth and putting me on the field my godfather once owned. The field was then, as it is now, a hardscrabble scratch of land, only back then it was surrounded by fenced-off farm animals and succulent fruit trees my friends and I would filch from. These days the field is an overnight parking lot for trucks, which serves the better purpose of patting down the grass and making the land, when empty, suitable for playing baseball. And that's what boys are doing today—playing baseball.

I stand on the edge of the field, which is on the outskirts of Santo Domingo, Dominican Republic, and watch them. I can tell they are poor, as I was when I was their age. But I cannot imagine my arms and legs were once the skinny stick figures that theirs are—hungry and undernourished. Yet I know I was just like them. I see myself in them, except when I peer into their eyes, eyes hungry with hope. For them this is a field of dreams. Will one of them be the next great Dominican baseball player? Will one of them be the next Pedro Martínez, or Albert Pujols, or Juan Marichal, or Sammy Sosa, or Adrián Beltré, or Robinson Canó, or David "Big Papi" Ortiz, or perhaps me? The list of players to dream about one day becoming is long. No country outside the United States produces more big-league players than the Dominican Republic—an island country that is about 5,300 square miles smaller than West Virginia.

For me, though, there never was a list. When I was a boy there were no Dominican players in Major League Baseball. When I started playing on that field there wasn't even a black player in the big leagues. I knew. I collected baseball cards with the pictures of players such as Joe DiMaggio, Gil Hodges, Phil Cavarretta, Carl Furillo, and Billy Cox, all of them white and from the United States. So when I was a boy I played the game simply because I loved it. To play it professionally wasn't even a thought, much less a dream. It would be more than a decade before someone went from our small island to Major League Baseball. That would be me.

I still can't believe it. *Me?* It seems incredible, even now, that I played seventeen years in Major League Baseball and managed for fourteen more; that I was teammates with two of the greatest players ever—Willie Mays and Hank Aaron; that I became a close friend of Roberto Clemente; that I was roommates with Hall of Fame players such as Juan Marichal, Willie McCovey, and Orlando Cepeda, as well as with Joe Torre, one of the game's outstanding players and a Hall of Fame manager.

I watch the boys today, and I feel sad for them. I wish they could play the game for the pure joy of it, the way we did. I know every generation believes it had it better than the generations that follow it. And I guess it is good that Dominican boys today know there is at least a pathway to the big leagues. But boys who are not even in their teenage years should not feel the pressure—and, believe me, there is pressure in my country—of having to make it professionally.

The only thing I envy about the boys who play on that field today is that they have real gloves, bats, and baseballs. We played with small, dry coconuts and thick sticks of wood that my father, with his carpentry skills, fashioned for us. Occasionally, there was a rubber ball. Sometimes someone would find—or more likely steal—a real baseball, which we would treat as if it were a gold nugget. Gloves? Our gloves were pieces of canvas ripped from the backs of trucks carrying goods and produce, and my mother would stitch them into a makeshift mitt. Mostly, we played bare-handed.

My eyes peer across the field, and the decades peel away. I see a coconut tree, smack in the middle of the field, where second base is. All those decades ago I took a machete to it. My boyhood friends helped me, but I was the ringleader and I knew I would get a whipping for it. My father, like most fathers on the island, would come home from a day of hard work and hang his leather belt on a nail. It symbolized his discipline, his authority. When you looked at that belt you thought twice about doing something wrong. But all I could think about was removing the obstruction of that coconut tree so we could play baseball. I had plenty of time to change my mind, too. After all, it took my friends and me a week of on-and-off *whack! whack! whacking!* that tree with a machete to weaken it enough to where a strong wind and our grunting pushes finally toppled it.

When my father learned of what I did, he marched me to my godfather—a big, benevolent man with kind eyes—apologizing and assuring him I would get a whipping. "No, no," he told my father. "They're just boys. They just want to play baseball."

My godfather was my father's best friend, and he also owned the local grocery store and often supplied my family with food on credit. And so, at his behest, I was spared a whipping, and the next day we were playing baseball again, only now on an unobstructed field—except for a cashew tree situated between left and center fields. Soon my eye was on it, my machete in hand. But I decided not to press my luck. We decided that balls—or maybe I should say small, dry coconuts or whatever other objects we used—hit to the cashew tree became ground-rule doubles.

As my eyes peer into the past, I wonder what my father would have thought all those years ago if he could have seen into the future. Would he still have thought about giving me a whipping? But how could he have known? How could he have dreamed that I would become the first Dominican to play in a World Series game? How could he have foreseen that three of his four boys—Matty, Jesús, and

I—would become Major Leaguers and that all three of us would historically share a big-league outfield together—something never done before or since? All three of us played in the World Series, the first time three brothers accomplished that feat. My son—my father's grandson Moisés Alou—also played in the World Series.

All totaled, my brothers and I played forty-seven years in the Major Leagues with a combined lifetime batting average of .291. We amassed 5,094 hits, more than any other brother combination in modern Major League history, even more than the DiMaggio brothers—Dom, Joe, and Vince. When my brother Matty won the 1966 National League (NL) batting title with a .342 average for the Pittsburgh Pirates and I finished second with a .327 average for the Atlanta Braves, we became the first—and only—brothers to finish one-two in a Major League batting race. And we weren't just one-two in the National League, we were one-two in all of Major League Baseball.

Baseball gave the three of us a better life, and it might have had a fourth Alou—my youngest brother, Juan—but history had other ideas.

Baseball came for me when I was attending the university in Santo Domingo, studying to be a doctor. The Giants' franchise, then in New York City, offered me 200 pesos to sign—the equivalent then of about $200. The thought of making a living playing baseball seemed ridiculous, but my family owed my godfather 200 pesos for groceries. I signed so my father could pay for the food he had gotten on credit. Two years later, in 1958, I became the first of what have now become hundreds of ballplayers to go from Dominican soil to Major League Baseball.

I want to be fair, however, to Ozzie Virgil Sr., who was the first player born in the Dominican to reach the Major Leagues. Few people outside of Ozzie's family were aware of him, though, since he moved from the island when he was thirteen and spent the rest of his years growing up in the Bronx borough of New York City, even serving in the U.S. Marines. Ozzie made it to the New York Giants two years before I broke in with the franchise in the first year the team began playing in San Francisco.

I believe our family's athletic ability comes from our father and our spirit—our drive and determination—comes from our mother. My brother Matty, who died in 2011, claimed my father played baseball but quit when he was fifteen, after seeing a friend die when he was struck by a bat. I don't know if that's accurate. Both my father and my brother Matty have died, as has my mother. What I can say for certain is that my father never threw a ball to me. We never played catch. He was too busy working as a carpenter and blacksmith, trying to put food on the table for a wife and six children in the fifteen-by-fifteen-foot shack we lived in. My father never even came to the United States to see my brothers or me play. He left the island only once, in 1964, when I took him to Caracas for a series between the Dominican Republic and Venezuela. Even then he stayed only a day, leaving for home because he was concerned that the few cows he had would suffer neglect in his absence.

On the day my father died at age eighty-nine, August 3, 1994, I was the first and only Dominican-born manager in Major League Baseball. My team, the Montreal Expos, also had the best record in baseball. By then my father, who was nicknamed Abundio on the day he was born, had lived up to that moniker. *Abundio* comes from the word "abundance," and what an abundant base-ball progeny he left behind. It's been written that you would need a scorecard to keep track of my family's baseball tree. In addition to my brothers and me, there is my son Moisés Alou and my nephew Mel Rojas, both of whom had successful big-league careers. Mel's son Mel Rojas Jr. is currently working his way up the Minor Leagues. Two of my father's other grandsons—Francisco and José Rojas—played Minor League Baseball. My father's sister's grandson was José Sosa, who pitched two seasons in the Major Leagues. I have a son, Felipe José Rojas, who also played Minor League Baseball and is now in charge of the Baltimore Orioles' baseball academy in the Dominican; another son, Luis Rojas, is a manager in the New York Mets' Minor League system; and another son, José Alou, was a Minor League player and is now a San Francisco Giants scout.

I have to laugh, too, because of how my friend and Hall of Fame pitcher Juan Marichal likes to say that my sister Maria Magdalena was as good a baseball player as any of us. Marichal got that information about my sister from very reliable sources—her brothers. She was good. We were all good. And we were all young once. Now I'm young only when I close my eyes and allow memories to fill my head. Or when I open them and look across that field and see my youth, and a story that was just beginning.

1

1935–1956

1

A Name

My last name is not Alou.

Baseball has given me so much, but this is the one thing it took away from me—my last name.

My father's name was José Rojas, and from his loins came five Major League Baseball players. I was the first and the first to go from the Dominican Republic's verdant land to Major League Baseball in the United States. Latin players were rare then, back in 1956, and the Latin tradition of placing the mother's maiden name *after* the family name wasn't well known. Somebody must have seen my paperwork when I arrived in Louisiana for my first baseball stop, saw that my name is Felipe Rojas Alou, and thus issued me my first jersey, which read "F. ALOU." At the time I didn't know enough English to explain the correction, so the name Alou stuck.

This never bothered my father, who had bestowed the name of his father on me. What did bother my father, and especially my mother, Virginia, is that I never became a doctor. It's what they wanted for me and also what I wanted for myself. It was what I was studying to become at the University of Santo Domingo when a scout for Major League Baseball's New York Giants noticed my athletic skills.

That I was even starting my education at a university was an accomplishment for the Rojas family. Like most Dominicans, especially Dominicans of that era who lived under the oppressive regime of the dictator, Rafael Trujillo, we were poor. I know it's a cliché for people to say they grew up not knowing they were poor. But believe me, we knew. Our home was the size of an average bedroom in the United States—fifteen by fifteen feet—some of it with an uneven cement floor, and the rest, particularly our kitchen floor, was dirt. My father built the home in 1934, the year before I was born in that house. It was painted blue with faint red trim, situated along the southern coast of the Dominican Republic in what is known as Kilometer 12, or Highway Sánchez. As the firstborn in my family, and as more siblings came into the world, six of us total, I grew up sleeping in a small bed with my brother Matty and sister Maria. We tore the sheets by pulling them at night and sewed them back together the next morning. What was worse is that it wasn't uncommon for one or both of them to wet the bed. So later, as more children came—Jesús, Juan, and Virginia—I slept on a thin mat on the cement part of the floor, no pillow, and was glad to do so.

An early event that drove home not only how poor we were but also the ways of the world arrived when I was about nine years old and my father got a little bit ahead with money. Back then U.S. dollars were the island's main currency, and my dad had been paid $11 for some work—a $10 bill and a $1 bill. My parents kept the money in their bedroom, hidden behind a picture of the Virgin Mary. To this day it's not uncommon in the Dominican Republic to see people traveling with a horse and buggy, selling fruits and vegetables. One day a woman passed by, and my father bought some tomatoes and green vegetables, using the $1 bill. Or so he thought. He actually gave the woman the $10 bill. Everything seemed normal. She even gave him change as if he had handed her a $1 bill. A little later my father searched for the $10 bill and couldn't find it. Panic set in. My mother called him careless, and an angry argument ensued. Soon they were both crying. We never saw the woman in the cart again. That's when I learned about life.

And then there was learning about death. I soon discovered that death, even the death of children, is a part of life. My father was a carpenter and blacksmith. As a carpenter he often built caskets. People would bring him wood to make a casket for a loved one. That was sobering enough to witness, but to see the tiny caskets he made, the size of my siblings and me, was heartrending. So many children died during that time because their parents didn't have enough money for medical care or the means of transportation to get them to a hospital. Or they got to the hospital too late. Even today there is a children's hospital in Santo Domingo where you see poor women outside, trying to get in to save their children's lives.

We were not immune from these types of tragedies. All of my siblings and I came into this world in that small fifteen-by-fifteen-foot house that had no electricity, running water, or any type of plumbing, and all with the same midwife—a big, stout lady, full of confidence, who wore a long, flowing dress. Her name was Bartolina, and from her hands came three Major League Baseball players, an engineer, and a veterinarian. It got so that whenever I saw Bartolina, I knew I was getting another sibling.

One day, though, about two weeks after Bartolina delivered a girl into our family, born between Matty and Jesús when I was around eight years old, I awoke to the sound of my mother sobbing. We knew the baby had suddenly started losing weight. Now she was dead in her crib. I can still see her sweet, serene face and recall how beautiful she was. I can also still see my mother's face, stricken with grief, looking at that precious baby with such profound sadness, weeping, tears rolling down her cheeks.

As a boy it triggered within me a desire to be a doctor, particularly one who would help people who didn't have enough money. None of the families where I lived could afford medical treatment, and if by chance you could, such treatment was usually too far away and the wait too long to do any good. Instead, we relied on island remedies and superstition. One time Matty fell out of a tree and broke his arm. A man came and massaged it and—supposedly— healed him. My mother knew all the herbs, teas, and various natural remedies to apply to an ailment. And if one of us kids was running a fever, we had a tin basin my mother would fill with cold water and put us in.

In spite of those hardships my upbringing was idyllic in many ways. There were a lot of relatives. My father had two sons before marrying my mother—Francisco, the oldest, and Joaquin Rojas. As for my mother, the family history is that my father helped my grandfather Alou build a well, and through that a friendship developed between my father and mother. When my father went to ask for her hand in marriage, the fear was that my grandfather would say no because my father was a Dominican and my grandfather was a Spaniard who had emigrated from the island of Majorca. At the same time the thought that my grandfather would say no because my father was black and my mother was white was not even a consideration. Interracial marriages were, and still are, common in the Dominican Republic. Years later, people made a fuss about Derek Jeter being an interracial player in the Major Leagues when he broke in as a rookie with the New York Yankees in 1996. But I was an interracial player in the Major Leagues in 1958.

My mother had seven siblings. I was the first grandchild and thus the first nephew born into her family when I entered the world at eleven pounds on May 12, 1935. I'm told all the Alou brothers and sisters used to fight over who would hold me. On my father's side of the family, I never knew my grandfather, but I do remember my grandmother. She was quite a lady. She smoked a pipe, and I vividly recall how she would take that pipe and a fishing pole and disappear for hours, almost always returning with some grouper for us to eat.

In the distance we could always hear the gentle sounds of the Caribbean Sea lapping against the shore. My father was a great fisherman, and I would often eagerly rise at 3 a.m. so I could go with him to the shoreline and try to catch enough fish to feed our family for that day. My father's fishing pole was bamboo, probably not much to look at today, but it was a prized possession and a serious sin if any of us kids thought to take it.

One day I took it.

About two miles from our home there was a rocky spot where the men fished. Although I was only around twelve years old, nobody noticed me as I rooted around the rocks to find some leftover dead baitfish the men discarded as unusable. My father's bamboo pole had a wire string and a large hook. I put a small dead fish on it and dropped it into the ocean and waited. After a while I got a bite and a fairly strong tug from a crevalle jack, a ravenous predatory fish that often feeds along reefs and shorelines. For a second the strong pull almost jerked the pole out of my hands. My heart leaped with panic. Evidently, my struggle was noticeable because one of my father's friends saw me and instinctively knew I shouldn't be there—and definitely not with my father's fishing pole. The fish wriggled away, which I was thankful for, because I might have lost that bamboo pole entirely. I, however, was not off the hook.

"Hey, what are you doing?" my father's friend demanded. "I'm going to let your father know you were here." From leaping with panic one second, my heart sank the next.

The waiting, anticipating my punishment, was worse than the whipping itself. I returned home and put the bamboo pole back exactly the way I found it. One day went by, then another. Maybe the man hadn't told my father, or, better yet, maybe he wouldn't. On the third day my father approached me, telling me he knew what I had done. I knew what the consequences had to be. He gave me three good lashes. That was my father. Mom would spank, but Dad would go for his symbol of authority, that thick cowhide belt, which he would hang on a nail when he came home from work. Dad was about five feet ten, a muscular and powerful man, and an extremely fast runner. Even into our teenage years, if he came after my brothers or me for some type of disciplinary reason, it was futile to try to outrun him.

Another whipping I received came from more innocent reasons. All these decades later, I can't even tell the story without laughing. Between the ages of ten and twelve, I along with two of my cousins and two of our friends had this ritual of going to the ocean naked. Anytime it would rain people would shut their doors to prevent water from coming in. That's when we would sneak out of our homes, strip off our clothes, and head down a worn pathway that cut through the brush toward the beautiful, but sometimes treacherous, Caribbean Sea. We would cling to the rocks to keep the waves from pulling us into the churning sea, feeling the saltwater splash over us while fresh rainwater fell on us from overhead. It felt so good—good enough for us to disregard that we were forbidden from going to the ocean alone, much less to shamelessly walk around naked.

We obviously had no telephones or any way of knowing what the weather would be like from day to day. Instead, we were always studying the clouds, something I still do today, and without a word we knew when the rain came it was time to discard our clothes and meet for our naked jaunt to the sea. We did it countless times, and we weren't careless. We had the timing down perfect, always making it back home, past all the homes with the doors still closed, before the rain stopped.

One day, though, our timing was off—way off. Just as we arrived at the ocean, the clouds parted, the sun emerged, and we were a long way from our homes, about a mile. It was the worst feeling. The trek back was agonizing, and we made it with our hands folded in front of our naked bodies, covering our crotches, like surrendering prisoners. As we passed house after house, all the doors were now open. I would have to pass them all naked because my house was the last one. As the other boys made it to their homes, I could hear their cries as they were getting their whippings, their yelps ringing in my ears as I trudged onward, like a condemned man, heading for the same fate.

Mostly I avoided whippings. My brother Jesús was another story, though. He got the most whippings, mostly because he had a quick temper and a bad habit of taking meat right out of the pot where it was still cooking over an open fire. He loved meat and always seemed to have a ravenous appetite. He would brazenly reach in bare-handed and take some, eating it before anyone could stop him and well before it was time to sit down for a meal. Out of the three Alou brothers who played Major League Baseball, Jesús was the one who grew the tallest and filled out the most: six feet two and about 195 pounds during his playing days.

I can remember only two times when I was not hungry enough to eat supper with my family. Once was another time when I sneaked off with my father's fishing pole, and with a friend I went down to the ocean. This time I caught a four-pound grouper. Of course, I couldn't bring it home, because this would expose me to the sin of taking my father's bamboo pole and ensure another whipping. So we went to my grandmother's house, where I knew I could sneak away with matches and a pan. My friend and I retreated into the woods, where we built a fire and cooked that grouper, eating as much of it as our bellies could contain. The other time I didn't have an appetite was when a cockfighting rooster I had, and had grown fond of, got killed by a passing truck. Not wanting to waste anything, my mother cooked it. When I saw my once proud rooster on a supper plate, I couldn't bring myself to take even a bite of him.

The worst day of my childhood was the day when we had no food to eat. As a parent now I can't imagine the stress my father and mother must have felt every day of our youth. Usually, though, there was enough for that day's sustenance. And although we didn't have much, I can assure you that if you came to my home, you were going to eat—boiled yucca, plantain, rice and beans, fish, avocado slices. Mango season was a highlight. It wasn't uncommon that by noon our house was a magnet for people, sitting around outside, talking, laughing, eating. I got to manage Vladimir Guerrero years later and got to know his family, and they were the same way: simple, generous, salt of the earth.

Everything back then seemed simple—simple and natural. Black coffee, rich in flavor, was a staple and something we drank almost as soon as we stopped feeding on our mother's breast milk. Coffee and dark, dense bread were often our breakfast. Creamy, sweet goat milk was readily available, too. Lunch was the main meal, and a main dish was fish with another island staple, rice and beans. Dinner was usually more fish along with boiled plantains; my mother could save a penny by not frying them in peanut oil, even though they tasted better that way. Chicken was an occasional dish. I never tasted steak until I became a professional baseball player in the United States.

Fruit was usually plentiful—grapefruit, orange, mango, papaya, soursop, coconut. I became adept at climbing coconut trees and, later, especially skilled at throwing rocks and knocking those tasty coconuts off their high perch. I'm convinced that my desire to nail a coconut hard enough with a rock built up not only my arm strength for baseball but also my accuracy. If I didn't hit a coconut hard enough to knock it off its perch, I would at least put a dent in it with enough rocks, deep enough that it would surrender its sweet water. When that happened we would stand beneath those coconut trees with our heads tilted back, like freshly hatched birds in a nest, catching the dripping nectar in our mouths.

Coconuts dropping from trees could be dangerous, too, if you weren't careful. Once, a coconut fell on my mother's arm, breaking it. At the time we didn't know it was broken. We only knew that my mother's arm gave her trouble the rest of her life. It wasn't until years later, when my brothers and I became Major League players and could afford to have an X-ray done, that we learned she had suffered a break.

One of the more dangerous things we did for food was hunt for crabs in the caves along the shoreline. You had to be careful in those caverns not to get trapped by a sudden strong wave or the rising tide. We were forbidden from going there, but Matty, Jesús, and I couldn't resist scavenging those caves for crabs. I can't tell you how many bites on my fingers I endured. One time when Matty was a little boy, a giant crab got hold of his forearm and wouldn't let go. Matty ran all the way home that way, yelling and yelping. Mostly, though, he was a very tough kid, a fearless boy who grew up to be the most fearless man I ever knew. He was a small guy—he only grew to be maybe five feet nine, probably shorter—but he would go up against anybody. And he was an excellent marksman, too. We used to fashion slingshots from any kind of twig that formed a V, attach some rubber from an old tire inner tube to it, and launch rocks at anything that moved or didn't move. Matty was good at both. He could hit a stationary object from a good distance as well as birds in flight. I admired his skill.

Matty also became a pretty good golfer as a boy. He caddied for the wealthy people at the Santo Domingo Country Club, bringing home whatever money he made to our parents. It was, and still is, a beautiful golf course, built in 1920 and designed by Robert Trent Jones Sr. On Mondays caddies were allowed to play about a half a round of golf. Matty was left-handed, which was considered a curse. For a couple of years, when he was two to four years old, my parents would tie his left hand to force him to use his right. But Matty was hardheaded and stubborn, and he wouldn't give in. He would try to eat rice with a fork in his right hand, and the rice would fall onto the floor. The poor kid. I felt sorry for him. But Matty never complained. He also never gave in. My parents didn't know they were trying to ruin a future batting champion. But when he got older and wanted to play golf with the other caddies, there were no left-handed clubs, so Matty learned to play right-handed.

While we were allowed to play and have a childhood, my parents were hard workers, and it was never any question in our minds and hearts as to how devoted they were to the family. My father had his carpentry and blacksmith shop next to the house. He was well respected and built many of the small shacks that passed as homes in our area. Whatever he built was always quality. There were times when I saw roofs on lesser homes flying away during storms. Not only did that never happen to our home, but, whenever violent storms arrived, our home became the default destination for shelter for some of our relatives.

My mother, a tough woman, used to crack rocks with a hammer for 3 pesos a truckload, 3 pesos being equivalent to $3 at the time. Mom's toughness sometimes surfaced in other ways. My father would often repair horse-drawn carts, and almost equally as often people didn't pay right away. One day a man who owed my father 8 pesos for fixing his cart came by, and my mother stopped him, stepping in front of his horse and grabbing it by the reins.

"Where is the money?" she demanded. "You say tomorrow, you say tomorrow, but tomorrow keeps coming and you don't pay! Pay or this cart is going to stay right here! You'll have to kill me first before you leave!"

I was just a boy, and I was scared, really scared. Then I saw the man pull the money from his pocket and pay what he owed.

I saw fear in my mother only once, when I was six years old. My father had gotten a job with one of the military generals to fix windmills. Often he would come home from his work as late as 11 p.m. Sometimes, because of the distance and the amount of work he had, he didn't come home at all. About twelve miles north of our home, the dictator's brother Hector Trujillo had a farm. There was a prison there where they would torture people. On one of those days when my father was away working, we heard news of a jailbreak and that the escapees were dangerous and might have weapons. Late that night, with my father still not home, a man abruptly appeared at our open door.

"*Buenas noches*," he said, meaning good night. It was a friendly greeting, and he seemed to have a kind face. But I could also see that he was wearing a prison uniform with the telltale black-and-white horizontal stripes and that my mother was shaking.

"Where is the man of the house?" he asked.

Shaking even more, my mother told him that he wasn't home. He was looking for clothes—a man's clothes he could change into. But the only clothes my father owned were on his back. The man was desperate.

"Look at what I have," he said, pulling at his prison uniform for emphasis, his eyes pleading. "And they are looking to kill me."

Finally, realizing my mother could not help him, he left, and as I heard him running through the brush I also heard shouting: "A suspicious person! A suspicious person!"

Looking back, he probably wasn't a criminal but rather a political prisoner, likely one who was caught and killed later that evening, if not the next morning. It proved to be a long night for us, especially because it was one of those nights when my father didn't come home at all. That was the last time my mother ever left our door either open or unlocked. Until the day she died in 2008, at the age of ninety-three, she always looked under her bed before going to sleep, sweeping a stick or a broom across the outer reaches, just to make sure. That might sound extreme, but even to this day I still have dreams about someone coming into my home, dreams that will awaken me in the middle of the night. Those dreams never go away, and none of those dreams are ever good.

The biggest fear any of us had on the island was of the dictator, Rafael Trujillo, and for good reason. Trujillo was brutal. Historians say his ruthless thirty-one-year reign, representing most of the rich and much of the military, was the bloodiest in all of the Americas, with some estimates saying he was responsible for the deaths of fifty thousand people. I saw the fear in the eyes of the men in my neighborhood. People disappeared. You heard about women, young women, being taken to him. My father was politically minded, and in that way he shaped me, too. In 1941, when I was six, Trujillo declared war against Nazi Germany, and my father was incredulous. "He's crazy," he said. "He's going to get us killed." Soon after, German submarines torpedoed and sank two Dominican merchant-marine ships that Trujillo had named after himself—the *San Rafael* and the *Presidente Trujillo*.

So I didn't have any doubt my father was against the dictator. Most everyone I knew hated the dictator. In the evenings, after my godfather would buy a newspaper, the men in my town would gather around and hear it being read. My father was often the reader, usually beneath a gas lamp someone would hold overhead. Whenever the conversation turned political, which was usually the case, the glances became furtive, the voices more hushed. Trujillo had *caliéses*, informants who would spy for him, all over the island. Sometimes you didn't know if your own neighbor was a *calié*. It was scary. People would disappear, never to be seen again.

As a boy I felt that fear. But I was still a boy, full of energy and occasional mischief. One time, testing our arms, Matty and I took target practice on anything that would pass by. On this particular day we threw rocks at an ambulance racing past us with its siren wailing. It was going too fast, though, and we missed it. Soon, a military truck rumbled by, with two soldiers riding in the back, carrying guns. From what we thought was a safe distance, we struck it with a couple of rocks. Big mistake. We saw that the truck was transporting boys, and we knew what that meant. Those boys were going to a notorious correctional institution in San Cristóbal, and this now meant we could be joining them. Two soldiers came after us. We took off running to a field—the same field where I cut down the coconut tree—and quickly integrated into a group of boys who were playing baseball. When the soldiers got to where we were playing, they demanded, "Did you see any guys running?" We all shook our heads no. The other boys had no idea why they were asking, but Matty and I knew, and our hearts were racing.

Finally, they moved on, and we continued to play baseball.

2

A Childhood

I never played organized baseball growing up. In the Dominican Republic of my childhood, in the poor town where I was raised, there were no equipment, no coaching, no true baseball field, no leagues, no parental involvement, and no dream of ever playing the game beyond my youth.

I was around fourteen years old when I got my first baseball glove. It was a gift from my mother's brother, Uncle Juan, who was a captain in the Dominican army and had a little bit of money. I went from playing baseball with my bare hands, or with strips of canvas sewed into a makeshift mitt, to a genuine Wilson glove. I held it to my nose, and to this day that smell, the smell of a real leather baseball glove, is even better than a new-car smell—no matter how expensive that new car is. My uncle instructed me to put oil on it, that it would preserve the glove, so that night I doused it with coconut oil. Later, as I slept contentedly, dreaming of what feats I could perform with this new leather appendage for my left hand, rats attracted by the coconut oil invaded my baseball glove and ate holes in it. The next morning, as I inspected the carnage, crestfallen, I saw that most of the pocket was eaten away. It would not stop me. I was determined to use that glove. My mother procured patches of heavy canvas and sewed it into the spots the rats had eaten, and I used that glove for the next several years.

This would have been about 1949, two years into Jackie Robinson breaking Major League Baseball's color barrier. We were especially aware of Jackie Robinson because in 1948, the Brooklyn Dodgers conducted their spring training at Santo Domingo, Dominican Republic—the capital city, which at the time the dictator had renamed Ciudad Trujillo, after himself. On March 11 we were bused from school to go see Jackie Robinson's Dodgers play the Dominican Republic All-Star team. I didn't even know what spring training was, but I knew this was something special. I was mesmerized seeing grown men play baseball with four real bases and wearing dazzling uniforms that shimmered in the spring sun. It was the first time I saw two baseball teams actually wearing uniforms—uniforms that contrasted each other with their different colors. The Dominican team lost, 4–3, thanks to a towering two-run, walk-off home run that a gigantic six-foot-five left-handed pitcher named Paul Minner hit. He was the same pitcher who two years earlier had surrendered the first home run in future Hall of Famer Frank Robinson's Major League career. But that didn't matter to us. We hated Paul Minner, reviling his name for years, because he was the man who hit the home run that beat the Dominican team.

I understood racism academically, in that I knew it existed, but I didn't understand it. I certainly didn't understand it coming from a family with a black father and white mother or from a country where race didn't matter. Early in Jackie Robinson's career, I remember seeing a photograph in the newspaper that showed him sitting alone, with white players sitting away from him. By now blacks were starting to trickle into Major League Baseball—and I do mean trickle. For years there were staunch holdouts, like the Boston Red Sox, who didn't field their first black player until Pumpsie Green made the roster in 1959, which turned out to be my second year in Major League Baseball. It was also in 1959 when Fidel Castro came into power in Cuba, which would greatly impact the Dominican Republic. Though integration was forging some headway, for a boy on a Caribbean island in 1949, the thought of going from Latin America to North America to play Major League Baseball was as foreign as we were at the time. We played for fun, and that was it.

Baseball in the Dominican Republic originally migrated from Cuba. Historians say the game was first played in Cuba in 1865, in Matanzas, which at the time was a thriving trade port on the island's northern coast, toward the western tip. Dockworkers were the first to play the game, doing so against North American ship workers. Early in its Caribbean evolution baseball was much more organized in Cuba than it was in the Dominican. So if you had some talent in the Dominican, you went to Cuba to play or perhaps into North America's Negro Leagues and even Puerto Rico. One of the top-flight players to emerge from the Dominican Republic early last century was Horacio "Rabbit" Martínez, born in 1912, who played both in Cuba and in the Negro Leagues. He was a great man—a man who profoundly impacted my life and the lives of my family.

My father was too busy trying to feed six children to ever play with us. I never once played catch with him. But he wanted us to play, and he would craft crude baseball bats for us in his carpentry shop. It was just a piece of wood, slightly thicker than a broomstick. Soon, as he gained a reputation for making the Dominican version of a Louisville Slugger, he made bats for other neighborhood boys. Prior to those homemade bats, we would usually play with hard, unripe lemons, hitting them with our hands. But when we had my father's homemade bats, we would play with small, dry coconuts, which lasted longer as a substitute for a ball.

There was one time when Matty and I happened to procure a real baseball. We had gone to watch a local ragtag team play a squad from Santo Domingo. It wasn't much to see, other than they were playing with a real ball and for money. They fashioned a baseball diamond from a cow pasture, the outreaches of which were over-run with underbrush. One ball was hit into those dense scrubs, and several fans spent quite a while searching in vain for it. The next day Matty and I returned to the scene, scouring the area, rooting around. It took us an hour, but we found the ball. For two poor boys like us, it was like a diver finding a rare pearl.

Whenever we or our friends did have a real baseball, we would use it until the cover started peeling off. Then we would wrap tape around it. I first learned how to throw a little bit of a breaking ball with a lemon, trying to mimic what I heard on the radio station from Cuba, listening to Winter League games and announcers describing pitches as *spinning, spinning*. Large rocks passed for bases, and usually we had only two bases. We didn't fully understand the rules of the game, but what we did know is that an open field ignited our imaginations. We had fun, and we played for hours.

Sometimes real life interrupted our fun. One day a military truck rumbled by our home, bellowing to a stop. Before Matty, who was about fifteen, knew what was going on, they grabbed him. I learned later that the dictator, Rafael Trujillo, needed laborers to work at the fairgrounds in preparation for the 1955 Fair of Peace and Fraternity of the Free World, which was behind schedule. The soldiers forced Matty to work all day without paying him a cent or even feeding him. Plus, he had to walk eight miles back home that night.

Another time when Matty disappeared, we didn't know what happened. It was a Sunday morning, and he left without saying anything. Lunchtime came, and he didn't come home. Dinner, no Matty. I could see my father pacing, worried. He went to the closest police precinct inside the city and told them he hadn't seen his son the whole day. On an island ruled by a ruthless dictator, it's hard to stay calm when your son suddenly disappears. Soon night fell, and still no Matty. At 10 p.m., we heard the gears of an open-bed truck grind to a stop in front of our home. There were fifteen guys bunched in the back of it. One of them was Matty, who bounded off as if nothing had happened. He had gone across the island to play in two sandlot baseball games, a five-hour trip each way. Normally, such an offense would be worthy of a whipping. Not that it would've mattered to Matty. He was fearless, a characteristic I saw years later in my son Moisés. I was afraid of the belt, but Matty wasn't. As it was, my father didn't whip him. We were all so glad to see our brother and have him back.

As I got older my dreams of getting an education and becoming a doctor started coming into focus. Because there wasn't a high school where I lived, I moved to Santo Domingo to live with Uncle Juan and attend high school there. This was only the second time I saw a baseball game played with two teams wearing different-colored uniforms and the first time I regularly saw it played with four bases. Because he was a captain in Trujillo's army, Uncle Juan earned a decent salary, mainly because Trujillo wanted to keep the soldiers who surrounded him happy. I would stay with my aunt and uncle during the week, and then Uncle Juan would give me bus fare on Fridays so I could go home and be with my family on the weekend. When I turned seventeen I decided I wanted to move back home while still attending school in Santo Domingo. It was a twelve-mile trip each way. I would get up at five in the morning and walk and catch rides along the way. I was never once late for school. Years later, my teachers would tell students who followed me that, despite my twelve-mile journey in the predawn hours, I was never late. There were other times when I would walk those twelve miles—and it was to play baseball against the city kids. During my teenage years my father somehow saved enough money to buy me a pair of baseball spikes from a pawn shop. I was so proud of them that one night I walked home from the city to my parents' home wearing those spikes. Good thing it was mostly along dirt roads. Sometime later, my father had to reclaim those baseball shoes and remove the spikes, because he didn't have a pair of shoes for himself.

All that walking proved beneficial, because in addition to having become a pretty good baseball player, I was a fast runner. I would often run instead of walk to wherever I wanted to go. People used to say about me, "That Felipe Rojas—he's always running." Although baseball was my favorite sport, I found myself drawn to other athletic endeavors. One day a group of high school friends and I were watching the track and field team. Some of the kids were retrieving the javelin that was thrown and walking it back to the coach. Not me. I picked it up, and instead of taking it back, I threw it. To everyone's astonishment it sailed over their heads by about twenty-five feet.

The coach approached me, saying, "Do you want to practice doing this?"

"Sure," I said.

Before I knew it I was on the track and field team, throwing the javelin, the discus, and the shot put and running the 100- and 200-meter dashes. With practice and learning the techniques, I improved my skills as both a runner and a thrower. My senior year in high school I threw the javelin 204 feet, which established a national record. My progression was so rapid that, while still a high school senior, I represented my country at the 1954 Central American and Caribbean Games in Mexico City—competing in the javelin, discus, and dash events. It was the first time I ever left our island and got an inkling that there was indeed a world out there, not just the images of it from scratchy radio broadcasts or hearing my father reading the newspaper under a gas lamp.

Soon, with the financial help of Uncle Juan, I was enrolled at the University of Santo Domingo, taking premed courses and pursuing my goal of becoming a surgeon and hopefully helping the poor people of my homeland. By now track and field was my passion, supplanting baseball. Although I was on the baseball team at the university, it was track and field I set my sights on, with the goal of representing my country at the 1956 Olympic Games in Melbourne, Australia.

It wasn't all sports and schooling, though. I learned the blacksmith and carpentry trade from my father and often worked long hours with him. Also, between the ages of fourteen and sixteen, I worked in a rock mine, my shift starting at 10 p.m. and ending at 6 a.m. It was arduous, brutally hard work, the most physically taxing work I've ever done in my life, which my father was also doing at the time. I made 12 pesos a week, the equivalent of $12, all of which went straight to my parents to help support the family. Not even one penny went into my pocket. There was no doubt that between the athletics and the hard work, I was growing into a strong man, about six feet tall, muscular, and with cheetah-like swiftness, like my father.

In 1955, when I was twenty, I was invited to represent my country in track and field at the Pan American Games in Mexico City. I was to throw the javelin, the discus, run the 200, and maybe compete in the pentathlon. Our country's baseball team was also there. It was my second trip off our island. During our stay two wrestlers, determined to escape Trujillo's dictatorship, defected. Because of that the watch over the rest us tightened, at times to a suffocating degree. We were also given strict orders to not mix with our female athletes. One of our baseball players, a big outfielder named Andres Aranda, didn't like the edict. Aranda was quick-tempered, as well as being a very strong white Dominican whom we called "Tarzan."

"I'm a man," he bellowed, "and these are women!"

At one point, because Aranda was so aggressively obstinate and so vocal about it, words were exchanged with a high-ranking officer in uniform, who went after Aranda to fight. Some punches were thrown, but thankfully a bunch of guys jumped between them, preventing the incident from really turning ugly. More words and threats spewed from Aranda, and it got him booted off the team for insubordination and sent home. That's when they came to me, because Aranda was the baseball team's left fielder and they needed someone to replace him. They didn't give me a choice. Baseball was growing in popularity in the Dominican Republic, and so my country's sports officials told me I was no longer on the track and field team. Instead, I was ordered to play baseball.

The best player on the team was Julián Javier, and he was on the radar of several pro scouts. He eventually signed with the Pittsburgh Pirates and played thirteen years in the Major Leagues with the St. Louis Cardinals and Cincinnati Reds. His son Stan Javier played seventeen years in the big leagues. I had a very solid showing, performing well, including going 4 for 5 in a 10–4 victory against the United States in the championship game, helping us win the gold medal.

Now the scouts were noticing me, which likely never would have happened had Andres Aranda not been sent home. It's one of those twists of fate, when a sequence of events gets shuffled in a way you never anticipated. What if those two wrestlers hadn't defected, leading security to tighten around us, which included forbidding us from socializing with the female athletes, angering Aranda, who caused a scene, which resulted in his being sent home and my moving into his vacated left-field spot on our country's gold medal–winning baseball team at those 1955 Pan American Games?

Once back in the Dominican Republic, my university's athletic director and baseball coach, Rabbit Martínez, approached me. As

I've mentioned, he was a well-respected baseball man who played in both Cuba and the Negro Leagues and was now a New York Giants scout. He told me he wanted me to become the first player he signed. Who knew then that I was going to open the door for my country?

I was a good player on my university team, but there were several other players who were as good or better. We had an incredible team. We could all hit for power. On the outskirts of our university field, about four hundred feet into left-center field, was a mango tree. I used to hit it on a fly ball and sometimes hit the ball over it. The other guys did, too. We didn't chop down the tree, though, like we did that coconut tree of my youth. But we would eat its succulent fruit. The difference between my teammates and me was that they came from well-to-do families. They were studying to become doctors, engineers, lawyers, and businessmen, and their families had the money to make those dreams come true. I was the poor kid from Kilometer 12 who was about to become even poorer.

My father lost his job. So did Uncle Juan, after he had the nerve to disagree with something Trujillo had done. It was something minor, not something that would get him either imprisoned or perhaps vanished altogether, but he did lose his job. As badly as I wanted to become a doctor, the means to do so were starting to look shaky.

A new Dominican league was forming, and almost all of my teammates from the Pan American Games were signing. The thought of playing baseball for money suddenly didn't seem so outlandish.

But the new Dominican league was not what Martínez had in mind for me. Martínez was working as a bird dog for a man named Alejandro "Alex" Pompez, a Cuban American who had owned a team in the Negro Leagues and was now a scout overseeing the New York Giants' Negro League and Latin American operations. Legend has it that Pompez—in addition to signing players such as Juan Marichal, Orlando Cepeda, and Tony Oliva—was the scout who discovered Willie Mays and had a hand in the Giants signing him. Martínez pushed me to Pompez. Selling me to Pompez, however, was easier than selling the notion of my leaving school for baseball to my parents. The first time Martínez went to my parents, he brought two of my teammates with him. As much as they tried to convince them of my talents, the answer was a firm no.

"I want Felipe to be the first player to go from our country to Major League Baseball," Martínez pleaded. "He's that good. He can make it."

"Baseball is not a profession," my parents countered, shaking their heads for emphasis, as if they were placing an exclamation point at the end of a sentence.

The resistance was even stronger from Uncle Juan, who was adamantly against my leaving the university and abandoning my path toward becoming a doctor. Shortly after that initial visit to my parents, Uncle Juan showed up on a late afternoon when I was playing dominoes with some of the guys. "Felipe," he called, "come over here." And then, in front of everyone, he announced, "You're not going anywhere. You're going to be a doctor."

It wasn't the first time Uncle Juan had done something like this. When he heard I was going to Mexico City for the Pan American Games, he tried to stop me. That day, because he still had his job, he showed up in his military uniform, getting out of his jeep with two other soldiers. He was stern, and with a voice like he was giving me a military order, he commanded me in front of everybody: "Felipe, you're not going to Mexico. It's going to get in the way of your studies. You're going to become a doctor!"

I loved him for that, and for other reasons, because I yearned to become a doctor. But I was beginning to see that money could be made playing sports. Already, my participation in athletics was helping to fund my schooling.

A couple of weeks after getting rebuffed the first time, Martínez returned to my parents' house, this time with three of my teammates. By now the Pittsburgh Pirates and Milwaukee Braves had heard about me. Al Campanis was also on the island, looking for players for the Brooklyn Dodgers. Campanis had an eye for talent, as attested by the fact that he signed two of the all-time greatest players—Sandy Koufax and Roberto Clemente. I believe Martínez, when he heard Campanis was in the Dominican Republic, was afraid he would find me, so he turned it on with my mom and dad. The teammates he brought with him were telling my parents, "Your son is really good. He's going to make money."

And then Martínez told them how much money I could make by signing—200 pesos. That might not sound like a lot, but to our family it was a fortune. That amount, 200 pesos, was the same amount my father owed my godfather, Bienvenido Ortiz, who was our grocer. The number immediately registered with me, because I heard my father on more than one occasion talk about how he needed to pay the grocer the 200 pesos he owed. I knew how much it was weighing on him. I also knew, with all the schooling I still had ahead of me, that I was years away from helping my family financially. This way I could help them right away.

I looked around our small home with a floor that was part uneven concrete and part dirt, lit by a lamp barely flickering, hardly able to illuminate the worn-out features on my parents' faces. "I'm going to sign," I told them.

My mind was made up, and I was almost a twenty-one-year-old man. Still, it wasn't easy. I wanted to become a doctor. My lifelong dream was to help people, to heal people, especially poor people. I thought of those tiny wooden caskets my father made for children and also of my sister who died.

Nowadays, signing a professional baseball contract is a cause for celebration. But there were no smiles on November 14, 1955, inside our tiny house, when my father finally agreed to cosign my contract, doing so after I promised, in front of my parents and Martínez, that if baseball didn't work out, I would come back and finish my education. The only reaction in my neighborhood came shortly afterward, when a sergeant at a local police station saw me and said, "You're going to go, but they're going to find out you're not any good." His words came out of nowhere, and they stung, but I wasn't deterred. Instead, I was determined.

Soon, there I was, Felipe Rojas, a poor kid from a poor island village, leaving the Dominican Republic for the United States of America, carrying with me the dream that I would make a name for myself, my family, and my country.

2

1956–1957

3

Coming to America

I arrived in America to a parade.

And then the rain thundered down, a torrent of racism. The parade was a literal one, twenty-five festive cars long, each bearing the name of one of the twenty-five roster players on the Lake Charles Giants baseball team of Louisiana's Class C Evangeline League, celebrating the start of the season. The thunderstorm was figurative but just as real.

It's ironic to think that Evangeline is a biblical word, coming from Greek, with the word "angel" situated in the middle of it. The word "angel" means "messenger," and the message I received was clear: I was not welcome, not in 1956 Louisiana, not with my dark skin color. For the first time I started to hear words like "monkey," "nigger," and "black son of a bitch," all in that lilting Louisiana accent—a syrupy drawl, the sound and cadence of which have never left my ears.

I knew racism existed, but nothing prepared me for this—certainly not my upbringing, being the son of a white woman of Spanish descent and a black father who was the grandson of slaves who were likely ripped away from Africa in the early 1800s to work Hispaniola farms. Even the several days I spent in spring training in Melbourne, Florida, before the Giants shipped me to Louisiana, didn't give me much of an inkling of what was in store. In Lake Charles, Louisiana, I learned firsthand about racism. I also learned the city had a favorite son, who coincidentally played for the Major League club—the New York Giants. He played shortstop, and I remember having his baseball card when I was a kid. His name was Alvin Dark.

There were three blacks on that Lake Charles team—Chuck Weatherspoon, Ralph Crosby, and me, the guy with F. ALOU on the back of his jersey. We all suffered the same fate, only mine was a notch worse. Not only was my skin too dark, but I was also a Latino, which meant I was viewed as a little less than equal in the black communities where I spent much of my time, trying to avoid trouble. And if there was anything I had, it was time—a lot of it. I spent a month in Lake Charles and barely played. I got only 9 at-bats in five games, all of them in Lake Charles, where I wasn't even allowed to dress with my teammates in the clubhouse. On the road opposing teams banned us from the field.

In those 9 at-bats I did get in, I recorded 2 hits and 1 RBI (run batted in). One of those hits came in my first professional plate appearance, when I laced a pinch-hit single to drive in a run. The next day we left on a five-day road trip, for which I was ill-equipped on so many levels. Not only was I not prepared to *not* play, but I was also practically penniless, with only the clothes on my back to carry me through those five days. By the time we got back to Lake Charles, I didn't know what was worse—the stench from me or from the unrelenting racism that lay in wait for me at every ball field, restaurant, and rest area.

Growing up in the Dominican Republic, we used to talk about how you had to be careful in America, so I knew, if only academically, about racism. But until now I had not seen the face of racism. I didn't know I would have to sit in the back of a bus. I didn't know I couldn't look at a white girl. I didn't know I couldn't eat in the same restaurants as whites. I didn't know I couldn't stay in the same motels. I didn't know I couldn't drink from the same water fountains. I didn't know I couldn't use the same bathrooms. On a road trip in Baton Rouge, I couldn't even enter the stadium through the players' entrance, much less enter the clubhouse. I had to sit in the bleachers in what was called the colored section. All of it was startling to me. Until you confront a lion, you don't know how ferocious he is.

About the only thing that tethered me to the humanity of man was the white family that housed me in Lake Charles. I'll never forget their kindness, not to mention their courage. They put themselves in danger by putting me in their home. They were circumspect about it, to be sure. When they drove me to the stadium, which was about a half mile from their house, I had to lie low, below the window, in the backseat of the car. The same thing happened when they took me home. I had to stay out of view until their car was safely tucked inside their garage, with the garage door shut.

Once a couple of my white teammates tried to walk me through the stadium gate in Baton Rouge, flanking me on each side, almost as if they were trying to smuggle me past security so I could make it to the clubhouse. Weatherspoon and Crosby, who were darker skinned than me, didn't even try to sneak in, heading instead for the left-field bleachers, where the black fans had to sit and where we, as opposing players, also had to sit. But a police officer spotted me walking in and stopped the three of us.

"He can't come in," he barked. "He has to go sit in the bleachers with the other Negroes."

And so I did, where I watched young men play baseball, knowing I was as good as or better than they were, knowing I had what it took to play and excel in this league. Early in the season at Lake Charles, there was a Baton Rouge player, José Garcia, who saw me warming up and came over and talked to me. Garcia was very light-skinned, so he passed as white. He told me, half jokingly, that he combed his hair a certain way to make sure he looked white.

"You can play this game; you have talent," Garcia told me. "But they're not going to let you play in this league. You need to go somewhere else, to another league, where you can show them you can play."

It was a waiting game. Louisiana was fighting the U.S. Supreme Court's 1954 *Brown v. Board of Education* ruling, which declared that state laws establishing separate public schools for white and black students were unconstitutional. Louisiana legislators were fighting back, trying to push through a bill that stated, "The Legislature of Louisiana does hereby solemnly declare the decision of the U.S. Supreme Court of May 17, 1954 . . . and any similar decisions that might be rendered in the connection with the public school system, public parks and recreational facilities . . . to be in violation of the constitution the United States and the state of Louisiana."

Meanwhile, I was miserable. I was eating food I didn't recognize, trying to learn a language I didn't understand, and enduring a raging racism that confounded me more than anything. And then there was that division in the black neighborhoods, where we were all dark-skinned, but we still weren't the same. Black ballplayers in those neighborhoods, whether it was Lake Charles or other places I played, had places to go that were not available to Latinos. So we were rejected by whites and looked down upon in black communities. It was as if we were always operating with two strikes against us.

One night, after yet another evening of not playing and sitting in the left-field section for coloreds, I decided to walk alone to the house where I was staying. In the canopy of darkness I didn't notice a black dog until it suddenly jumped a low fence and barreled into my side, almost knocking me down. Great, I thought, even the dogs don't want me here. That same night the news arrived that Louisiana's racist legislature had won, voting 119–0 to impose its archaic segregationist laws. It was official. The people they called Negroes and colored were not welcome in the Evangeline League—not in Lake Charles and not anywhere else where the league's teams played.

I understand that for years there was even a notation in the Evangeline League's record books that read, "Baton Rouge forfeited April 28 game to Lake Charles, refusing to play in violation of segregation law because Lake Charles had two Negro players."

The Giants sent those Negro players—Chuck Weatherspoon and Ralph Crosby—to Class C leagues in Missoula, Montana, and Salinas, California, respectively; they sent me, F. ALOU, the colored kid from the Dominican Republic, to Cocoa, Florida. Little did those people know that out of the twenty-six players who officially spent time on that 1956 Lake Charles Giants roster, I was the only one who would make it to the Major Leagues. Not that it mattered to them back then.

After arriving to a parade, I was now departing on a Greyhound bus.

4

Just Give Me a Chance

There were no major highways, so it took almost three days to travel from Lake Charles to Cocoa. I survived the journey by sleeping very little and eating exactly 50 cents' worth of peanuts from bus-stop vending machines and drinking water from fountains designated for colored people. I also stubbornly defied the Greyhound bus driver, who persistently pointed with a jerking motion toward the back of the bus. It wasn't that I was making a social statement; rather, I was so panicked I would miss the Cocoa bus station that I would hover in the seat behind the driver, asking in my fractured English whenever we stopped: "Cocoa. Me Cocoa. Cocoa?" I think his annoyance eventually translated into pity. Either that, or he got tired of pointing to the back of the bus.

For the first time since I arrived in America, I was homesick. I missed my homeland, my family, my culture, my food. Thoughts of returning to the Dominican Republic, returning to school, and resuming my studies in pursuit of a medical degree filled my head. Not only was I going from Lake Charles to Cocoa, but I was also going from the Class C Evangeline League to the Class D Florida State League. To make matters worse, I was supposed to have started my pro career in Danville, Virginia, which was a Class B team in the Carolina League, but because of visa problems I didn't arrive on time, which was why I was sent to Lake Charles. Even with my limited understanding of the English alphabet, I knew that was going backward.

What I lacked in the native language of America I made up with my knowledge of geography. Florida, I knew, was the southernmost state, a connection to the Caribbean. So when the Greyhound bus crossed the border and I made out the sign that said WELCOME TO FLORIDA, I was overwhelmed with the notion that I could stay on the bus and ride it all the way to Miami and from there return home.

But there were three strong reasons I knew I was going to get off that bus in Cocoa. My father was finding only odd jobs to do, not really working. I felt the responsibility of feeding seven people back home. I thought of Rabbit Martínez and Alex Pompez and how they put faith in my becoming the first player to go from the Dominican Republic to Major League Baseball. I gave them my word. I signed a contract. I couldn't do something so dishonorable as to let them down by quitting. And finally, in connection with that, I wasn't just representing my family and the reputation of the men who signed me; I was representing an entire country.

On the third day, in the still darkness that is 4:30 in the morning, the Greyhound bus wheezed to a stop in what seemed like the middle of nowhere.

"Cocoa?" I asked.

"Cocoa," the bus driver replied, nodding.

I was the last person off the bus, tentatively stepping into the blackness. I thought Cocoa was a city, but as I looked around I didn't see anything that resembled a city. The bus station was a bench. With no place to go and the sun still hours away from appearing, I snaked my arm through my suitcase handle, laid down on the bench, and allowed some much-needed sleep to overtake me.

I awakened to the blinding brightness of day and a warm blanket of humidity. Looking around I still saw no city. The only thing I knew about this new team I was to play for was its name, the Cocoa Indians, and that it had two Latin players—Julio Navarro and Héctor Cruz. I met both of them in Melbourne, which was about twenty-five miles south of Cocoa, when I first arrived in America. I didn't have an address or a phone number, so I started walking.

I would see people and say, "Navarro? Cruz?" The only replies I received were puzzled stares.

Suddenly, as if she appeared from the mist, a beautiful black woman slowed her car down to a stop and leaned out the window. "Where are you going?" she asked.

I replied by taking a pantomime swing with an imaginary bat. "Navarro? Cruz?" I asked.

"Ballplayers?" she quizzed.

I nodded. "*Biesbol*," I said.

She said something I couldn't understand, leaned over and opened the passenger door, and motioned for me to get in. A few minutes later, we arrived at a house. It couldn't have been any later than 8 a.m., but that didn't matter to her. She awoke the occupants, who poked their sleepy faces out the window, beaming when they saw me.

"It's the Dominican!" Navarro called out. "Hey, Dominican, what are you doing here?"

The Cocoa Indians played in St. Petersburg the night before, and Navarro and Cruz had been home only a few hours. They were still glad to see me, though, and, boy, was I glad to see them. Navarro could speak English and Spanish, and he told the woman he knew of a family that would take me in as a boarder. She took me there, deep into the black section of town, where a kind woman named Blanche showed me a tiny room. I collapsed on the bed, fully clothed, and slipped into a deep sleep. That room became my first real home in America, and Blanche and her husband, Singletary—I never knew their last name—became surrogate parents.

I awoke at 4 p.m., and it wasn't too long afterward when Navarro and Cruz stopped by on foot, and we walked a half mile to Provost Park, where the Cocoa Indians played. It was a rickety structure with a steamy clubhouse that was more like a cave, dank and dingy, with barely enough room to dress. Making matters miserable were the mosquitoes, which swarmed with unrelenting vengeance, descending on exposed flesh like kamikaze fighter pilots.

Still, I was happy. Finally, I could play baseball and play every day. Thus, in 1956, I launched my professional career. Buddy Kerr, the Indians' manager, greeted me with a sincere handshake and smile and told me I was the regular center fielder. I got my first hit that night and felt settled in. In retrospect, it was to be one of the greatest seasons I had as a professional.

Early on, my teammates chided me for my swing, calling me out for what they called an ugly hitting style. "Maybe so," I would reply. "But I keep getting hits, more than anyone else."

I clubbed 169 hits over 445 at-bats for the Indians that season, good enough to lead the Florida State League with a .380 batting average and a .582 slugging percentage. We also went 90-50, best in the league, which was quite an accomplishment, because the Indians were in last place when I arrived. I could have batted—or perhaps it is more accurate to say I *should* have batted—.400 that season. After all, I was hitting .433 with about a month to go in the season. But the pressure got to me, and, frankly, I choked. Still, leading the league with a .380 batting average was quite an accomplishment.

I say I clubbed 169 hits that season because I've always believed that hitting a baseball is an aggressive endeavor. That's the way all of us Alous approached it. We never had a hitting coach in the Dominican Republic, yet the three of us—Matty, Jesús, and I—were all solid Major League hitters. Combined, we accumulated 5,094 hits (2,101 from me, 1,777 from Matty, and 1,216 from Jesús). My son Moisés, a fierce hitter, surpassed us all with 2,134 hits. That's 7,228 hits from the only four men to have played Major League Baseball with the name ALOU on the back of their jerseys. All of us had an attitude that a bat is an offensive weapon. It's an aggressive weapon.

My brothers and I had that mind-set growing up. We would spend hours in our yard hitting—or should I say attacking?—any small object we could find and throw. The rule was that if you didn't strike out, you could keep hitting—and the three of us liked to hit. That was a contest mostly between Matty and me, only because Jesús often preferred to go fishing rather than join us. But when Jesús made it to the big leagues, he was known to swing at anything near the strike zone, doing so with enough success to spend fifteen years in the Major Leagues. The Alou brothers were not hitters looking for walks. Over a 162-game season the three of us combined to average only 26.3 walks and 41 strikeouts to go with a .291 batting average. In fact, Jesús not only finished his career in 1979 as a Houston Astros player *and* batting coach but also had a walk rate of 3 per 100 plate appearances, the lowest in the twentieth century for someone who played a minimum of 1,000 games. Some hitters bring a bat to the plate, and it looks like they're trying to defend themselves from the baseball. Not the Alous. We approached the plate as the aggressors.

In relation to this I believe in hitting—not swinging. You have to hit. Yes, your swing is important, but you have to learn to hit with your swing, even if it's ugly, like mine was. I also believe a lot of batters take too many pregame swings. Because of that not many hitters are good late-game hitters. They leave a lot of energy in the batting cage. Look at the New York Mets' hitters in the 2015 World Series. To me it looked like they took too many pregame swings during the season, especially late in the season, and it showed.

I also believe every hitter has a way of hitting, that he was born with a swing. His swing is like a fingerprint. No two hitters have the same swing. I also believe not everyone has the same answer when a pitch is thrown. In order to arrive at your answer, you have to be able to anticipate pitches—not guess, anticipate. If you guess, you're going to get beat. Anticipation means remembering what happened in your last at-bat, or yesterday, or last week, or last month, and then using that information. If you guess, you're going on no information.

Because I could hit right away as a professional player, I felt mostly accepted by my teammates. And Cocoa turned out to be a paradise for me. The fishing, the weather, the vegetation—it reminded me of home. I quickly discovered some wonderful fishing spots, the kind Florida was known for back in the 1950s. When I wasn't playing I would be the guy you would see walking through town shirtless, carrying a string of fish. I quickly discovered, too, why I had awakened Navarro and Cruz that first morning. Because of the team's limited budget, we rarely stayed in a motel. Instead, we would cram sixteen players, along with our manager and equipment, into the club's two station wagons and sometimes drive all night back from road games. And we would do so not on the highways that now exist in Florida, but often along two-lane roads, sometimes arriving back in Cocoa when the sun's first morning rays started to shoot across the horizon.

The only place we stayed overnight was in Gainesville, Florida. Typical of everything else in the South at that time, there was a motel for the white players to stay in and something barely livable for us in the black section of town for the COLOREDS—that word I kept seeing everywhere, usually in all capital letters. I never knew the quality of the motels where the white players stayed, but I was petrified of the boardinghouse where we stayed in Gainesville. It was in the boondocks, on the other side of the railroad tracks—dirty, filthy rooms filled with cockroaches and mosquitoes. And it felt as if it were held together with matchsticks. We stayed on the second floor, where we could see below through holes, afraid to walk because of the concern we would step on a rotting section of wood and crash to the first floor. We had to take every step gingerly, gently applying enough pressure until you felt comfortable taking another step.

My salary was $275 a month, and I used it for my basic expenses and to purchase a so-called Hollywood course that would teach me to read, write, and speak English. I was determined to learn my new language. The rest of the money I sent home to my parents. I soon found out, though, that there were other sources of income. Those fans in Cocoa had a habit of passing a hat around if an Indians player did something extraordinary. One night early in the season, we were losing 2–0 to West Palm Beach when I came to the plate with two men on in the bottom of the ninth—and hit a game-winning three-run home run. Afterward, those great Cocoa fans gave me $89. I treated Navarro, Cruz, and our second baseman, a black player named Jim Miller, who was now sharing my little boarding room with me, to hamburgers and cake. It soon turned into a ritual for Navarro to entreat me at our home games to "hit a home run for us tonight. We're short on money and we're hungry."

While being able to hit right away helped me get accepted by most of my teammates, it also got me thrown at probably more than the average player—and definitely more than white players. It was obvious, and it was difficult to hold back from retaliating. Navarro was always in my ear, telling me not to strike back.

"Patience, Felipe," he would implore. "You must have patience."

I tried, but I wasn't always successful. Here I had come from a Caribbean country that, to Americans, probably seemed behind the times, but every day I was faced with this centuries-old notion that the color of a man's skin made him superior or inferior to another man. I wasn't accustomed to it, nor did I ever want to get comfortable with it. If that meant being ignorant in certain situations, then so be it. Black players like Chuck Howard and my roommate Miller could immediately smell trouble brewing and intuitively knew to leave. I didn't seem to have that instinct. Or maybe it was something I refused to learn.

It was customary after road games for the team to stop at a restaurant on the way back to Cocoa. Blacks and Latinos would have to wait outside for our meal, often in a backyard area, fed through a back door, while the white players would go inside. I never once ate inside the same restaurant with any of my white teammates. One night as the white players filed into a restaurant in West Palm Beach named Le Vagabond, a waitress met Miller, Howard, and myself at the station wagon in the parking lot and told us she would serve us there. This was unusual. Normally, it was some of our white teammates who brought our meals to us. No sooner had we thanked her when a man who apparently was the proprietor emerged from the restaurant, yelling. "Don't you know where their place is!?" he screamed at the waitress.

That was all Miller and Howard needed to hear, and they took off running. The man's rant continued, and although I didn't understand all the words he was saying, I picked up enough to know what was going on. I sat there fuming, trying to hear Navarro's mantra—"Patience, Felipe, you must have patience"—instead of this white man's angry, racist words. Finally, he left. I sat there, no longer with an appetite, waiting for my teammates so we could get back on the road and back home. A couple of minutes later, a police car wheeled into the parking lot. Two policemen emerged and walked toward me. With my limited English I made out one of them telling me to get out, and if I didn't get out he was going to pull me out of the car.

In that moment I swear I was ready to die. I was tired of the humiliation. Tired of the abuse. Tired of capitulating. When one of the officers reached through the window and tried to grab my arm, I cursed him in Spanish with such ferocity that I think it startled him. At the very least it caused him to back away. By now some of my teammates had retrieved our manager, Buddy Kerr. I could see the humanity in his eyes, the raw sadness over what I had to endure.

"I can't do anything here, Felipe," he said. "They want you to leave."

I shook my head, my arms folded across my chest, my jaw clenched. I believe at that moment Buddy Kerr learned what kind of man I was. He stopped asking me to leave, and instead he climbed into the station wagon, turned the ignition key, and drove the car across the street, where we waited for the other players to finish eating before heading to Cocoa. That night, covered in a blanket of such overwhelming despair, I couldn't sleep.

There were times when what kept me going was Buddy Kerr's kindness. He played shortstop for nine big-league seasons, mostly with the New York Giants. He would pull me aside and tell me I had what it took to make it, to not give up, to not let the racial slurs and slights defeat me. "You have what it takes," he would implore me. And those times when pitchers would throw at me, Kerr never hesitated to defend me, often doing so on the field, threatening the opposing team and pitcher. What a man. I appreciate more today his courage and decency.

But there was only so much that he, or anyone, could do. Even pitchers on my own team would throw at me, aiming for my head during batting practice and acting as if the ball had gotten away from them. I knew better. I once overheard some of my teammates telling opposing pitchers what pitches I hit well and what gave me trouble. It was all I could do to stop myself from drawing them into a fight.

Whatever fury I felt I channeled it into my game. I developed the confidence that even if a pitcher knew my weaknesses, he still wasn't going to get me out. That confidence bred more confidence, and there was one particularly hot streak when I got 15 hits in 19 plate appearances. My average peaked at .433 before plummeting late in the season. Even though I knew I was playing well, there was no newspaper in Cocoa for me to check statistics and see just how well I was doing. One afternoon when I was at a restaurant in what was called the colored section of Daytona Beach, I got a newspaper and began deciphering names and numbers. I saw that a Daytona Beach Islanders player named Don Dillard had wrestled the batting title away from me on the strength of a 5-for-5 performance the night before in Cocoa. The realization of it all startled me at first, and then it motivated me. My batting average had been going backward, but that night I went 5 for 6, while Dillard went 1 for 4. I overtook him and held on to win the batting title—my .380 average edging Dillard's .375 finish. I also led the league with 48 stolen bases, finished third with 21 home runs, and knocked in 99 runs. I did all that after missing about a month of the season while sitting in Lake Charles. But I did get that 1 RBI in Lake Charles, which combined with Cocoa gave me an even 100.

It's a good thing I had such a solid season with the Cocoa Indians, because when I returned home I learned that the Giants had not paid the $200 signing bonus. I wonder sometimes, had I hit .180 instead of .380, if that check would have ever come. It arrived soon enough when I informed the Giants that payment was due.

My arrival in the Major Leagues would be coming soon, too.

5

Moving Up

My first offseason from professional baseball was eventful. Evidently, news of my successes in the Florida State League rippled through my country, and I was bestowed with a banquet in my honor. I was given many gifts, but there was one I received from a close friend, Roque Martínez, that I thought ridiculous at the time—a Bible.

I had no desire for a Bible and didn't think I had any use for it. Owning a Bible at the time was also forcefully frowned upon by the Catholic Church, which held sway over the country, second in power only to the dictator, Rafael Trujillo. The church particularly told parents not to allow their children to read the Bible, an edict I knew my Catholic mother took seriously. When I returned home I furtively hid the Bible in my suitcase and forgot about it.

What was most on my mind that offseason was a girl named Maria Beltré. I first saw Maria when she was six and I was thirteen. My father built her family's home in Haina. Because of the age difference we really didn't move in the same circles. But now we were spending a lot of time together, mostly at her home, where we would sit and talk. In rare bold moments I would reach out and hold her hand. I was thrilled when, after we talked about marriage, my father talked with her father and both families gave their consent.

Almost equally thrilling was news from the Giants that they assigned me to their Class Triple-A American Association farm team in Minneapolis—the last league before the Major Leagues. When I packed to leave for Minor League spring training in Sanford, Florida, I saw in my suitcase what I had completely forgotten about that offseason—the Bible. I knew I couldn't leave it behind, for fear my mother would find it. So off to America it went with me.

After spring training I arrived in Minneapolis in time for an exhibition game against the Milwaukee Braves. The perimeter of the ball field showcased mounds of freshly shoveled snow that had fallen the night before. I already didn't like the cold weather. And then, when a ball reached a mound of snow in the outfield and I had to reach in to get it, I got that icy sensation from touching snow for the first time in my life. I especially didn't like that. The only thing I did like about being in a northern state was rarely seeing signs indicating where COLOREDS could eat, drink from a water fountain, or use a bathroom.

I had a good spring training, hitting .387, and the crazy thought occurred that perhaps no matter what league I played in, I would be a .380-or-better hitter. That bubble burst quickly in the American Association, which I learned was a significant talent jump from Class D ball. Battling the cold and better pitching, I struggled. After a month that saw my batting average settle at an anemic .211 with no home runs, I was shipped to Springfield, Massachusetts, in the Class A Eastern League.

I was with the Minneapolis Millers long enough, though, for two lifelong relationships to take root. I became friends with a kid from Puerto Rico whom I had met a few years earlier, when he was sixteen and I was eighteen and our two countries played against each other in a juvenile all-star baseball series. I remembered him as a chubby kid, with bad knees from birth, but what a talent. He could hit and hit for power, had a slick glove, and even with bad knees could run. We also crossed paths for a few days a year earlier when I first arrived in America at Melbourne, Florida. He was one of the few Latino players on the Minneapolis team, and we bonded, becoming buddy buddies, inseparable. His name was Orlando Cepeda, and in that brief time we spent together I was like a big brother while he taught me pointers about hitting.

The second relationship I developed was with the Bible my friend Roque Martínez left me. I found comfort in it initially because it was written in my native Spanish. But I couldn't understand its message. Even so, what I did understand I found inspirational. I discarded any feelings of guilt the Catholic Church instilled in me for even possessing a Bible. I went from reading it furtively to reading it faithfully. Its message slowly took root, providing a stability that would ground me for the rest of my life.

When I told Cepeda that the Giants were sending me down to the Class A team in the Eastern League, he went to his room and cried, and over the next week he cried some more. He asked the Giants to not send me down. He even had thoughts of asking them if he could go with me. Thankfully, the latter didn't happen, because Cepeda hit .309 with 25 home runs that season. The next year with the San Francisco Giants, he was the National League Rookie of the Year, en route to a Hall of Fame career.

I was sad to leave Cepeda behind but happy to find my old friend Julio Navarro in Springfield. I also found the weather there to be just as cold as Minneapolis. But I knew there would be no excuses. I redoubled my efforts and poured myself into baseball. And when I wasn't playing, I was usually reading that Bible or writing letters home to Maria.

As in Cocoa the year before I had a good first game that helped me settle in—lacing two hits and making a really good running catch in the outfield.

One of the things that plagued me early in my career was an absentminded habit of forgetting to bring my gear with me on road trips. It happened in Cocoa and now again with the Springfield Giants. It was decided on this one road trip, when I forgot my gear, that I would wear the uniform and shoes of one of my teammates—a pitcher named Chet Vincent. I really felt guilty, because it meant Vincent wouldn't play during that road trip. I sought redemption on the baseball field, feeling an obligation to excel. And I did. In one doubleheader I banged 7 consecutive hits, knocked in 7 runs, and stole 4 bases.

In addition to Navarro, I became fast friends with another Puerto Rican—a middle infielder named José Pagán, who would go on to have a fifteen-year Major League career.

Aside from the team finishing twenty-nine and a half games out of first place, it was mostly a good season for me. I say *mostly* because I suffered an injury that hounded me the rest of my career. As it did in Cocoa my batting average soared and then plummeted. I was hitting .389, running like the wind, stealing bases, tracking down balls in the outfield. My strategy at the plate was basically to put the ball in play and run like hell. More than once I saw the surprised look on an infielder's face when I would beat a throw to first base.

One time my speed got the best of me when I managed to score from first base on a single. When I crossed home plate, running furiously, I felt something pull in my right leg and went sprawling flat on my face. After sitting out for three days, and with my leg still pulsating pain, I returned to the lineup. I wasn't the same, and soon I was relegated to pinch-hitting duties and part-time play. My batting average nose-dived before settling at .306 for the season. Worse still, my leg never felt the same, and I never again had the same speed at my disposal that made me an elite base stealer and a standout in track. Eventually, in 1964, I had an operation on my leg that almost prematurely ended my career.

When I returned home that winter I thought I had gone backward. But then I learned the Giants were promoting me to their top farm club—the Phoenix Giants in the Class Triple-A Pacific Coast League, again one step away from the Major Leagues. As it was, that would be the last offseason I would spend in the Dominican Republic as a Minor League player.

The Promised Land waited.

1958–1963

6

The Rookie

There are pivotal points in life that embed themselves like a book-mark, forever glued to a page of your personal history. There is every-thing in your life that happened before that and then everything that happens after. It is that dramatic. Critical. Indelible. Unforget-table. For a baseball player, it is the day you are told you are going to the Major Leagues.

I was playing for the Phoenix Giants in the Class Triple-A Pacific Coast League, and we were in Seattle on one of those rainy days Seat-tle is famous for. We had been there for two days, but because of all the rain we had not played an inning. I was playing well overall—batting .319 with 13 home runs, 16 doubles, and 42 RBI through June 7, barely more than a third of the way through the season.

A few days earlier, I messed up. Actually, first baseman Wil-lie McCovey and I messed up together. We flew with the team from Phoenix to Los Angeles, where we had a four-and-a-half-hour layover before we were to fly to Portland to play the Bea-vers in a series. Because the layover was so long, McCovey wanted to see his sister, who lived in a black section of LA. She insisted we come, telling us she would feed us some collard greens and authentic southern cooking (the McCoveys were from Alabama). I'm glad we went because it was some really good food, but we ended up staying too long. Heading back to the airport, already running late, we were caught in LA traffic when I saw a TWA airplane soar over us.

"That is our flight," I told McCovey, and sure enough it was.

The club wasn't pleased, and our penalty was that we had to pay for our own flight to Portland. To this day, if I have a flight, I'm always one of the first persons to the gate.

After Portland we were in Seattle. Sitting in my hotel room with the rain pattering outside, I saw a pair of dusty shoes someone left under my bed. As I examined them the phone rang, and it was my manager, Red Davis.

"I have a surprise for you," he said.

"What?"

"They want you in the big leagues, and they want you to leave today."

I was shocked, not only because I had been in trouble a few days earlier, but also because I didn't think I was ready, and even to this day I wish I spent the entire season in Phoenix. It wasn't a lack of confidence. I had confidence. It was *understanding*. I was no fool. I had problems with the fastball, particularly fastballs inside. I also knew I was not that good against left-handed pitchers. The only left-hander I knew growing up was my brother Matty, whom my parents tried to force into becoming right-handed. Because left-handedness was considered a curse in my country, I hardly faced any left-handed pitchers until I turned pro, and I knew that was a weakness.

It seems kind of funny now that I was looking at a pair of dusty old shoes when I learned of my call-up because it was only days earlier when a conversation about shoes injected me with a booster shot of assurance about my playing abilities. McCovey and I had rented rooms in a Phoenix home, and it was immediately obvious that his passport to the big leagues was already stamped. It wasn't a matter of *if* McCovey would make it, but *when*. It also wasn't a question of whether he would have a good career, but rather just how great of a career he would fashion for himself. Willie Mac, as we called him, could do it all. I realized that the first time I laid eyes on him, during spring training in 1957. There was a ton of talent in camp. I could see competition from every side, from everywhere I looked. But some players really stood out. Willie Mac was one of those guys. He could run—he was a skinny kid—play a slick first base, hit for average, hit it out of an airport, and hit it *hard*. You didn't need a

readout of exit-velocity speeds to know that baseballs rocketed off his bat. McCovey, all six feet four of him, stood at the plate like a coiled cobra, ready to strike. It was fearsome to witness, and I was thankful I wasn't a pitcher having to face him.

Trying to save money, especially since I was regularly sending checks home to my family, I bought an inexpensive pair of shoes, Thom McAn's. They felt like two boards on my feet that wouldn't give—stiff, heavy, and perilously slippery. McCovey, on the other hand, was buying nice shoes, Stacy Adams and Florsheims—stylish and expensive stuff for a Minor Leaguer.

"Willie Mac," I said to him one day, "you shouldn't be spending so much money on shoes."

He looked at me and smiled. "You should quit buying cheap shoes, Felipe," he said. "You and I are going to make money in the big leagues." Hearing those words from a player whose skills eventually took him to the Hall of Fame . . . it was as if he were stamping my passport, too.

I loved living in the same house with McCovey. Before the season we went half in on an $80 used car, $40 each, even though I had not yet learned how to drive. It was a big old car, but cheap, not just in cost but in quality as well. The radiator was like a colander, leaking water. It was a twenty-minute drive to Phoenix Municipal Stadium, but it took us longer because we had to stop three or four times at filling stations to refill the radiator, and even then it was smoking when we got to the stadium. Everything shook in that car, including us. Willie Mac, just a twenty-year-old kid, spent the entire season in Phoenix, mainly because Orlando Cepeda, who also played first base, was with the big club, putting up numbers that would win him the National League Rookie of the Year Award. Afterward, he sold the car for the same $80 he paid for it and sent me a check for $40. That was Willie Mac. A sweetheart of a man.

That offseason in '58 and again in '59, I talked McCovey into playing winter ball for my Santo Domingo Escogido Lions team in the Dominican. Willie Mac won a lot of games for us, homesick the whole time. As for me, I was home, which always felt comfortable

and translated onto the field. Those two seasons I won the Winter League batting titles.

After my call-up I was rushed to the airport so quickly I didn't have time to tell McCovey goodbye. I met the Giants in San Francisco, and although I knew I was in the big leagues it still felt like the Minor Leagues. The Giants were playing their first season in the old Seals Stadium in the city's Mission District. It had been a Minor League ballpark—the Seals also being the only pro team Joe DiMaggio played for other than the New York Yankees—with its seating capacity bolstered to 22,900 to accommodate the Giants' first two seasons before Candlestick Park would be finished. It didn't look much different from the Pacific Coast League stadiums I had played in.

Maybe it was because I wasn't overwhelmed with my surroundings that I started off so well. Batting leadoff in my first Major League game, I turned on a slider and lined a single to left field on the first pitch in my first at-bat. In my second at-bat I hit a double to left field. In my third at-bat I knocked in a run with a sacrifice fly to right field. In my final at-bat I popped out to shortstop Roy McMillan in shallow left field. I finished my MLB debut 2 for 3 with an RBI in a 6–3 loss against Cincinnati and pitcher Brooks Ulysses Lawrence. A right-hander, Lawrence was a former Negro League player who was pitching for what was renamed the Cincinnati Redlegs from 1953 to 1958 because of the McCarthyism communism hysteria that swept through the country.

I got two hits again the next day, a hit in my third day, and another in my fourth day—this one my first big-league home run, which came off of the Pittsburgh Pirates' Vern Law, the man credited with coining the phrases *Experience is a hard teacher because she gives the test first, the lesson afterward* and *A winner never quits and a quitter never wins*. Of course, I wasn't about to quit. With six hits and a home run in my first four Major League games, I was just getting started.

I didn't think much about being a part of history, part of that inaugural Giants team in their first year in San Francisco after the

franchise moved from New York. I do remember thinking the Giants should have built their new stadium right where Seals Stadium sat. It was a perfect location in the city, and for whatever reason it wasn't that cold or windy there at night.

Almost immediately, I fell in with some Japanese fishermen, and we used to fish along this patch of land south of the city. One day someone said, "You know this is where they are putting the new ballpark."

"You're kidding me," I said. "Here?"

I was incredulous. It was almost impossible to fish there, so I couldn't imagine trying to play baseball there. One minute it could be calm, and the next minute the wind would blow so strongly you would have to pack up and go home. The temperature could—and would—plummet, getting downright icy, even in the summer, with the water slashing angrily about. I couldn't believe the difference several miles made between where Seals Stadium sat and where Candlestick Park would inhabit. We started playing there in 1960, and the Giants called Candlestick Park home—much to the chagrin of many ballplayers—for the next fifty-four years.

Along with not really grasping being a part of history, I didn't think of myself as a pioneer, either, and if I did, it was because of the environment from where I emerged. In barely two years and a month, I had gone from a rural speck of land on a Caribbean island, where athletically I was mostly known for being a javelin thrower, to Major League Baseball. I believe there was a divine dictate involved, because there is no logical way to explain how someone could come from someplace where there were no baseball fields and no role models to playing in the big leagues. To realize now that I'm the first player to go from Dominican Republic soil to Major League Baseball humbles me.

It was later when I became aware of Ozzie Virgil Sr., who was born in the Dominican Republic three years before me and made it to the big leagues two years before me. The reason I wasn't aware of him is because Ozzie left our country when he was thirteen, moving to 169th Street and 3rd Avenue in the Bronx, New York, where he graduated from high school and then joined the U.S. Marines. He also played his early winter-ball seasons in Puerto Rico, where I heard his father was from and where his son Ozzie Virgil Jr. was born, rather than in the Dominican Republic.

I finally met Ozzie in 1956, when he returned to the Dominican Republic to play in the Winter League. I learned a lot about baseball from him. I also learned that he was from the island's Monte Cristi province. I feel a special kinship with Ozzie. He is the first Dominican native to play in Major League Baseball, and I'm the first to have gone from the Dominican Republic to Major League Baseball. He is also kind enough to refer to me as the first everyday player from the Dominican Republic. Ozzie, who batted .231 with 14 home runs and 73 RBI in his nine journeyman seasons, is one of the classiest, most dignified men I know, a real gentleman. He also owns the distinction of being the first black player for the Detroit Tigers, breaking their color barrier in 1958.

In San Francisco I reconnected with my old pal Cepeda. He got me to move in where he was living, with Rubén Gómez, the Puerto Rican pitcher who had a house with his wife, Teresa, and their two children on De Long Street in Daly City. Teresa was like a mother to Cepeda and me, cooking for us and making our beds, and Rubén was like a father.

From the first day I arrived with the team, Al Worthington, a big right-handed pitcher, started talking to me about Jesus Christ, and I started listening. I was also reading more and more from the Bible. And then there was Orlando Cepeda, who introduced me to the vibrant and eclectic San Francisco nightlife. While Worthington was telling me in one ear about Jesus, Orlando was telling me in my other ear, "Felipe, you won't believe how beautiful the women are here."

San Francisco was a great city—very integrated, populated with people from all over the world. Chinatown. Japantown. Mexican. Ethnic foods. People on the streets all night long. Beatniks at North Beach. Columbus Avenue. Fisherman's Wharf. It was alive, breathing an air all its own. I went a few times to Joe DiMaggio's restaurant on Fisherman's Wharf, but once they found out I was a ballplayer for the Giants, they wouldn't let me pay. So I stopped going. I didn't want anyone to have the impression that I was trying to get free food.

One of Cepeda's favorite hangouts was this Mexican joint called Sinaloa that had everything—food, drink, live music, dancing, and the beautiful women Cepeda told me about. He would take me there and to other places that played live jazz—especially Latin jazz. We would listen to, and sometimes hang out with, guys who became legends of the genre—musicians like Cal Tjader and Mongo Santamaría.

Cepeda especially loved bongo music . . . to a fault. We roomed together on the road, and it was common for players to bring a phonograph player and a radio with them. Cepeda would play that bongo music all night in our hotel room, the turntable playing a record over and over again in a loop. I couldn't sleep. Finally, when I could hear Orlando snoring, I would lift the needle, only to hear him bark, "Hey, whaddaya doing? Leave my music alone." He would say it in a friendly way, a brotherly way, but still serious. So back the needle would go on those records. I learned every one of those songs, every beat of the drum, by heart.

After my second season I had to get another roommate. In his autobiography, *Baby Bull*, Orlando writes candidly about his drug use during his playing career and later his conviction for drug trafficking and the prison time he served. I never saw Orlando using drugs when we were together, but I knew something was up, something that was heading in the wrong direction for him. One night during the 1959 season we were staying on the twenty-fourth floor at Milwaukee's Schroeder Hotel, and Cepeda was either hallucinating, having a bad dream . . . I'm not sure what. But he was trying to jump out of the hotel window. It took all of my strength to stop him. He wasn't called Baby Bull for nothing. It scared the hell out of me. I still shudder when I think about it today. Even though we were like brothers, the team eventually roomed us with different people.

The only player who didn't have a roommate on road trips was Willie Mays, for the obvious reason that he was Willie Mays. Willie took a liking to me right away. He would make rookies bring him stuff and carry his gear, his luggage, things like that—the normal, innocuous initiation rites. But he never did that to me. He started calling me Chico that first season and still calls me Chico to this day. Whenever I hear someone call out, "Hey Chico," I know Willie Mays is in the room.

From the first time I saw him play, it was evident to me that Mays was a superior player, as was Cepeda. Their talents rose above everyone else's. I knew that no matter how hard I worked at it, I would never be as good as they were. Those were just the facts. I remember looking at those guys and some of the other National League players—Hank Aaron, Roberto Clemente, Duke Snider, Frank Robinson, Eddie Mathews, Stan Musial, Ernie Banks, Richie Ashburn, and others—and thinking to myself, *You've got to be kidding me!* What incredible talent. I knew, though, that I could still be a player. Yes, they were better than me, but I was better than other guys in the big leagues. I believe it's important to know where you fit, and I felt like there was a place for me in the organization. You have to understand that, and then you have to go to work and be the player you can be, finding where you can contribute.

That year my contribution began as an everyday starter in the outfield. Thanks to my speed I batted leadoff and hit over .300 my first month before tailing off and becoming a platoon player. I recorded 182 at-bats, hit 4 home runs, knocked in 16 runs, and batted .253. It was a beginning, but there were signs I was having problems, and it wasn't only with left-handed hurlers. Pitchers started figuring me out after my fast start, which was not only the six hits in my first four games. It also was a game, one week after I was called up, where I went 3 for 4, stroking a single, double, and triple, scoring twice and knocking in a run. What pitchers deciphered is that I was a better breaking-ball hitter than a fastball hitter—especially fastballs inside, which I started seeing a steady diet of. I was suddenly getting jammed inside, inside, inside. Pitchers would feed me fastballs inside and then fool me with a breaking ball away. It was merciless. They were determined to run me out of the big leagues with that inside fastball. My batting average nose-dived, and I went from starting to platooning to hearing rumors that I was going to be shipped back to the Minor Leagues.

Meanwhile, Willie Mays's greatness didn't surprise me. He merely lived up to everything I heard about him and what little I witnessed of him before my call-up in 1958. A year earlier, I played against Mays when he was barnstorming in the Dominican Republic with an all-black team. I hit a ball into the gap in left-center field that I didn't think a man could get to. But Willie made this spectacular diving catch, leaving me slack-jawed.

Since I was moving up the Giants' farm system as a center fielder, a sportswriter before one of those barnstorming games asked Willie, "Do you think Felipe Alou will replace you in center field?"

"I hear he's pretty good," Willie replied in that high-pitched voice. "How old is he? I hear he's going to be a good player."

That was Willie Mays, ever gracious, never controversial, basically ignoring the question. There were times when he would tell us black and Latino players, while rubbing his own black skin on his forearm, "You have to be careful with this." He didn't go any further than that, and the message was obvious. Instead of going forward and being a militant, Willie was a pacifist.

I saw Mays battle Philadelphia's Richie Ashburn for the batting title that season. Both were line-drive hitters, though Mays had much more muscle. Willie went 5 for 10 in our last two games of the season against St. Louis. One problem: Ashburn went 8 for 13 in his last three games against Pittsburgh, edging Willie for the batting title—.350 to .347. Not to be overlooked that season is that Stan Musial trailed them with a .337 batting and Hank Aaron at .326. Incredible. I feel very fortunate to have played during the era that I did.

And then there were the pitchers. As with the hitters, these were men. No boys here. And no dilution of talent, either—not with only eight teams in the league. I was with real baseball players, grown men with families, with children to feed. Don Drysdale threw at me. Warren Spahn once hit me in the neck. It's a game, but this was no game.

Soon, I would be one of those men with a family and children to feed. Maria and I were regularly writing letters to each other. It was the only way to communicate, since her family, like most Dominican families, had no telephone. That offseason another turning point in my life arrived. Maria and I got married in Santo Domingo, setting the stage for what would become my most tumultuous season in the Major Leagues, which I also believe set the stage for my eventual trade from the Giants.

7

Roberto Clemente

Orlando Cepeda did two monumental things for me: he was instrumental in turning me around as a Major League hitter, which affected the rest of my playing career, and he introduced me to Roberto Clemente, which affected the rest of my life.

Even in a cosmopolitan city like San Francisco, there was still a division between being black and being black Latino. It was slight, but it was there. The black players had places to go, and we had different places where we would gather.

One of those places for us was an apartment on Lombard Street where two older Puerto Rican women lived. They would have the Latino players over, like family, and Orlando Cepeda and José Pagán used to go there often. A few days after I arrived in San Francisco, the Pittsburgh Pirates were in town, and Cepeda wanted me to meet Clemente at a little gathering these older Latino women were having. I wasn't expecting much. Cepeda was my friend, and I could sense a strain between him and Clemente. The two of them had an intense rivalry—both being from Puerto Rico and both having competed against each in the Puerto Rican Winter League. Clemente played for the San Juan Senators and Cepeda for the Santurce Crabbers, which was a fierce rivalry not unlike the Giants and Dodgers—only in the same city. While there was a mutual respect, there was always that palpable tension between the two, born from their competitive fires.

The tiny apartment was filled with the scent of Latin food, rice and cod, as well as with Hispanic players from the Giants and Pirates. Among us all one player stood out—Clemente. His presence commanded the room. We started to talk, and before long that's all I was doing—talking to Clemente. Or maybe I should say—listening. Everything about Clemente radiated passion—his voice, his words, even his gestures. The way he was on the field was exactly the same way he was off the field. The early evening morphed into late evening, and still we were talking. I was so absorbed in what Clemente was saying that I didn't notice it was midnight and we were the only two guys left. Everyone else had gone either home or back to their hotel. There wasn't much talk about baseball. Instead, it was about race, culture, language, social issues, the disadvantaged, how the Latino ballplayers were treated by the American media, how Puerto Ricans were treated like second-class citizens in America. I was taken aback. I had no idea Clemente was so involved with the poor, the oppressed. It was incredible. That's when I became aware of Roberto Clemente the man.

A week later, we were in Pittsburgh. I just had that 3-for-4 game in Philadelphia, where I hit a single, double, and triple in my last three at-bats. In my first at-bat at Pittsburgh's Forbes Field, I homered over the scoreboard in left field, which meant that over two days and four consecutive at-bats, I hit for the cycle. In my next plate appearance, feeling good, feeling *en fuego*, I hit a screaming line drive to right field that had base hit plastered all over it. Out of nowhere the right fielder flashed into the scene, diving, outstretched, spearing the ball for an out. That's when I became aware of Roberto Clemente the ballplayer.

Clemente and I shared some of the same frustrations with Major League Baseball and the media. Because Latinos either didn't speak English or didn't speak the language very well, we were often made fun of. They would quote us verbatim, but they didn't do that with the American players. They cleaned up their quotes. I saw it as a lack of respect. It wasn't as if the media were trying to learn Spanish. Still, we tried to be helpful. We tried to communicate. We thought the media wanted information, not to make fun of us. Clemente and I often had discussions about the disparity, the double standard.

Like his personality, Clemente was exuberant and flamboyant

on the field. You noticed him immediately, and you didn't want to take your eyes off him. It was a joy watching him play, even if you were watching from the other dugout. This was especially true if he was roaming that vast right-field patch of real estate at Forbes Field, which stretched from 376 feet down the line to 462 in center field. Clemente knew every crook, corner, and cranny, every bounce and ricochet, and he commanded whatever was hit into his domain like a maestro directing an orchestra. He would field a ball and without looking turn and throw to a bag, putting it right there for the fielder. Perfect. He could play blindfolded, and he had a gun for an arm. Even watching him run was mesmerizing— long strides that looked disorganized, yet so fast. Clemente ran as if a pack of dogs were chasing him, all arms and legs. And his slide was spectacular. It wasn't a slide to hurt anyone, but it was aggressive. Nobody ever accused Roberto Clemente of not hustling. He was always overhustling.

What they did accuse him of was being a hypochondriac, of not playing hurt. I've learned through the years that as hard as it is to put yourself in another man's shoes, it's impossible to put yourself in another man's body. People don't know the kind of injuries and pain Clemente played through. He was in a serious auto accident in 1954 that left him with chronic back problems. He also suffered from bone chips, once had a deep thigh bruise that led to hemorrhaging, the lingering effects of malaria and insomnia—the list of physical ailments and setbacks was long. Yet he played. Whenever I hear it said that Clemente didn't play hurt, my response is, how did he accumulate 3,000 hits by the age of thirty-eight?

Not only was Clemente the first Latino—and the eleventh player all time—to log 3,000 hits, but he was also the first Latino inducted into the Hall of Fame. For all of us Latin American players, Roberto Clemente was our Jackie Robinson.

I never understood the media's criticism of Clemente, although in a way I did. He was a vocal defender of Latinos and militant about it. That got him a lot of criticism and even some enemies. But what I didn't understand is why the American media ask Spanish-speaking players to speak English and then make fun of them for attempting to do so. The media would routinely quote Clemente in his broken English, in his pidgin English, and do so literally. It infuriated him. As an example let's say Clemente said, "I got a hit." They would quote him phonetically and spell hit *h-e-e-t* in the newspaper to accentuate that his pronunciation of English words was off. For whatever reason there was always a jealousy of Clemente, from the media and even from some Latino ballplayers. And he was hypersensitive and a very proud man. It was not a good combination.

Today, Major League Baseball has the Roberto Clemente Award, voted by the fans and media, given annually to the player who "best exemplifies the game of baseball, sportsmanship, community involvement and the individual's contribution to his team." But Clemente's work in Latin America, much less in North America, wasn't heralded much when he was a player. I remember going into communities in Pittsburgh with him, listening to him counsel young men and women against premarital sex, out-of-wedlock pregnancy, and drug use. He did that and countless other things in America. Yet the media focused on his injuries, his broken English, and his flamboyant play, which they wrongly interpreted as Clemente being a hot dog and a showboat.

Like us Alou brothers, Clemente was aggressive at the plate, attacking pitches. I asked him once why he checked his swing so much, which he always managed to stop, and he told me, "I'm always swinging at the pitch."

As big as Clemente's talent was, the biggest thing about him was his heart. Roberto was not political. He was better than that. He was social. He inspired me on the social side of life, with his care for Latin America. This guy was incredible.

We used to talk quickly here and there during the season, and sometimes he drew me into social events. In the offseason, when he was in Puerto Rico and I was in the Dominican Republic, he was always involving me in charity events. During the 1972 offseason Clemente wanted me to play in charity games to benefit children that pitted Dominican Republic all-stars against Puerto Rican all-stars. He scheduled one game in the Dominican and another in Puerto Rico. I told him, "Roberto, I'll play in the game here in the Dominican, but I'm not going to Puerto Rico to play. I have a fishing trip planned. I cannot go." He pressured me to also play in Puerto Rico, but, if anything, I was about as stubborn as he was.

After we played the game in Santo Domingo, Roberto asked me if I could bring some of the other Dominican players to the airport for the trip to San Juan. It was the least I could do. Earlier that year, when I was playing for the New York Yankees, the great catcher Thurman Munson heard I was looking for a new car. Thurman knew people who could get him cars at Detroit's factory prices. He bought me a '72 Oldsmobile Toronado, paying $4,000 for it, and I paid him back and shipped the car home to the Dominican Republic. I loaded up a bunch of players in that Oldsmobile Toronado that Munson, a man who died seven years later in an airplane accident, had gotten me. When we arrived at the airport Roberto was waiting.

"Well," he said, "you're here at the airport, and we have a charter flight. You are going to San Juan with us."

"Roberto," I said, "I told you I have a fishing trip planned."

"Felipe, you have to come. You are the biggest attraction on the Dominican team. This is for charity."

Thinking that I could wriggle out of this by another means, I said, "I don't even have my papers with me. I can't go without documentation."

Roberto took me around the customs area, past security, and said to some people at the airport, "This is Felipe Alou." Somehow he bypassed customs and immigration and got me on that flight. Without even having a change of clothes, I stayed in Puerto Rico for two days and played in the game.

That was Roberto Clemente. He overwhelmed me with his character. His personality. His leadership. He was the man.

About a month later, on December 23, 1972, a catastrophic earthquake struck outside Managua, the capital city in Nicaragua, killing about ten thousand people and leaving an estimated quarter of a million people homeless. Clemente played in Managua in 1964, in the International Series, and developed a connection with the people. In fact, he was in Managua just a few weeks before the earthquake struck. He organized three flights with relief supplies—food, clothing, and medicine—but soon learned that corrupt officials were selling the supplies and profiting from them rather than giving them to the people in desperate need. So he decided to personally go on the fourth flight. Knowing Clemente, I know what he was thinking—that nobody would try to pull a fast one with the supplies if he was shepherding it to the people.

Eight days after the earthquake, on New Year's Eve, I was pulling my aluminum boat toward a fishing trip, listening to the radio. Through the crackle of static an announcer interrupted the program with the news that a plane carrying both relief supplies and Roberto Clemente crashed after takeoff into the Atlantic Ocean off the coast of Isla Verde, Puerto Rico. Only thirty-eight, Roberto Clemente was dead.

I pulled off to the side of the road and cried.

Beginning of the End

My second year with the San Francisco Giants was the beginning of the end, a year that reverberated with problems and controversies, the aftereffects of which rippled through the years. That's not what I see now, with the benefit of twenty-twenty hindsight; it's what I saw then.

Freshly married in the offseason, I arrived in Phoenix for spring training in 1959 with Maria, which was immediately met with resistance from the Giants' traveling secretary. Since Maria had no phone where she lived in the Dominican Republic, we spent the previous season writing letters. I didn't want to go through that again or go through the hassle and expense of international phone calls. Mostly, I simply wanted my wife with me, and I thought it was the right thing to do. The thought that it would get me in trouble had not crossed my mind.

But the Giants had scheduled me to room with other players, so they had to do some shuffling and didn't like that. They were also annoyed that I didn't given them any notice that I was bringing my wife. This all was compounded when Maria had the gall to cook in our room with an electric stove. Evidently, the smell of Caribbean food bothered some people—though not the Latinos. Juan Marichal was in camp that spring, still a year away from his Major League debut, and he would stop by to eat, enjoying the type of food he was used to eating back home in the Dominican Republic. Soon, though, the Giants moved Maria and me to a Mexican neighborhood in Phoenix. While Maria's cooking was a welcome visit to my taste buds, the way we were treated as a newly married couple left a bad taste. It was probably during that spring when Maria became pregnant, which also set the stage for another butting of heads with me and the Giants' management.

Baseball-wise, things were getting better. I was still a platoon player, but I was starting to put the puzzle pieces together that are necessary if you want to have a meaningful Major League career. It still amazes me that everything I did as a hitter, even early in my pro career, was self-taught. No wonder I had some holes in my swing. I was getting better with left-handed pitchers, given that I was seeing more of them than I had ever seen before. In fact, I got so proficient hitting against left-handers that over the course of my career, the best success I had happened to come against a left-handed pitcher. I think you've heard of him—Sandy Koufax.

I punished Koufax. And I don't mean that boastfully. I mean it with the utmost respect. Koufax, in addition to being one of the greatest ever, was also one of the nicest guys. At Candlestick Park the visiting team had to pass by the home-field dugout. Even when he was pitching Koufax would talk to us as he passed. He was a real gentleman. And then he would go out on the pitcher's mound and break your bats. So I have a lot of respect and reverence for Koufax. But I did punish him.

It's one of those beautiful baseball oddities that as a hitter, you can have enormous success against one of the greatest of all time and then struggle against a journeyman pitcher—and vice versa. I used to see the ball well off Koufax's hand, yet to me he had the best fastball and curveball in the game. How do you square that? The most home runs anyone ever hit off Koufax is seven, and only four players accomplished that feat—Hank Aaron, Frank Robinson, Ernie Banks, and me, Felipe Alou, the only non–Hall of Famer in the group. Once, I even hit two home runs in one game off Koufax. And here's the irony: after struggling early in my career with left-handers and fastballs, I guarantee you all seven of those home runs I hit off Koufax came on fastballs.

It took me a while, though, to figure out the inside fastball. Getting a steady diet of them combined with curveballs away almost ended my Major League career before it had a chance to even get going. Baseball is ruthless that way. Once your opponents decipher your weakness, they keep attacking it again and again, and I was getting eaten up by those inside fastballs. Coaches know strategy. But it's up to pitchers to execute that strategy. My best chance was when pitchers didn't execute.

Everything begins and ends with the fastball, so as a hitter you try to determine the quality of a pitcher's fastball early in his career and early in a game. You look for it on the on-deck circle, not only from the pitcher himself but also from how the hitter in the batter's box is handling it. We had to go by our eyes. Back in the 1960s we didn't have radar guns measuring the speed of pitches and posting it on scoreboards.

I remember when I was with the Atlanta Braves, I struggled in an at-bat against a young New York Mets pitcher. Hank Aaron, a student of the game, noticed.

"Felipe," he asked, "is this guy throwing hard, or were you late?"

"He's throwing *hard*!"

The pitcher was Nolan Ryan.

Orlando Cepeda was the first guy who helped me with adjusting to the inside fastball, and he helped me a lot. "Felipe, you're opening up too soon," he told me. "The way you're attacking a fastball gives you no juice."

Cepeda broke it down for me. "When a catcher has a 100 mph fastball coming at him, he *receives* it. Then the pitcher throws an 80 mph changeup, and he *receives* it the same way. Catchers wait for the pitch to get there, and their hands don't change. You need to be the same way as a hitter. Wait. Don't jump ahead. Good hitters, instead of going forward, go backward to wait for the ball. The hand is quicker than the eye. Trust your hands. If someone shoots a bullet for you to hit, you don't move forward to hit it, you stay back, and you have a better chance to hit it. You have to stay back to hit a baseball. Even if you don't have enough time, you'll still have enough time to dink it for a hit." It was invaluable advice.

And then I heard it again. We were at old Busch Stadium during a series in 1959, and once again I wasn't in the lineup. While I was walking across the field pregame, feeling dejected, the Cardinals' hitting coach, Harry Walker, saw me.

"Hey, kid. Come over here," he said. I was carrying my baseball bat, and Walker took it from my hands. "Kid, what a runner you are. You can really run. You have an arm. You have the ability to play the outfield . . ." He paused, looking down at my bat he was still holding in his hands. "Don't let this piece of wood take you out of the game. With all the athletic tools you have, don't let it take you out of the game. I wish I had the privilege to work with an athlete like you, to work with your hitting."

Then he told me the same thing Cepeda told me—to wait on the pitch and not open up too soon on the inside fastball. Now I had two people telling me the same thing, and I made sure to tell Cepeda about the conversation.

If that wasn't enough, there was one more person who reiterated the same message—Roberto Clemente. "Don't be afraid to be jammed," he told me, which I respected from Clemente because he didn't have the same power as Cepeda.

That offseason in winter ball I purposely positioned myself closer to the plate to get used to seeing inside fastballs, forcing myself to employ the techniques and tips I was learning. I hit .359, which gave me a lot of confidence that I carried into the next season.

It was a process and it took a while. On the big-league level, it especially clicked for me on September 3, 1960, in a nationally televised Game of the Week showcase against the Los Angeles Dodgers. Once again, the pitcher was hammering me with fastballs, jamming me inside. I turned on one of them in the fourth inning and crushed a home run. As I rounded third base I glared into the dugout and at Dodger manager Walter Alston. "Keep pitching me inside!" I yelled.

We won that game, 1–0. And by the way, the pitcher I hit that home run off of was Sandy Koufax—the first of the seven I connected on him.

After that the Dodgers and other teams started pitching me as they would a real hitter—in and out, elevating, changing speeds. I knew then that I had earned respect.

Respect from the Giants was a different matter. I was playing well in 1959, starting and batting leadoff more and more. Maria was now about five months pregnant, and I had a doctor's appointment with her on July 30. I told our manager, Bill Rigney, about it and that I would be a little late to pregame warm-ups. Since I didn't have a car or know how to drive yet, I took Maria on municipal buses to her doctor's appointment and then got to Candlestick Park just as the guys were coming in from taking infield. I went to my locker and saw the name of one of my old teammates from the Phoenix Giants there—José Pagán. I looked at Andre Rodgers's locker, and the name of my old roommate from Phoenix was there—Willie McCovey. Several feet away Rodgers was sitting at an empty locker with his head hanging low.

Eddie Logan, the clubhouse man, was at my shoulder. "The manager wants to talk to you," he said.

I still hadn't put it all together. I walked into Bill Rigney's office. He was sitting there, his hat still on, as I stood near his desk. "Philip," he said. Rigney never called me by my name, Felipe. It was always Philip, which always annoyed me. "Philip, I'm sorry to tell you this, but we're sending you to Phoenix."

The words were not even out of his mouth when I thundered back: "I am not going to Phoenix!"

I could see it set Rigney back for a few seconds. Finally, he recuperated. "You're not going? What are you going to do?"

Though I was a little slow at first, it was all clear to me now. The Giants were bringing up two dark-skinned players in Pagán and McCovey, so two dark-skinned players had to be sent down—Rodgers, a Bahamian, and me. Was there a specific quota? I don't know, but that was the suspicion with a lot of us Latino players. What I did know is that I was playing well and didn't deserve to be sent down. And I wasn't going to go.

"I'm going home to the Dominican Republic," I said.

I could see in Rigney's eyes that he knew I wasn't bluffing. "Tell what you're telling me to Horace Stoneham," he said, referring to the team owner. A phone call revealed that Stoneham wasn't around, but his nephew and team vice president and general manager Chub Feeney was. It didn't matter who I talked to. I was hot.

I got up to Feeney's office so quickly that he was still talking to Rigney on the phone when I walked in. He cut the conversation short and hung up the phone.

"Are you going to the Dominican?" he asked.

"Yeah."

"What are you going to do?"

"I'm playing well," I said. "I'm hitting close to .280. There are a bunch of guys hitting about .240. Send one of them down. My wife is pregnant. It's 115 degrees in Phoenix. I'm not going to Phoenix now. I'll go next season. I'll spend all of next season there if you want me to. But I'm not going now."

"Can't you send her home and you go to Phoenix?" Feeney asked.

"No, sir."

"What are you going to do in the Dominican?"

"I really don't know, but what I do know for sure is that I'm going."

Laughing, Feeney said, "What are you going to do, cut sugarcane?"

"I don't know," I snapped back. "But if I do, I'm going to be the best sugarcane cutter on the island."

I reiterated to him that my wife was pregnant and I didn't want her in 115-degree weather. If they wanted me in Phoenix, I would spend all of next season there. Just not now. Not under these circumstances. Feeney wouldn't budge and neither would I, so I left.

I had no money to pay the clubhouse guy, which is customary for ballplayers to do, so I went to the United California Bank on Montgomery Street, where I had an account. I withdrew all my money, about $300, and closed my account. All the while I kept asking myself, *Felipe, what have you done? Felipe, what have you done?* I took a bus back to the stadium, paid the clubbie, and went to our apartment. Maria was obviously shocked to see me. The game was on, with Willie McCovey on his way to going 4 for 4 with two triples in his Major League debut. I paid the landlord and told her I was leaving, explaining to her that the Giants wanted me to go to the Minor Leagues and I wasn't going. That's when Maria heard what was going on, that we were going home, and I could see she was happy. The landlord called a cab for us, and it arrived at our apartment complex at the same time as our clubbie, Eddie Logan, did. The Giants sent him to see if this crazy kid was really going to leave. He was sitting in a truck, parked behind the cab, I guess spying on me.

"Hey, Eddie, tell them I'm leaving," I shouted, before pointing to the car in front of him. "And by the way, that is my cab."

Anybody who knows me knows that when I say something, I'm going to do it. In my mind I was going back to school and become a doctor.

Our flight was at 10:20 p.m., and Maria and I got to the airport at 3 p.m. We already had tickets because it was mandatory then, if you came to the United States from another country, to have a return ticket. We took an American Airlines flight, a propeller plane, to Denver and then headed to New York, arriving the next morning. During a four-hour layover in New York before catching our Pan Am flight, a man came looking around and then looking at me. I was the only black person at the gate.

"Are you Felipe Alou?" he asked.

I nodded.

"I'm a scout for the Giants," he said, "and they want you to go back today."

"Tell them I'm going home," I said.

He tried to talk me out of it, but he could see from my determination that it was a waste of time.

The Giants must have called Rabbit Martínez, my old university coach who was their scout, because he was waiting for me at the airport in Santo Domingo. He took me to my parents. Just as Maria was the day before at our apartment, my parents were shocked to see me, especially my dad. Only two years earlier, after hitting .380 in Cocoa, Florida, and also being named the Winter League Rookie of the Year in the Dominican Republic, I proudly announced to him, "I am going to be in this business for a long time."

There were some long conversations with Martínez, at times

heated. He finally convinced me to go back. He told me the Giants were going to retire Hank Sauer and make him a hitting coach, opening a spot for me on the roster.

I know that might sound cold, that because of me, Hank Sauer, the 1952 National League Most Valuable Player (MVP), saw his playing career come to an end. But Hank Sauer was forty-two years old, occupying the bench on a regular basis. Into August he had all of fifteen at-bats that season, with only one hit—a home run. Hank, to his credit, was good about it. Until the day he died in 2001, whenever Hank would see me he would always kiddingly say, "You retired me and made me a coach."

Of course, he knew it was time to retire, and so did the Giants. Why that wasn't the original decision was obvious to me. In 1959 America no team in Major League Baseball, including the San Francisco Giants, wanted to field too many black and Latino players. At least the Giants were ahead of the curve with the amount they did have on the roster. After all, it wasn't until 1959, twelve full years after Jackie Robinson broke the color barrier, that the Boston Red Sox had their first black player—Pumpsie Green.

Coincidentally, the day I left the team was the day before the Pittsburgh Pirates came into San Francisco for a three-game series. With the Pirates, of course, was Roberto Clemente, with whom I enjoyed such long and deep conversations concerning the unfair treatment of blacks and Latinos. I returned to San Francisco in time for the last game of the three-game series, already in progress. I hit a pinch-hit single to, of all people, Clemente in right field. It scored the tying run from third, and we ended up winning, 5–3.

Getting that hit was a brief respite from the tension that now existed between me and the front office and Bill Rigney, whose disdain for me was palpable. After that incident, I was relegated mostly to the bench, batting only seventy-one times in the last sixty games, typically as a pinch-hitter, which I wasn't very good at. I never felt secure. I felt as if I was under a sentence.

We, just the Latinos, talked about it, what had happened and how it looked as though there was a quota system. The conversations didn't linger, but my feelings did. I was convinced the Giants were going to do one of two things with me—send me to the Minor Leagues permanently or trade me. I knew they wouldn't release me, but they could bury me. Somehow, some way, I was going to pay the price for having left the ball club and flying home to the Dominican Republic. I was black and Latino and I had played with fire, and I knew it.

Dawn of a Decade

Much has been said, written, and studied about the dawn of the decade that was the '60s and the seismic changes it brought. Perhaps a prescient speech delivered during that summer's 1960 Democratic National Convention best summed up the earthquake and subsequent tremors about to hit America. "Today, our concern must be with the future," a young charismatic speaker said. "For the world is changing. The old era is ending. The old ways will not do."

More than a half century later, those words from John F. Kennedy ring louder and truer than they did then.

The world was changing, America was changing, my country was about to change in a big way, and change was coming to Major League Baseball. The Latino influx and its prevalent and pervasive influence were coming and coming on strong. Six Latinos landed on the Giants' roster by 1960—me, Orlando Cepeda, José Pagán, Ramón Monzant, and two newcomers: Juan Marichal and my brother Matty Alou.

And more were coming, not only to the Giants but to other organizations as well. In 1960 one of my other brothers, Jesús Alou, was working his way up the Giants' Minor League system. He played the year before for the Hastings Giants, a Class D team in Nebraska—as a pitcher. Then one day Jesús, perhaps with the type of defiance his older brother was already exhibiting, announced he was no longer a pitcher but would be a hitter. It was a smart move, and I doubt anybody resisted him. Jesús pitched five innings for the Hastings Giants that season and was torched for 8 hits to go with 12 walks and 11 earned runs. His earned run average (ERA) was an ugly and inauspicious 19.80. He did get 3 at-bats that season, bang-ing 2 hits. So Jesús knew what he was doing, switching from the pitcher's mound to the batter's box.

In 1960 a Latino also led an MLB team to the World Series title, hitting .314 with 94 RBI during the regular season and then .310 in the Fall Classic. That player was Roberto Clemente. Yet two of his white teammates finished one-two in the National League MVP voting—Dick Groat and Don Hoak. Clemente finished eighth. Groat, an average-fielding shortstop, did lead the league with a .325 batting average, but he hit only 2 home runs and recorded 50 RBI. Hoak batted .282 with 16 home runs and 79 RBI. Even Lindy McDaniel, with his 12-4 record pitching for the St. Louis Cardinals, finished ahead of Clemente in the MVP voting, coming in at the fifth spot, three higher than Roberto.

You could deny awards and accolades, but you could not deny that our influence and at times our dominance in baseball were coming, and it was going to change the game. One year later, in 1961, Clemente became the first Latino to lead the National League in hitting, batting .351. In 1964 Clemente led all of Major League Baseball with a .339 batting average, and a Dominican, Rico Carty, with whom I later became teammates on the Atlanta Braves, finished second at .330. Third was Hank Aaron (.328), and fourth was a Cuban, Tony Oliva (.323).

Then there was the real breakthrough season, 1966, when these three players finished first, second, and third in hitting, leading not only the National League but all of Major League Baseball: Matty Alou, .342; Felipe Alou, .327; and Rico Carty, .326.

Never before, or since, have three Dominicans finished first, second, and third in a batting race. And when you also consider that finishing fourth through seventh that year were Dick Allen (.317), Roberto Clemente (.317), Frank Robinson (.316), and Willie Stargell (.315), it meant that MLB's top seven hitters that season were black.

The following year, in 1967, the NL's top three hitters were from three different Latin American countries: Roberto Clemente, Puerto Rico, .357; Tony Gonzalez, Cuba, .339; and Matty Alou, Dominican Republic, .338.

It was Harry Walker and Clemente who helped make Matty the great hitter he became. When Matty joined the Pirates in a December 1, 1965, trade at the age of twenty-eight, Walker and Clemente took him under their wing. Walker was the Pirates' manager, and he encouraged Clemente to be more of a leader. So he was, especially with Matty, who tried to be a home run hitter with the Giants. It never worked. Matty was small and light—about 160 pounds—with a short, compact swing. In his six seasons of attempting to hit home runs for the Giants, he had all of 12—total. Walker and Clemente worked with Matty day after day that first spring training, gradually transforming him into a line-drive hitter who sprayed the ball to all fields. Walker tirelessly pitched batting practice to Matty while making him swing with a heavier 38-ounce bat, forcing him to hit down on the ball instead of trying to elevate. All of it helped him become a great line-drive hitter.

The result was that .342 Major League–leading batting average, which was 111 points higher than what he had registered the previous year with the Giants. He also batted over .300 six more times during the next seven seasons. The only time he failed to hit better than .300 during that stretch, he registered a .297 batting average.

In typical aggressive Alou fashion, Matty attacked pitches. Critics called him a wild swinger. I was asked about that for an *Ebony* magazine article after the 1967 season, to which I said, "He's the only wild hitter who hits .300 every year." *Seriously?* They were going to criticize Matty for being a so-called wild swinger? *Really?* In those four seasons after Clemente and Walker straightened him out, Matty had a stretch where he hit as follows:

1966: .342 (led MLB)

1967: .338 (third in MLB)

1968: .332 (second in MLB behind Pete Rose; I was third at .317)

1969: .331 (fourth in the NL, fifth in MLB)

But, yeah, people were criticizing him for being a wild swinger. Incredible.

Meanwhile, in 1960 I was still mostly a platoon player, still feeling entrenched in Bill Rigney's doghouse, still waiting for an opportunity to be an everyday contributor. As we approached the All-Star break, only two games over .500, a sportswriter asked Rigney about our struggling team. "Are you going to make any moves the second half?"

"I'm not making any moves," Rigney replied. "I don't have any players."

That didn't sit well for those of us who were sitting on the bench. For sure, it bothered me. Right after Rigney said that Jim Marshall, a first baseman, outfielder, and pinch hitter who was spending most of his time riding the bench, looked at me and a few other backups and asked, "Did you see what the skipper said in the paper?" It was a rhetorical question, no reply necessary.

Maybe our owner, Mr. Stoneham, heard, too. Because it wasn't long afterward that he fired Rigney and named Tom Sheehan the interim manager. Sheehan, sixty-six, was the scouting director and a former Minor League manager who pitched six nondescript seasons in the Major Leagues—one of which was a 1-16 campaign for the 1916 Philadelphia Athletics. Mostly, he was a buddy of Stoneham's.

A sportswriter asked Sheehan the same question. "Are you going to make any moves?"

"I'm going to find out what this kid Felipe Alou can do," Sheehan replied. "I'm going to play him every day."

And he did. McCovey was struggling, batting .247, so Sheehan benched him, moved Cepeda from left field to first base, and put me in left. In my first game under Sheehan, I got my first extra-base hit of the season, a double.

Things were progressing. I was an everyday player, married, soon to be a father . . . and also learning how to drive. Taking the municipal buses around the city was getting old. It was time to get behind the wheel. My brother Jesús used part of his $1,500 bonus when he signed in 1958 (five times more than what Matty got and $1,300 more than I did) and bought a car in 1959—a used red and white Chevrolet Impala. He drove that car everywhere in the Dominican. Even if we were only going three blocks, he would say, "Hey, let's drive." Sometimes the family would all climb in just to go for a ride.

It triggered in me the need for my own car. I bought a black Pontiac Catalina in San Francisco and had it shipped home through the Panama Canal. I did this before I even had a driver's license or knew how to drive. It was José Pagán who taught me, doing so on those hilly, narrow San Francisco streets. He would try to teach me on empty roadways, because I had a bad habit of slamming on the brakes whenever I saw a car coming in the other direction, even though the car would be in its proper lane with usually a divider between us. It always startled me nonetheless. Once when he was teaching me, Pagán's two boys—nicknamed Tony and Monchi—were in the backseat. Neither one of them was any older than four. Sure enough, a car came from the other direction, properly in its lane, but I panicked anyway, slamming on the brakes. Poor Tony and Monchi flew from the backseat, one of them over me and the other over Pagán, and banged into the windshield. That was it for the driving lesson. "Get out and let me drive," Pagán said.

I felt bad about it, but he was nice. "Felipe, you have to relax," he kept telling me. "You have to trust the other driver. You can't slam on the brakes every time you see another car."

Pagán was a great teacher, and the streets of San Francisco were a great textbook. But it still took me the entire season to learn how to drive.

It took me longer to learn how to tie a necktie. We had to dress respectfully before and after games—gray slacks, black blazer, white shirt, necktie, and a handkerchief. It was expensive to be a big leaguer. Cepeda used to tie my necktie for me, and I would usually not untie it. Instead, I would loop it on and off from my neck. Because of doing that, and relying on Cepeda, it took me years before I could tie my own necktie.

With Matty being a late-season call-up, me finally establishing myself as an everyday player, and Jesús working his way through the Minor Leagues, it took financial pressure off our family. I had already moved my parents and younger siblings from our fifteen-by-fifteen-foot home to a bigger home in the San Juan Bosco neighborhood in Santo Domingo—a more comfortable three-bedroom house with a refrigerator, running water, and electricity (more often than not). It got the family out of the darkness of the countryside into more light. Next door was the Caraval family, with some really pretty daughters. Our family introduced one of the girls, Alma, to Marichal. They eventually married and remain married to this day, with six beautiful children of their own—five daughters and a son.

Marichal was an integral part of the Latino movement in Major League Baseball. Of all the Latino players, it was Marichal whom *Sports Illustrated* chose to put on its August 9, 1965, cover, sporting that trademark high leg kick, with the headline "Latin Conquest of the Big Leagues."

The Giants called up Marichal in July of that 1960 season, about the same time I became an everyday player, and he exploded onto the scene. I knew him and knew of him, and I knew what to expect. Still, he opened a lot of eyes when, in his July 19 Major League debut against the Philadelphia Phillies, he took a no-hitter into the eighth inning—retiring the first nineteen big-league batters he ever faced—before Clay Dalrymple hit a single to center. Marichal finished with a one-hit shutout, recording twelve strikeouts in a 2–0 win.

It was only the beginning. By the end of the decade he won more games than any other pitcher in the '60s, notching 191 wins—27 more than Bob Gibson, 33 more than Don Drysdale, and 54 more than Sandy Koufax. While Clemente became the first Latino inducted into the Hall of Fame, Marichal became the first Latino pitcher—and the first Dominican—inducted.

I first became aware of Marichal when he was pitching for the Dominican Republic Air Force, by orders of the dictator Trujillo's son Ramfis, and he was an eye-opener even then. We played Winter League ball together, too. His older brother Gonzalo taught him how to play baseball, but Juan had God-given abilities nobody can teach—intelligence, balance, control, and toughness.

He was a long shot to make the big-league team at the start of the 1960 season, but an unfortunate incident in spring training ensured he would need more time in the Minor Leagues. Marichal was pitching batting practice without a screen, which was normal then, and he didn't put on an athletic cup because he had developed a rash. Big mistake. The first batter hit Juan's first pitch right back at him, a line drive that struck him square in the balls. I wince just recalling it. To this day Marichal says it's the worst pain he ever felt. He spent three days in the hospital, mostly with an ice bag on his swollen right testicle. The day the hospital released him the Giants sent him to their Minor League camp in Sanford, Florida.

It's a shame, because I thought Juan was good enough to make the team out of spring training. I wanted him with us, breaking bats. Instead, he got hit in the balls. By the time he did get to us he was eating up the Minor Leagues. He finished the 1960 season with us by going 6-2 with a 2.66 ERA.

During those early offseason years with the Giants, Marichal would come by our house in the Dominican and run with my brothers and me to stay in shape. He loved to run. We would fish and scuba dive together, too. One time when we were spearfishing out in that beautiful Caribbean Sea, Juan started hollering. He was in excruciating pain from a sudden leg cramp, probably from all that running, and was struggling to stay afloat. I swam over, grabbed him tightly, and dragged him back to the boat. He claims to this day that I saved his life.

Marichal was famous for his pitching style—that big, dramatic leg kick. Early in his career a sportswriter asked him about it, noting how it was similar to Warren Spahn, who threw the same way from the left side. "Oh, yes," Marichal said. "Warren Spahn throws just like me."

The way he said that—"Warren Spahn throws just like me"— provoked media criticism. Spahn was a legend who was winding down his Hall of Fame career. After that people started calling Marichal cocky. But I knew Juan and that was him—a very confident, in-your-face guy. Extremely competitive. He wasn't trying to put anyone down, especially Warren Spahn. He would say things like that out of his incredible confidence.

Sure enough, almost three years to the day after his one-hitter debut, Marichal and Spahn united for the most epic pitching battle I've ever seen and probably the greatest pitching duel the game has ever seen. Only Carl Hubbell, coincidentally thirty years to the day earlier, had a better individual pitching performance—throwing an eighteen-inning shutout for the New York Giants. But never before or since has there been a better duel than the one Marichal and Spahn put on display in a game between us and the Milwaukee Braves on July 2, 1963, at Candlestick Park. They both pitched a scoreless game into the sixteenth inning—Marichal high-kicking from the right side and Spahn high-kicking from the left side. Willie Mays finally ended it with a walk-off home run against Spahn to give us the 1–0 victory. Historians say Marichal threw 227 pitches to record his sixteen-inning shutout, while Spahn threw 201 pitches. Marichal yielded 8 hits and Spahn 9 (one of them to me, a two-out single in the bottom of the ninth).

Our manager, Alvin Dark, tried to take Marichal out in the ninth inning. Juan flatly refused. Pointing to Spahn on the mound, Marichal told Dark, "You see that man? He's forty-two years old. I'm twenty-five. There is no way I am coming out of this game as long as that old man is still pitching." Although Spahn was forty-two, he also hit the hardest ball off Marichal that game—a seventh-inning double off the right-field wall. It was the only extra-base hit Marichal yielded. Spahn was an outstanding hitter for a pitcher, finishing his career with thirty-five home runs. Dark tried again in the twelfth inning to relieve Marichal, but Juan stubbornly refused to come out. The tension in our dugout was now almost equal to the tension in the game. After our last out in the bottom of the fourteenth inning, Juan thought he saw a relief pitcher coming from the bullpen, and he quickly grabbed his cap and glove and ran to the mound.

After retiring the Braves in the top of the sixteenth inning, with the score still tied 0–0, Marichal lingered on the field near first base, waiting for Willie Mays to jog in from center field. He stopped Willie, threw his arm around his shoulder, and said, "Alvin Dark is mad at me. He's not going to let me pitch any longer."

Mays reassuringly patted Marichal's back and said, "Don't worry. I'm going to win this game for you."

One out into the bottom of the sixteenth inning, Mays hit the first pitch he saw from Spahn straight into the wind. The ball cleared the left-field wall for a home run. It was the only hit Mays recorded that night.

Author Jim Kaplan wrote a book about that game, appropriately titled *The Greatest Game Ever Pitched: Juan Marichal, Warren Spahn, and the Pitching Duel of the Century*. In it Kaplan quotes another Braves starting pitcher, Bob Sadowski, saying that after the game, Spahn was the last player to the clubhouse because of doing interviews. "When Spahn arrived," Sadowski said, "everyone stood, applauded, and lined up to shake his hand. If you didn't have tears in your eyes, you weren't nothing."

Seven future Hall of Famers played in that game—Juan Marichal, Warren Spahn, Willie Mays, Orlando Cepeda, Willie McCovey, Hank Aaron, and Eddie Mathews. Incredible. As a postscript, sitting in the stands at Candlestick Park was a twenty-eight-year-old Braves fan named Bud Selig. The former baseball commissioner still talks about that game. We all do.

The turning point for Marichal came after the 1961 season. Following that impressive start, when he went 6-2 with a 2.66 ERA in 1960, Marichal was so-so in 1961, going 13-10 with a 3.89 ERA, struggling against lefties. Afterward, he told me he was heading to the Dominican Republic to play in the Winter League and develop a pitch to get left-handed hitters out. And he did. Marichal basically invented his own screwball that he threw over the top. It looked like a curveball to left-handed hitters. He also developed pitches from other arm angles, sometimes even sidearm without that high leg kick. But it was inventing that screwball that helped elevate him to greatness.

"Compadre, I got it," he told me one day. "I got the pitch for lefties." That's when he became a complete pitcher, going 18-11 in

1962 before rattling off six seasons of 20 wins or better over the next seven years.

We didn't play in the Winter League in the 1960 offseason. Instead, the Giants were asked to play a series of exhibition games in Japan. We started the road trip playing two games against U.S. soldiers on a military base in Honolulu, Hawaii, before flying to Tokyo, where we were greeted by dignitaries and kimono-clad girls. It was exotic, intoxicating, magical. I was playing well, feeling confident, looking forward to carrying my success overseas and my newly established role as an everyday player into the 1961 season. I felt like one of the guys.

We played a 7–7 tie exhibition game when Sheehan assembled us for news from back home. His stint as interim manager was over. The Giants had hired a permanent replacement—Alvin Dark. The news shocked me and maybe even shook me. Dark had never managed. At thirty-eight, Dark had just completed a season mostly playing in the infield for the Milwaukee Braves. We actually acquired him in a trade for Andre Rodgers. As a player, seven seasons of which were with the New York Giants (1950–56), Dark gained a reputation for being a hardworking, no-nonsense guy, with a desperate desire to win.

That was all well and good. What shook me is knowing he was from Lake Charles, Louisiana, and how it was his name I heard constantly when I came to America in 1956 and spent a miserable month in that southern city, enduring all sorts of racism before being told I had to leave because people of my skin color weren't allowed to play baseball alongside white men. Now I was hearing the name Alvin Dark again.

I knew more changes were coming.

And it had me worried.

10

Dark Days

I have a mind that is difficult to turn off. I've been told I overanalyze things. I'm sure that worked to my advantage later in my career as a manager, but as a man, and as a player on that 1961 San Francisco Giants team, I couldn't help but dwell on the fact I left the club two seasons earlier and that for the upcoming season our manager was a man from Lake Charles, Louisiana—the city where I first encountered the repulsive reality of racism.

I knew during spring training in 1961 that Matty was going to make the team and he was going to be a player. I also knew Jesús was coming and he too was going to be a player. With Willie Mays entrenched in center field, and rightfully so, and Harvey Kuenn in his prime, I knew there was going to be a logjam in the outfield and somebody was going to have to go. With my active mind working overtime, I reached the conclusion it would be me. When? I didn't know. But I knew it would be me.

My immediate concern was Alvin Dark, who wasted no time confirming my darkest thoughts, setting the tone almost from day one with the Latino players. As I recall there were eleven Latinos in spring training, five of whom made the team—Juan Marichal, Orlando Cepeda, José Pagán, Matty, and me. José Cardenal was there that spring, too, on his way to becoming a big leaguer, mostly with the Chicago Cubs, where he became the all-time most favorite player of a young girl there who would grow up to become Michelle Obama. One day, early in camp, Dark gathered us Latinos in short center field. His message—more like an edict—was short, but definitely not sweet.

"I don't want you guys speaking Spanish while in uniform," he said. "Some of the guys don't like it when you speak Spanish."

I didn't doubt that. There was a pecking order in baseball as well as in society. First-class citizens were the whites, second-class citizens were the blacks, and the third-class citizens were the Latinos. So I'm sure there were complaints from players—both white and black. But I believe it was mostly Alvin Dark, a rigid former marine with all his insecurities as a new thirty-nine-year-old manager. I believe it made him uncomfortable not knowing what we were saying, and it was obvious he was trying to enforce his authority. It was a ridiculous decree, and it angered us—especially Cepeda.

Cepeda pointed to Matty, who knew very little English. "How am I going to speak to him without speaking Spanish?" he demanded.

As he was saying this, I was thinking to myself, *How can I explain to my father that I can't talk to my own brother in Spanish?*

Cepeda was belligerent in his defiance, and the rest of us followed his lead. We started speaking in Spanish to each other right in front of Dark, doing so louder and louder, emboldened by our collective voices. And what we were saying—in Spanish—is that we were going to continue talking to each other in Spanish. We walked away from him, exaggeratingly speaking in our native tongue with ever-increasing mocking volume. We were never told not to speak Spanish with each other again. But the damage was done, a fissure created.

No slight went unnoticed, especially to Cepeda. He started noting that whenever Dark had a clubhouse meeting, he avoided the Latino players—unless he wanted to yell at us, which was often. Dark frequently questioned our desire, our effort, our mental capacity. After one game where I struck out three times, Dark said I didn't hustle, to which Cepeda opined, "I guess after you strike out, he wants you to slide into the dugout to break up a double play." Cepeda said this to me in Spanish, though his sarcasm could translate into any language.

There were other signs of tension. As he did the spring before, Marichal was pitching batting practice early in camp. One day the first guy in the batting group I was in was Eddie Bressoud, who was about to lose his starting shortstop job to José Pagán. Marichal broke Bressoud's bat with his first pitch. Walking away, Bressoud grumbled, "Those kids pitching in winter ball come in here and make us look bad. They should bring those kids in later." "Those kids" could have been rephrased as "those Latinos."

Bressoud was a good guy, though. He was mostly frustrated that Marichal broke his bat and likely concerned that he was losing his starting job. Alvin Dark, however, was more difficult to figure out— more complex. He was a devout Southern Baptist who would take me and other Latinos and blacks to church. Sometimes he would start workouts later on Sundays, so we could go to church first. He was extremely religious, a believer, yet he fell like many of us do. During the 1962 season, while married, Dark started seeing an attractive redheaded woman named Jackie. We first saw them together on a road trip in Chicago, riding an elevator toward his hotel room late one night. Dark eventually divorced his first wife and married Jackie, which is something he chronicles in his autobiography, calling himself a hypocrite.

Dark also had a bad temper, sometimes peppering his tantrums with profanity. His lack of knowledge with Latinos made his profanity dangerous. In America calling somebody a son of a bitch doesn't carry the same heat that it does in Latin America. Don't say anything about the mother to a Latino, because if you include the mother, you're going to be in trouble. If you call a Spanish player a son of a bitch, all hell is going to break loose. I feared that was going to happen with Dark and one of our Latino players.

One time Dark's temper really cost him—badly. It came in a June 26, 1961, game against the Philadelphia Phillies at Connie Mack Stadium. We lost 1–0, leaving twelve runners on base—nine in the last three innings. Losing ate at Dark. He abhorred losing. In the clubhouse afterward he heard a couple of guys joking and laughing, and it enraged him. He picked up a steel metal stool and flung it across the room. As the stool was on the fly, I could see blood dripping from it and the tip of Dark's little finger falling off. Dark grabbed his hand, and immediately there was blood all over his uniform.

Our pitching coach, Larry Jansen, his eyes wide with horror, pointed at the finger lying on the clubhouse floor. "Cap, Cap, look . . . ," Jansen said. Then he sat down, and I thought he was going to faint.

Dark lost the tip of that finger permanently, although our team trainer, Frank Bowman, preserved it with alcohol in a pickle jar.

We played the Phillies two days later in a rain-delayed affair, with the lead ebbing back and forth and the clock ticking toward 1 a.m., which was important because the city of Philadelphia had an ordinance stating that no inning could start after that time. In the fifteenth inning we scored three runs to take a 7–4 lead.

Mike McCormick was on the mound in relief of Jack Sanford, who had been a little wild, giving two runs back to the Phillies while leaving a runner on third. McCormick was one out away from nailing the game down when our catcher, Hobie Landrith, overthrew McCormick in tossing the ball back to the pitcher's mound. The ball skittered into center field, and the runner on third scampered home to tie the game at 7–7.

McCormick got the last out, but now it was past 1 a.m., meaning the game would end in a tie. It was the longest march back to the clubhouse. The hallway at Connie Mack Stadium was so narrow you had to walk in single file. We were like a line of condemned prisoners.

In the clubhouse Dark took some stomping steps, and I thought he was going to explode again or maybe call a team meeting. But he said and did nothing.

I heard Dark got better control of his temper in his later years, especially when he was managing the freewheeling Oakland A's to a World Series title in 1974. But with us it never seemed to get better, only worse. And it could be petty, almost personal. Dark forbade Cepeda from playing his Latin jazz music in the clubhouse, which was one thing. But then he tried to prevent Cepeda from taking his record player with him on road trips—which, for the sake of getting a good night's sleep, I would not have minded one bit. It wasn't right, though. Dark sent the clubhouse man, Eddie Logan, to Cepeda and told him not to bring his record player with him on a road trip we were about to embark on. Cepeda forcefully told Logan to tell Dark that if his record player couldn't go, he wasn't going either. That was the end of it. The record player, and Cepeda, went on the road trip—and I lost several more good nights of sleep.

Cepeda claims that Dark's bigotry fostered division in the clubhouse and cost the Giants a couple of pennants. I don't know about that. There is no doubt Dark mismanaged his power and that he struggled with managing people, but he did excel in managing—in the strategic part of the game. I know he made me a better ballplayer. I always say I graduated into a big leaguer under him.

It wasn't only Cepeda who noticed all the racial slights or became angry over them. He was just more inclined to want to turn those slights into a confrontation—physical, if necessary. Once when we were in Pittsburgh on a road trip, Cepeda and I went to a restaurant next door to our hotel. It was a Saturday night after a day game, and we were dressed in new suits we had purchased from a Jewish tailor in Philadelphia whom many players patronized. Walking into the restaurant we asked for a table for two.

"We don't serve Negroes here," the headwaiter at the door said.

"That's okay," Cepeda replied, "because we don't eat them."

When Cepeda and I started talking to each other in Spanish, the man, thinking he had mistaken our intentions, added, "You looking for a job? We have nothing for you. If you're looking to wash dishes, you might try the restaurant down the street." Cepeda was hot, and he wanted to retaliate and fight. Instead, we went back to the hotel and ordered room service.

Sometimes—oftentimes, really—the racism was *that* overt. Other times it was subtle. And then there were the times when it appeared to be there, but really wasn't. I felt that way many years later with Al Campanis. In 1987, on the fortieth anniversary of Jackie Robinson breaking the color barrier, Campanis was a guest on the ABC News program *Nightline*, hosted by Ted Koppel. Koppel asked Campanis why there had been so few black managers and no black general managers. Regrettably, but not reprehensibly, Campanis replied that blacks "may not have the necessities" to be a field manager or general manager.

I say "not reprehensibly" because I knew Al Campanis, and I knew he was not a racist. And if anything, I had every reason *not* to like him. Campanis, who played alongside Jackie Robinson with the Montreal Royals, was once a superscout and topflight manager in Latin America. Known as a keen evaluator of talent, he discovered and signed Roberto Clemente as well as Sandy Koufax and Tommy Davis. After I hit .380 in the Florida State League in 1956, Campanis was asked that offseason when he was in the Dominican Republic for the Winter League why he didn't sign me to the Brooklyn Dodgers.

"We believe this guy is just a Double-A player," he said.

When he said that, I really hesitated. It damaged my confidence. For him to condemn me like that . . . well, it took me a while to recuperate from that dictate from Al Campanis. So I had good reason not to like him. Instead, through the years I came to really like him, admire him, and respect him.

I observed him a lot in the Dominican Republic—how he would mingle with people, eat with people. He would be in the boondocks, where nobody would ever know how he acted, and he was always one of the people. In my country, to a man, we knew Al Campanis was not a racist. So when he said those things on *Nightline*, it shocked me. It also broke my heart. Sure, the statement he made was wrong. Nobody would deny that. But being wrong did not make him a racist. Campanis also said I was nothing more than a Double-A player, and he was wrong about that, too.

Alvin Dark, on the other hand, was a racist. I believe his racism was part of what led the Giants to trade me after the 1963 season, when I finally challenged him on being a bigot. It eventually caught up with Dark in 1964, when he was infamously quoted in New York's *Newsday* as saying this about blacks and Latinos: "We have trouble because we have so many Negro and Spanish-speaking ballplayers on this team. They are just not able to perform up to the white ballplayers when it comes to mental alertness. You can't make most

Negro and Spanish players have the pride in their team that you can get from white players."

It would be Dark's last season managing the Giants. He was fired, not because of the bigoted quotes attached to him but because of his affair with Jackie. Still, it was the comments he made to *Newsday* that shadowed him all the way to his grave. That's a shame, because during his lifetime Alvin Dark changed. He was a racist, but he did not die a racist. One by one, through the years, he apologized to me and others—even Cepeda—for the things he had said and done. He became a different man, better.

In Phoenix in the spring of 1987, we had an old-timers' event celebrating the 1962 World Series. Dark was there, and he individually pulled several of us black and Latino former players aside and apologized for how he had treated us. When he and I talked I could see the sincerity in his eyes and hear his heart speaking in his words. It was legitimate. There was no doubt about that. He was sorry. Alvin wasn't an old man then, but he was sixty-five, with many more yesterdays than he had tomorrows. I'm sure he was reflecting on his life, and I believe he didn't want to die with the things he had said and done as a young man still on his account.

If we're honest, we're all probably prone to be prejudice. I know that even before I met him, I already had negative thoughts when Alvin Dark was announced as our manager. In my mind he was a racist until he proved otherwise—and unfortunately he didn't, not in the time I played for him. But the way he changed and comported himself later in life allowed my mind to turn off those thoughts and my heart to open up. He became a good man, the Christian man he always aspired to be. Several months before he died at age ninety-two, I spent some meaningful time with him at his home, and he again touched me deeply with the words he said and the regrets he still carried.

Today, my feelings for Alvin Dark are only tender.

11

Death of a Dictator

I wish I could say that the most unsettling thing that happened in 1961 was Alvin Dark's arrival. But it wasn't. Instead, what shook me the most was the thunderclap news that arrived on May 30. Rafael Leónidas Trujillo Molina—a.k.a. the dictator—was dead, assassinated outside Santo Domingo when his blue 1957 Chevrolet Bel Air was ambushed with a hail of gunfire.

Inside, I rejoiced. Outwardly, I was stoic. I knew enough not to exult or comment publicly, aware that the arms of Trujillo were longer than the distance between Santo Domingo and San Francisco. Even from the grave, Trujillo could—and did—do damage.

We lost a doubleheader to the Cincinnati Reds at home that day. I kept my thoughts and emotions together enough to get 2 hits over 8 at-bats. Matty got 1 hit in 5 at-bats—a solo home run. Juan Marichal uncharacteristically, though understandably, lasted only four innings, surrendering 7 hits and 5 earned runs along with 2 walks. Marichal struggled a lot that season, going 13-10, so I can't 100 percent attribute his poor outing to being distracted by the news. But I feel comfortable in saying Trujillo's assassination left the three of us Dominicans shaken.

Not that our Cuban compadres throughout baseball were any less distracted. The botched Bay of Pigs invasion in Cuba, intended to assassinate Fidel Castro, arrived only forty-three days earlier—on April 17, 1961.

It was a scary time. I knew Trujillo's assassination would result in repercussions, with both the guilty and the innocent paying. But I never bargained that those repercussions would last years, evolving into a civil war and an unwelcome occupation of my country by the United States. Before it was over, the years of roiling turmoil would touch the life of even our youngest brother, Juan, perhaps altering a path that might have taken him to Major League Baseball as the fourth Alou brother.

Meanwhile, the immediate repercussions reverberated violently throughout our island. The next day I watched the Universal Newsreel report, which was a popular mode of communication then, often played at movie theaters. The short film screamed the headline ASSASSINATION! TRUJILLO KILLED: ARMY IN POWER.

The announcer reported the news this way: "A thirty-one-year reign of terror and bloodshed comes to an end in the Dominican Republic, as dictator Rafael Trujillo is shot down by seven assassins. His victims were numbered in the tens of thousands during his iron-fisted rule of the island nation, a rule that produced fabulous wealth for a few and the grimmest of poverty for the majority. He ruled by the gun and died by the gun. And now the scramble for power begins."

Although Trujillo is said to be responsible for tens of thousands of murders, it was the brutal killing of three beautiful women—the Mirabal sisters—that was the tipping point that led to his assassination. There were four sisters, who in lore came to be known as the Butterfly Sisters, and they openly opposed the dictator. In addition to their vocal opposition and distributing anti-Trujillo pamphlets, they also were involved in clandestine activities. On November 25, 1960, three of the sisters were returning from visiting their politically imprisoned husbands when Trujillo's henchmen intercepted them along a lonely rural road. The sisters and their driver were brutally clubbed to death in an open field. It is believed that perhaps one or more of them were raped. Their bludgeoned bodies were then placed back in their jeep, which was run off a mountain road into a ravine, attempting to make it look like an accident. Everyone knew better, and even in Trujillo's inner circle there was outrage. Six months later, Trujillo was gunned down.

Immediately after their father's assassination, two of Trujillo's sons—Leónidas Rhadamés Trujillo Martínez and Rafael Leónidas Trujillo Martínez—chartered an Air France jet and returned from where they were living in Paris. The more notorious of the two sons was Rafael, better known as Ramfis. Assuming power, Ramfis rounded up hundreds of people—essentially anyone who was even remotely assumed to be involved in the coup. Inhumane tortures and sadistic killings followed, indescribably hideous, some at the hands of Ramfis himself. Perhaps the most detailed account of that era is recorded by journalist Bernard Diederich in his book *Trujillo: The Death of the Dictator.*

Diederich recounts how one of the political plotters, Miguel Ángel Báez Díaz, was viciously tortured and kept naked with other prisoners—a ploy implemented to prevent them from using their clothes to hang themselves. For no apparent reason Báez was one day given a hearty meal to eat. When he thanked his jailers afterward, he was told that what he had just eaten was his son's flesh. Shocked, Báez hunched in the corner of his filthy cell. "You don't believe it?" the jailer chided. He then brought Báez the head of his son on a tray. Báez died on the spot of a heart attack.

In the hours and days after Trujillo's assassination, my mind raced back through the years. From the day of my birth he was the only ruler I knew in my country. I thought of my father, my godfather, and the other men in my town reading a newspaper under a handheld gas lamp, furtively discussing politics, their eyes darting, always worried about Trujillo's spies—the *caliéses* or SIM, which stood for Servicio de Inteligencia Militar, or Service Intelligence Military. People disappeared. One of those people was a second cousin, Raúl Rojas, a leftist who opposed the dictator. Raúl was a taxi driver, and he and his girlfriend and his car disappeared in the middle of the night—never to be found. We later heard some people say they saw a SIM vehicle stop him and his taxi on a highway next to the ocean.

I thought of my grandfather Mateo Alou, my mother's father, who worked for Trujillo as his gardener. He first came to Cuba from Spain. It was part of the family's lore that Mateo Alou fathered two chil-

dren in Cuba, Magaly and Martin Alou, who became famous sing-
ers. When I was a boy we used to listen to them sing on the radio.
My grandfather came to the Dominican Republic around 1900. After
Hurricane San Zenon—the fifth-deadliest Atlantic hurricane on
record—ravaged the island in 1930, he became Trujillo's gardener, the
caretaker in charge of a lush compound about a mile long and a half
mile wide. It had trees, gardens, animals . . . a real paradise. Many of
the trees my grandfather planted still sway in the Caribbean breeze.
I can still vividly see him riding to work on the back of a mule.

My dad wanted to name me Mateo, after him. "No, name him
Felipe, after your father," my grandfather insisted.

When the next son was born, my father told him, "Now I'm nam-
ing this one after you."

"No, no," my grandfather protested but with a smile. "That is a
bad-luck name."

"You're not bad luck," my father countered.

I thought about that on November 3, 2011, when my brother
Mateo "Matty" Rojas Alou died at seventy-two. Other than our
sister who died as a baby, Matty is the first and only one of us six
siblings to pass away.

So many memories. So many things your mind races back to when
your country's only ruler, the man your grandfather once worked
for, is assassinated.

I saw Trujillo several times from a distance and met him twice.
Once, as a schoolboy, I was in an Independence Day parade, known as
the 27th of February. It was mostly a military spectacle, with soldiers,
police, and students. We wore our school uniforms and marched like
soldiers along George Washington Avenue. The training took months.
As we passed Trujillo on the parade route, when we were about forty
feet from him, we were to turn toward him and bow our head.

I met him for the first time during the Winter League in 1956,
right after my first professional season in Cocoa, Florida. I was playing well enough to eventually be named the Winter League Rookie
of the Year. Trujillo would go to a ballgame once in a blue moon,
and he was there one day at the stadium named after him—Estadio

Trujillo. I was in my baseball uniform, about ten minutes before game time, when I heard my named called.

"Felipe Rojas!"

Soldiers came into the dugout with machine guns. I saw other plainclothes officers hovering nearby. I thought they were arresting me. "The *generalissimo* wants to see you."

As I walked up to the El Presidente Suite, my cleats scraping against the cement steps, fans saw me and started applauding. When I reached the suite Trujillo extended his hand. He was dressed impeccably in a white suit and black tie.

"*Lo Felicito*" (I congratulate you).

"*Gracias*" (Thank you).

He wished me well on my career, and that was it, a brief encounter, but that's all you need to look into a man's eyes, to measure his countenance, his bearing, his soul. I saw a man in charge of himself. Arrogant. He was put together. His face demonstrated power—good-looking, intelligent-looking, but with evil eyes. I felt my blood accelerating. I felt as if I were in the presence of a monster. I never have to wonder if I've seen the face of the devil. I believe I've already seen it.

That scene played out much the same way at a Winter League game two years later, with Trujillo once again wearing a white suit and black tie. He threw out the first pitch that day to Joe Pignatano, a catcher for the Los Angeles Dodgers. The only difference was that in 1958 I knew there were rumblings to kill him. He had spies—his *caliéses*—all over the city, killing people. You had to be careful.

Nothing about seeing Trujillo face-to-face surprised me. His mug was everywhere, after all. His picture hung in most every home—more out of fear rather than reverence—accompanied by the words *En esta casa Trujillo es el jefe* (In this house Trujillo is the boss). My dad never hung that picture in our home.

I saw and met his son Ramfis several times, too. I believe he was just as evil.

In the offseason we used to play exhibition games at the air force base in San Isidro. It was all in fun, the games pitting us in a tournament against teams from the navy, air force, army, and the police. One day, with a real tough sun hanging overhead, we were playing in front of Ramfis, the general, and the chief of staff. A ball was hit to center field, deep to the warning track. The poor outfielder couldn't pick up the ball from the sun. It hit him on the head and bounced over the fence. The impact dazed him, and our trainer, who was there from America, ran to aid him. Just when it appeared he would be fine, two soldiers materialized, each one grabbing him by the arm and ushering him off the field. The error evidently embarrassed Ramfis, and I heard later the center fielder was imprisoned. That's what life was like under the Trujillo regime—imprisoned for misjudging a fly ball.

Earlier in 1958 we were playing the Dodgers in a game at the Los Angeles Coliseum. There was a dark-haired man with a mustache in the box seats pregame. He was sitting with a beautiful woman, and I heard some American players mentioning her name—Kim Novak. She was an actress who was currently starring alongside James Stewart in the Alfred Hitchcock movie *Vertigo*. But I didn't know her and I didn't know the man, either. At least not initially. Besides, everyone was shooting glances at Kim Novak—not him.

A security guard approached me. "A man in the stands wants to talk with you," he said.

I ignored it, figuring the man was what ballplayers call a greenfly—someone who likes to buzz around players and bother you.

A little while later, I was told again this man wanted to talk to me. I looked at him, looked again at the dark hair and mustache, and I could tell he was Latino. Then it struck me. It was Trujillo's son Ramfis, who had been living life large—a jet-setting playboy dating starlets and residing mostly in Spain, France, and Italy.

When I went over and talked to him Ramfis told me he was having a party that night on his ship—the *La Fragata Presidente Trujillo*—and he wanted me to attend. "I'll send someone to pick you up," he said.

I told him the game was finishing late and that I had a curfew with the Giants.

"Do your best to come," he implored. "I've been telling people you'll be there."

I never made it.

News reports that said the party aboard the ship cost $10,000 in 1958 money reached the Dominican Republic. Given that most people were living in dismal poverty, it wasn't received well. Ramfis's dalliances with Hollywood starlets were also chronicled in a May 19, 1958, *Time* magazine article, which reported, "'A wonderful gentleman,' said Kim Novak, her hazel eyes wide and dreamy. 'A real good-will ambassador for his country. He likes hamburgers and so do I.' Zsa Zsa Gabor swooningly agreed: 'One of the finest men I've ever met.'" The article went on to say, "Such character references are not easy to earn, but Hollywood thought it knew how Lieut. General Rafael ('Ramfis') Trujillo Jr., 28, eldest son of the Dominican dictator, got them. At a Los Angeles foreign-car agency, where he bought a $12,000 Mercedes-Benz to replace his old Cadillac, Ramfis shipped off another $5,500 Mercedes to Zsa and an $8,500 model to Kim Novak."

I'm sure that didn't go over too well in my country, either.

The following year, at a Winter League game, Ramfis arrived and sat in the El Presidente Suite—again with Kim Novak. This time she was wearing a dress so short you could see her underwear. He didn't call for me, nor did I go to him.

Ramfis's attempts to secure control of the Dominican Republic eventually failed. Late in 1961 he went into exile in France, traveling there with his father's casket aboard the famed yacht *Angelita*. It is said the casket was lined with $4 million in cash, along with jewels and important documents. He settled in Spain, under the protection of another dictator—Generalissimo Francisco Franco.

Eight years after his father's assassination, while driving his Ferrari 330GT outside Madrid, Ramfis was critically injured in a car accident, dying of pneumonia eleven days later. It is said that his brother Rhadamés was executed by a Colombian drug cartel in a South American jungle sometime around 1994.

Violent ends for violent people. But it was the violence that occurred on May 30, 1961, when the dictator Rafael Trujillo was assassinated, that shook me the most.

12

The Road to the World Series

In spite of all the problems we had during Alvin Dark's inaugural season in 1961, I knew 1962 was going to be a good year for us. I knew we had a team strong enough to go to the World Series. It wasn't just that we had five future Hall of Famer players in Willie Mays, Willie McCovey, Orlando Cepeda, Juan Marichal, and a young pitcher up from the Minor Leagues named Gaylord Perry. We had other good players, too, and I would like to think Matty Alou and I were two of them. The 1961 season finally established me as an everyday player. I recorded a respectable .289 batting average, with 18 home runs and 52 RBI. Now I was ready for more.

One of the early repercussions from Rafael Trujillo's assassination was mounting civil unrest and mob violence in the Dominican Republic, which forced us to play a truncated Winter League season. I used that limited time wisely, purposely standing closer to the plate in my ongoing quest to conquer the inside fastball.

At spring training everything clicked, as if all the puzzle pieces finally fit. I recall that Dark played me in every game, which wasn't the normal thing to do, and I rewarded him with the best spring of my career, hitting .461.

"Felipe, are you tired?" Dark asked me one day.

"No," I said. "Keep playing me. I want to carry this into and through the regular season." And I did.

The stats might say that my 1966 season with the Atlanta Braves was better, but I believe 1962 was the best season I had in the big leagues—a .316 batting average, with 25 home runs and 98 RBI.

Whereas I used to be a leadoff hitter, Dark shuffled me all over the lineup, hitting first, second, third . . . everywhere but eighth. A sportswriter asked him about it one day. "How come you're using Felipe Alou everywhere?"

"Felipe Alou is a time bomb in the lineup," Dark replied. "He can surprise you anytime, anywhere in the lineup."

Boy, my chest puffed out after reading that in the newspaper. It really boosted my confidence. I felt great, as opposed to what Bill Rigney did two seasons earlier, when he told a sportswriter at the All-Star break that he wasn't making any changes with our struggling lineup because he didn't have anybody on the bench to turn to. I took that personally. I believed Rigney singled me out, that his comments were directed specifically at me.

It was a lesson I carried with me years later when I became a manager. I learned that when you're managing people, what you say to the media impacts a player—especially a young player. You can send messages through the media, but not destructive ones. You can say things like *We're not hitting* instead of *A couple of guys are not hitting*. If I'm struggling as a hitter, nobody has to tell me. It's everywhere—on TV, on the radio, in the newspaper. As managers we have to be careful that we don't aggravate the situation.

It probably helped that I wasn't giving Dark many opportunities to doubt me. I started the season with a twelve-game hitting streak that saw my batting average soar to .438 with 4 home runs and 14 RBI. One of those homers was a moon shot at Cincinnati's Crosley Field, where they had a large clock with the words OFFICIAL WATCH situated above the scoreboard in left field. My home run busted the *W* in that sign, which stood 50 feet off the ground and 328 feet from home plate. No wonder Dark said what he did about me: "Felipe Alou is a time bomb in the lineup."

That doesn't mean it was always smooth sailing with Dark. We lost one day to the Houston Colt .45s, a woeful expansion team that later became the Astros. Those early seasons in Houston, before the Astrodome was built, the Colt .45s played at old Colt Stadium, where it seemed as if all the mosquitoes in Texas flew in for the games. That night we suffered a bad loss to a bad team in a bad ballpark;

afterward Dark was in one of his dark moods. There was a spread of food on a clubhouse table—a postgame feature relatively new to baseball. In a spasm of startling rage, Dark jerked the tablecloth and knocked over the table, sending food everywhere.

Three thoughts raced through my mind. The spread was provided for us by this nice white couple, and to this day I wonder how they felt seeing all their hard work ruined by an immature fit of anger. I thought about how we had come to rely on the postgame clubhouse food—especially the black and Latino players, since it was still tricky finding restaurants that would serve us, especially late at night. Mostly, I thought about hungry and starving people, like those in my Dominican Republic homeland.

The visiting clubhouse at Colt Stadium was makeshift, with a dirt floor, and after Dark sent the food flying I saw a boiled egg rolling along it. I picked it up, dusted off some dirt, and started eating it. Looking Dark square in the eyes, I said, "You're not supposed to throw food away. When people are starving, you don't throw food away." The room fell silent. It was tense. But I made a statement I thought needed to be made.

Because we were winning, and winning a lot, the problems that season were few and the mood mostly upbeat. In the Bible it says love covers a multitude of sins. Well, in a big-league clubhouse, winning covers a multitude of problems.

Speaking of the Bible, I was delving deeper into my faith. I had already connected with the Fellowship of Christian Athletes, and now I had fallen in with a man who introduced me to the Pocket Testament League. I was speaking in churches and prisons and working in the offseason with missionaries in Latin American countries.

I was a young father, too. My firstborn, Felipe, was a baby, with Maria, José, and Moisés soon to arrive.

That doesn't mean my teammates and I weren't prone to our own immaturities, typical of young men in their twenties thrown together to live, work, and travel on a day-to-day basis. We were ballplayers, full of machismo and short on experience, which is never a good combination.

One of the dumb things we were doing was playing chicken with our automobiles. We would climb in a couple of cars and race down Army Street—now called Cesar Chavez Street—toward the San Francisco Bay. Usually, the main culprits were Carlos Virgil (Ozzie's brother), José Pagán, and Juan Marichal, who enjoyed fast cars and speed. I never drove, but I foolishly rode along. They would race down Army Street straight for the bay, with neither driver wanting to give in and slow down. Only when it was imminent that we were going to die, or at the very least plunge into the bay, would they hit the brakes. A few times I would get out of the car after our wild ride, trying to calm my adrenaline rush, only to see that we had stopped only feet from the seawall. We felt invincible.

The cops, as they tend to be with professional athletes, were more fans than enforcers of the law. One time Marichal and I were riding to the airport, and we were late for our team flight to Los Angeles for a series against the Dodgers. Typical of Marichal, he was speeding, and it led to that dreaded sound of a police siren.

The officer recognized us. "You with the team?"

"Yes."

"Why are you driving so fast?"

Marichal explained that we were running late to the airport for our team flight. Fumbling for a U.S. driver's license he did not have, Marichal first handed the officer a lottery ticket and then his Dominican Republic driver's license.

"Don't worry. Don't look for it," the officer finally said. "I'm going to let you go because you're with the Giants. Go ahead and catch your flight." He might as well have also added, *And beat those Dodgers!*

Earlier in the season Marichal and I bought handguns in Houston—Marichal a Smith & Wesson revolver and I a Browning .380 pistol. We were planning to take them back with us to the Dominican Republic.

We were in Cincinnati on a road trip, and, common for teams at the time, the white players and coaches stayed on one floor and the blacks and Latinos on another floor. Marichal and I were rooming together, and Willie Mays, who always had his own room, was across the hall. Like a couple of big, fun-loving kids, Mays and Marichal would wrestle each other. The doors to our hotel rooms were open that day, sort of like a loose setting in a college dorm. Mays was straight across the hallway, waiting for room service to arrive, since he rarely ate out because of the crush of people who followed him.

He walked across the hallway into our room, wanting to wrestle. Marichal obliged, and they started to grapple—these two strong men, future Hall of Famers. After a struggle full of grunts, Marichal pinned Mays to our hotel room floor. Getting up, Mays wanted to wrestle again. They did, and this time Mays pinned Marichal. Getting up again, Marichal wanted to go a third time for a tiebreaker, but Mays wanted to stop. Marichal goaded him for another contest, but Mays refused.

Jokingly, Marichal picked up his Smith & Wesson off his bed and said, "You want to wrestle with this?"

"Put that thing away—don't play!" Mays said, his normally high-pitched voice an octave higher than usual.

Marichal later learned that there was a single bullet in one of the chambers. It was a sober reminder that even though we were young and having fun and feeling invincible, we still needed to be careful.

But that's the kind of team we had, guys who could joke and kid and even wrestle with each other. Given that we were a team with a mixture of whites, blacks, and Latinos, more so than any other big-league club at the time, we genuinely enjoyed each other and wanted to be around each other. We had what teams call chemistry. Again, winning helps create that closeness.

I didn't maintain the torrid pace I started the season with—there would be no challenges to becoming the first batter to hit better than .400 since Ted Williams in 1941—but I did go on a sizzling hot streak where I got nine hits in nine consecutive official at-bats.

The streak started in September, and by then I had made my first All-Star team. I wasn't the starting right fielder, however. That honor went to Roberto Clemente. But I did pinch-hit a sacrifice fly, knocking in one of our three runs in a 3–1 victory against the American League.

My streak started September 8, against the Chicago Cubs. I started 0 for 2 before pounding three straight singles. I would get six more consecutive hits—going 9 for 9—before recording an out. This is how the streak went:

September 8: I hit three singles versus the Cubs after going 0 for 2 at Candlestick Park.

September 9: I went 4 for 4, with a double and a home run to left field off Cubs pitcher Bob Anderson, who used to give me a lot of trouble. That night I spoke at a church in Palo Alto, about thirty-five miles from San Francisco. Some of my teammates didn't like that I was spending more and more time speaking at churches, thinking that I was taxing myself too much, but I didn't allow that to dissuade me. There were about two thousand people in attendance, and I didn't notice one particular face until after I was done speaking—Alvin Dark. When our eyes met he beamed one of the biggest smiles he ever gave me.

September 10: I went 2 for 2 with two walks against the Pittsburgh Pirates, again at Candlestick Park. Guys were now pitching around me, and I drew the walks from Harvey Haddix and Roy Face, the only walks they surrendered that day.

September 11: The Pirates started knuckleball pitcher Tom Sturdivant. I always hit knuckleballers and Sturdivant well, and by now I was seeing the ball like a grapefruit, so I felt confident. I should have known something was up, though, when I looked to the sky pregame and saw a buzzard circling overhead. My first at-bat, with a runner on second, I hit a rocket between third base and shortstop, probably the hardest-hit ball of the streak. Third baseman Dick Schofield lunged for the ball and was able to knock it down with his glove. It went straight to shortstop Dick Groat. Because the ball was hit so hard, Groat had time to barely throw me out at first base. Too bad, because in my other two at-bats I got a single and a home run off Sturdivant to boost my batting average to .327.

Then, as if in a finger snap, I sank into a slump. I went 0 for 4, 0 for 4, 0 for 3, 0 for 4, and 0 for 1 over the next five games, going from seeing the ball like a grapefruit to crying for a base hit. Finally, on day six of my drought, I got a single . . . off Tom Sturdivant. I was 0 for 17 at that point. My hitting streak and my hitting drought both ended against Tom Sturdivant. That's baseball.

I learned something from that experience, something I took with me when I became a coach and a manager. I learned that when you're hot and you're on base a lot, you get tired—especially if you're a hitter *and* a base runner, as I was. Baseball is a grind, and fatigue in general is an ongoing opponent. The day after my 9-for-9 hitting streak ended, Willie Mays collapsed from exhaustion in our dugout at Cincinnati's Crosley Field, with my brother Matty replacing him in center field. That's why I have the utmost respect for Pete Rose. I don't know what he took, and I don't care. All I know is that Pete Rose hit a lot, was on base a lot, and ran the bases a lot, and he was never tired.

They say that in baseball good pitching beats good hitting. I'm not so sure about that, because when you're hot as a hitter, it doesn't seem as if anybody can get you out. Mays had a saying: "When I'm not hitting, I don't hit nobody. But when I'm hitting, I hit anybody."

One of the hottest hitters in baseball that season was Frank Robinson. He batted .342 while leading the National League in runs scored (134) and doubles (51), along with what modern metrics have introduced to us—on-base percentage (.421), slugging (.624) and on-base plus slugging (1.045). Two other statistics from that season were also telling—Robinson led the league in intentional walks (16) and being hit by pitches (11).

Pregame on the same day Mays collapsed in our dugout, we were in Cincinnati for the start of a two-game series against the Reds, and I overheard Alvin Dark telling the pitchers and catchers how they were to handle Robinson, who was really doing damage against us and was notorious for defiantly crowding the plate. "Pitch him inside, hit him, walk him—but whatever you do, you're going to pitch him inside!" Dark said. Our pitcher was the veteran Billy Pierce, who was having a great season. First at-bat, first pitch, Pierce goes inside, and Robinson crushes it for a two-run homer. Third at-bat, first pitch, Pierce goes inside again, and Robinson hits a rocket for a solo homer. Three at-bats, two home runs.

"F—!" Pierce shouted as Robinson circled the bases. "I'm going to pitch him the way I want!"

He didn't get the chance. Thanks to Robinson's two bombs, Dark lifted Pierce after six innings, relieving him with Don Larsen. It was the first and only time I ever heard Pierce curse, so I knew he was upset. The game will do that to you.

As with hitters, who can go on hot streaks and then suddenly turn cold, the same happens with ball clubs. I was on that 9-for-9 hitting streak in the middle of a seven-game winning streak for our team, a stretch that also saw us go 16-3 over nineteen games. Then, in that inexplicable way that is baseball, we lost six straight.

On September 20, in the throes of that losing streak, we crossed paths with the Los Angeles Dodgers at our hotel in St. Louis. They had arrived from Milwaukee and had an off day, while we were finishing a two-game series against the Cardinals. We were playing poorly, and the Dodgers won eight of eleven games to build a four-game lead over us. With only nine games left in the season, I think most of us believed it was over. I'll admit I thought it was. A lot of us—including me—already sent our families home in preparation for the offseason.

To be successful you have to have chemistry and teamwork. A team can lose that without even knowing it. And we had lost it. Good players alone don't make a good team. If you don't have chemistry, teamwork, and togetherness, you're not going to win. We had it at the start of the season, but that desire got lost, and to this day I don't know why or how it happened. Little did we realize that our manager noticed it, and he was about to do something about it.

In the hotel lobby in St. Louis some of us ran into Dodgers relief pitcher Ron Perranoski, and he jokingly said to me, "You might as well go home to the Dominican Republic. We have this pennant race sewed up." Tommy Davis, a good guy and a great hitter for the Dodgers, echoed the same thought. "I guess we'll see you guys next year," he said. It was a friendship statement, not a dig. Not disrespectful. I don't know whether Perranoski's and Davis's words reached Alvin Dark's ears, but what I do know is we lost to the Cardinals in a walk-off that night and Dark called a team meeting the next day in Houston.

"Guys," he said, "we have a chance to win this."

I don't think anyone believed him. He added that we were also going to conduct team practices every day before our games. That didn't go over well. A lot of us thought it was a punishment.

At the first practice Orlando Cepeda showed up in one of those heavy workout jackets you wear early in spring training, when the weather is still cold. It was his way of showing up Dark. But Dark ignored him. Cepeda was complaining. I was complaining. We were all complaining. But Dark adamantly and ardently practiced us every day, imploring us that we could still win the pennant. It woke us up. We won six of our last nine games. Meanwhile, the Dodgers stumbled to a 2-7 finish.

It didn't help the Dodgers that Sandy Koufax was struggling with a vascular injury—numbness in his left pitching hand, particularly in his index finger, which left it cold and white. Koufax was 14-4 in July, with 209 strikeouts, when the Dodgers shut him down after he took his fifth loss on July 17—lasting only an inning against the Reds. They say he crushed an artery in his palm that season and at one point his index finger split open. These days you shut down a pitcher the rest of the season—especially someone of Koufax's stature. But the Dodgers brought Sandy back in September. He still wasn't right, finishing 14-7 after two more losses—one of them in a three-game playoff for the pennant and both of them ugly.

We were one game back going into the last game of the season. Dark had benched me the previous three games. He was playing Matty more, though, who rewarded him by going 14 for 27 in the six games he played in over the last eight days of the regular season. But now, in that regular-season finale, Dark benched both me *and* Cepeda. I had 97 RBI and Cepeda had 113 RBI and 34 home runs. Cepeda saw it as an insult, a slight, a slap in the face, but truthfully Cepeda struggled in September, batting .232 with only 3 extra-base hits—2 homers and 1 double. I believe sitting us was more a testament to our depth. How many managers could say they were able to bench one Hall of Famer (Orlando Cepeda) and start in his place another Hall of Famer (Willie McCovey)? And Dark's options in the outfield with me on the bench were Matty Alou and Harvey Kuenn, who had been the American League batting champ three seasons earlier, hitting .353. I'm a proponent of the designated hitter, and it sure would have been nice to have been able to DH someone like Cepeda, McCovey, or me.

Our lineup was good enough to beat Houston 2–1 in a day game at Candlestick Park, thanks to Willie Mays and the solo home run he hit in the eighth. We rushed to the clubhouse afterward, crowding around a radio to see what would happen with the Dodgers. It was gut-wrenching, a scoreless tie going into the eighth inning, with the Dodgers' Johnny Podres and the Cardinals' Curt Simmons throwing gems. Finally, St. Louis catcher Gene Oliver delivered an eighth-inning homer. The run held, giving the Cardinals a 1–0 victory and the Dodgers their fourth consecutive loss. The regular season was over, and we finished in a flat-footed tie with our archrival—both teams finishing 101-61. A three-game playoff would decide who was going to the World Series.

Pandemonium exploded in our clubhouse. Player after player went to Alvin Dark and hugged him. He believed in us, and he was right.

We didn't have too much time to celebrate, though. Game One of the three-game playoff was the next day. Thank goodness it was at home in Candlestick Park.

Historically, there has always been a simmering animosity between the Giants and the Dodgers, the rivalry having traveled the distance from New York to California. Earlier in the season, before a series against the Dodgers at Candlestick Park, Dark ordered the groundskeepers to speed up the infield by cutting the grass short and also slowing the base paths by watering them down—both designed to neutralize the Dodgers' vaunted speed. The Dodgers complained and retaliated by stealing our weighted practice bat. We returned the favor, stealing their weighted practice bat.

Now here we were again, with a three-game playoff destined to send one of us home and the other to the World Series. It was the same as eleven years earlier, in 1951, when it was the New York Giants and the Brooklyn Dodgers and Bobby Thompson hit the "Shot Heard 'Round the World"—a ninth-inning Game Three walk-off homer to win it for the Giants. Just as in 1951, the Dodgers held a substantial lead in the pennant race, only to have the Giants catch them. Would eleven years later provide a West Coast part-two déjà vu?

The Dodgers started Sandy Koufax, and it was clear from his first pitch this wasn't vintage Koufax. Even Sandy admitted that years later, saying, "I had nothing at all." He battled, though, tenacious, and that's when I really saw what kind of man he is. But the nasty bite wasn't there on his curveball, and his fastball had an uncharacteristic flatness to it, transforming it from overpowering to predictable. Still, Koufax got our first two hitters out in the first inning—Harvey Kuenn and Chuck Hiller. I came up with two outs and mashed a double to left field. Willie Mays followed with an opposite-field home run to put us up 2–0. Koufax then induced Cepeda to groundout unassisted to first base. In the second inning Jim Davenport greeted Koufax with another home run, followed by a line-drive single from Ed Bailey, and that was it. Koufax came out, and the Dodgers burned through five relievers the rest of the way. We won, 8–0, but I'll admit I felt sorry for Koufax. I think a lot of us did. Sandy was always such a gentleman.

Game Two was at Dodger Stadium, and on the way to Los Angeles the talk was that this was all business. No going out. No girlfriends. Everybody abided by the edict. The game turned into a bit of a slugfest. I got a couple of hits, including an RBI double off Don Drysdale that scored Cepeda. In all fifteen runs were scored. Unfortunately, only seven came from us in an 8–7 loss. The big blow was a bases-clearing, three-run double off the bat of Lee Walls. The ball rocketed over Willie Mays's head, and I thought for sure Willie would catch it. He didn't. Every once in a while moments like that would remind me that, as great as Willie was, he was still mortal.

Now it was down to the deciding Game Three, also at Dodger Stadium, with Juan Marichal going against Johnny Podres. We took a 2–0 lead in the third, but the Dodgers retaliated with a run in the fourth, two in the sixth, and another in the seventh to take a 4–2 lead.

It was that tack-on run in the seventh inning that especially bothered me, because of the way the Dodgers' third base coach, Leo Durocher, acted when they scored it. After Maury Wills lined a one-out single, he stole second. Then, with two outs, he took off for third. Catcher Ed Bailey's throw was wild, and as it got away from our third baseman, Jim Davenport, Wills raced home. That would have been bad enough, except that Durocher ran all the way down the line with him and slid as Wills slid home safely. Thinking they had the game won, Durocher got up laughing, like it was a show, a joke. I never wanted to win a game as badly as I did that game.

When I came off the field after the bottom of the eighth, with the score still 4–2, I went straight for the clubhouse and did something I've never done before or since—I prayed for us to win. I felt I needed a quick connection with Jehovah God, a few seconds to visit with him before going into combat.

I returned to the dugout just in time to see Matty lead off the ninth inning by lacing a line-drive single to right field. The inning produced another single, four walks (one by me), a wild pitch, an error . . . and four runs to give us a 6–4 lead. Historians had a field day with that, since it was also four ninth-inning runs the Giants scored in the 1951 playoff to give us a 5–4 victory against the Dodgers. In our case Billy Pierce came in to pitch a scoreless ninth inning to secure the win and the pennant.

I ran in from right field, jubilant, celebrating with my teammates. At the same time I caught sight of some of the Dodger players, forlorn, heads bowed, a few showing tears. As I did with Koufax, I felt sorry for them. For us, though, it was pandemonium again in the clubhouse. I found another quiet spot, this time in the shower area, and bowed in another prayer. I emerged to see someone offer Alvin Dark a paper cup filled with champagne.

"No, thanks," he said. "I don't need any help to be happy at a time like this."

He was right.

Coming together and winning as a team, accomplishing what we believed we were capable of doing when we were in spring training seven months earlier, was such a pure joy, and nothing artificial could add or subtract from that.

But more work in the form of the New York Yankees waited, as did their opening-game pitcher, Whitey Ford, who was riding a then record thirty-two-inning scoreless streak in the World Series. Anticipating after we beat Koufax that we would win the playoff series, the Yankees flew ahead to San Francisco. We, however, still had to travel back from Los Angeles. There were reports that fifty thousand fans were waiting for us at the airport, some of them blocking the airfield. Our pilot circled for an hour and twenty minutes before deciding to land at a maintenance depot a mile from our gate. The fans still found us, swarming our bus, smashing some windows in their raucous celebration. We didn't get home until about four in the morning.

Awaiting us several hours later were Whitey Ford, the New York Yankees, and Game One of the 1962 World Series.

13

1962 World Series

How do you go from the incredible high of beating your archrival in a three-game series to several hours later being ready to play Game One of a World Series? You don't. And we weren't.

To this day, if you wear a Giants uniform and you beat the Dodgers, there is a special sense of satisfaction—even if it's a spring training game. So after beating the Los Angeles Dodgers with that ninth-inning, come-from-behind rally, it felt as though we had already won the World Series. We sensed the fans felt that way, too. There was a buzz for Game One of the World Series at Candlestick Park. No question. But it wasn't the same buzz.

We were tired. Our energy—physically and emotionally—was down. Meanwhile, the New York Yankees were rested and eager. Our pitching staff was depleted, forcing us to start relief pitcher Billy O'Dell. The Yankees had Whitey Ford on the mound, riding the crest of thirty-two scoreless World Series innings.

Some of the other Latino players and I chatted before the game—in Spanish, of course—and we wondered what could be more exciting, more electric, than what we had just experienced against the Dodgers. I heard some of the other guys saying things like, "What more can we do?"

After seeing two future Hall of Famers in the playoff series—Sandy Koufax and Don Drysdale—we got our first look at another one in Whitey Ford. It was apparent from the first pitch that Ford, while not a hard thrower, was the type of pitcher who allowed you to get yourself out. Anything that looked like a strike was a ball, and anything that looked like a ball was a strike. He had a sinker, a changeup, and a big roundhouse curveball—a lot of movement with a lot of pinpoint control. His pitches headed straight for the strike zone and then, once you committed, faded away or dropped out. And Whitey never gave in. Even on a 3-0 count, when most pitchers give you a fastball, he would still make his pitch, and he would throw it on the black part of home plate.

Maybe that explains how, while we were able to get ten hits and draw two walks against Ford, we still managed only two runs. It didn't help that we had no pop in our bats—just one extra-base hit, a double from Chuck Hiller. The Yankees managed only one more hit, and only two extra-base hits, but they also worked five walks against our pitchers.

Things might've been different had I gotten to one of those extra-base hits. In the first inning, sandwiched between striking out lead-off hitter Tony Kubek and cleanup hitter Mickey Mantle, O'Dell surrendered a pair of singles to Bobby Richardson and Tom Tresh. With two outs and runners on first and second, Roger Maris smashed a long fly ball to right field. I chased it to the warning track, leaped . . . and felt it graze off my glove as both the ball and I fell to the ground. I think I might have saved it from being a home run, but the hit still did damage. With the runners going on two outs, both easily scored, while Maris pulled into second for a double.

I did save us some possible calamity in the third inning when I made a diving catch on a sinking fly ball off the bat of Tresh. We also battled back with runs in the second and third—I contributed a single in the middle of our third-inning rally—to knot the game at 2–2. But the Yankees scored four runs in the last four innings to win 6–2.

In Game Two I felt we were up for business. I believe there was a realization that if we played the way we played against the Dodgers, we could win this thing. We had Jack Sanford going in Game Two and Juan Marichal scheduled for Game Four. We thought we had better pitching. But we didn't know about Ralph Terry, although we should have. Terry was an average pitcher before the '62 season, with a Major League record of 48-49. His claim to fame was surrendering Bill Mazeroski's walk-off World Series–winning home run for the Pittsburgh Pirates two years earlier, in 1960. But he had his best season in '62, winning a league-leading twenty-three games, and for my money he was the best pitcher for the Yankees in that World Series. Evidently, others agreed with me, as he became the World Series MVP.

Terry limited us to five hits and two runs over seven innings in Game Two, but thankfully Sanford pitched a three-hit shutout to give us a 2–0 victory, tying us at a game apiece with a day off and the Series heading to New York.

After getting a hit in each of the first two games, I went hitless in Game Three. Bill Stafford had a tough sinker and a slider away, and I couldn't get a pitch to hit all day. I did make a leaping catch to rob Elston Howard of an extra-base hit. We still lost 3–2, our pair of runs coming on Ed Bailey's two-run homer in the ninth inning, scoring him and Willie Mays, who led off the inning with a double.

I don't know why, but it was during Game Three that I got reflective. Kids today in the Dominican Republic dream and strive for the World Series. But I never did growing up. My field had no dreams— only lemons and limes and coconuts and makeshift mitts and playing purely for fun. I believe God puts you in positions, and I was thankful for that, thankful for where I was. But it struck me that only seven years earlier I was studying to be a doctor at the University of Santo Domingo. That was my world. Now I was in the World Series.

Game Four had Marichal going for us . . . and then disaster struck. It was billed as a classic pitching duel—Marichal versus Ford. We were winning 2–0 going into the fifth inning. Tom Haller hit a one-out single, followed by another single from José Pagán. With runners on first and third and one out, Marichal, a decent hitter, stepped to the plate.

Alvin Dark gave him the bunt sign, and Marichal squared before letting the pitch go by—ball one.

The bunt sign was on again, and again Marichal squared before letting the ball go by—ball two.

Now Marichal had the take sign—ball three.

Marichal faked a bunt—strike one.

Marichal faked a bunt again—strike two.

What followed was a strategic decision that we'll always scratch our heads about. With a 3-2 count, Dark signaled for a suicide squeeze, which meant Haller would be racing home and Marichal absolutely had to put the bat on the ball. It was a stupid call. We thought it was stupid then and still believe that today.

No doubt Dark thought Ford, on a 3-2 count, would deliver a cookie right down the middle. But that wasn't Whitey Ford. In retrospect, I believe Ford outsmarted Dark. One of the things that separate great pitchers from the rest of the pack is that great pitchers sense plays, and I'm convinced Whitey Ford sensed a suicide squeeze. He threw Marichal a nasty pitch, out of the strike zone—a pitch that dived into Marichal's ankles. There is no way a pitcher with Whitey Ford's control would miss the strike zone that badly. He had just thrown two pinpoint strikes. I believe he purposely threw down and in, impossible for Marichal to bunt. But with Haller racing in from third—and as a catcher he wasn't exactly a speedster—Marichal was forced to stab at the ball with his bat. The impact produced a loud *thwack!* It sounded like the ball hit all bat, but it hadn't. The baseball smashed Marichal's index finger so hard his fingernail fell off, and he was immediately removed from the game. Adding insult to injury, the ball went foul, which meant Marichal struck out.

Marichal has always said that up until then he was pitching the best game of his life—four shutout innings with four strikeouts, two of them against Mickey Mantle. We ended up winning 7–3, but we lost Marichal for the rest of the Series.

Because we sent our families home late in the regular season, anticipating that we wouldn't catch the Dodgers, Juan and I were living together in my apartment, driving together to the games at Candlestick Park. His disappointment was profound. Giants owner Horace Stoneham had some connections in Japan, and he had an herbal salve flown in overnight. They put it on Marichal's index finger and wrapped it, hoping for a miracle cure. They took it off several days later, before Game Seven, and it looked worse than when he first injured it.

For the time being, we were tied 2–2 in the World Series.

Game Five had to wait a day in New York because of a rainout. With an extra day's rest, Ralph Terry pitched another solid game, with Tom Tresh hitting a double, a home run, and a sacrifice fly to knock in three of the Yankees' five runs. I had a triple and a single, but we scored only three runs, losing 5–3. Down 3–2 in the Series, it brought us to the brink of elimination.

It would be four days before we played another game. After the rainout in New York, we returned to San Francisco for, of all things, what meteorologists say was one of the worst storms to hit the area in a century, claiming at least forty-six lives. The deluge was so severe that several names were attached to it: the "Columbus Day Storm of 1962," the "Big Blow," and "Typhoon Freda." For us, it was one huge rain delay, as it dumped almost five inches of water in the Bay Area, flooding streets and wreaking havoc. We ventured farther inland to get in some practice as we waited it out. When Game Six finally arrived, MLB tried to dry the field with hovering helicopters and by pouring gasoline on the infield and lighting it on fire. It helped some but not enough. We felt the sogginess beneath our feet the next two days.

As good as Whitey Ford is, he lasted only two outs into the fifth inning of Game Six. We tagged him for nine hits and five earned runs. I got two of those hits, knocking in a run and scoring another. We won 5–2, setting the stage for Game Seven.

We were hoping Marichal could start, and to this day we wonder what the result might've been had he not smashed his finger attempting an ill-advised suicide-squeeze bunt. I would occasionally ask him how it felt, and his reply was always glumly the same: "It hurts."

Because of losing three days to an epic rainstorm, we had to face Mr. Ralph Terry again, and once again he was on top of his craft, carrying a perfect game into the sixth inning, until our pitcher Jack Sanford broke it up with a single to center field. Sanford also pitched superbly, yielding only a run through seven innings. Our main problem was that going into the ninth inning, we managed only a pair of hits and no runs.

Trailing 1–0, Matty led off the ninth with a perfect pinch-hit drag bunt between the first and second basemen. I was up next and received the bunt sign. I hit twenty-five home runs and knocked in ninety-eight runs that season and had been asked to bunt maybe twice. Now I was bunting for the first time in the World Series. I squared and pushed a bunt down the first base line. It stayed fair for a bit, but the first baseman, Moose Skowron, let it roll foul. I blame the wind. But that's still no excuse. Even though I hardly bunted all year, you have to be ready to bunt in the World Series—and I wasn't ready. It still pains me that I didn't get that bunt down, and I consider it one of the lowest points of my professional career, something I'll take to my grave because I failed in that situation.

I got the hit-and-run sign before the next pitch, which came in high. With the infield charging, expecting a bunt, I fouled it straight back. I took a big roundhouse cut at the third pitch and missed. Strike three. That at-bat still haunts me. I failed to advance my brother with a bunt, and then I struck out. Little did I realize it would be the last pitch and the last at-bat I would ever have in a World Series.

Chuck Hiller followed with another strikeout. With two outs in the bottom of the ninth inning in Game Seven of the World Series, Willie Mays stepped to the plate, representing the winning run. Typical of Willie, he came through in the clutch, lining a pitch down the right-field line. "I was thinking home run," Mays said later.

Too bad he didn't hit one, because this is where I'm convinced the soggy field came into play. Under normal circumstances, maybe Mays's hit would've traveled all the way to the fence. But it didn't. Roger Maris cut it off and fired the ball to Bobby Richardson, who relayed it to the catcher, Elston Howard. The soggy field also slowed my brother, as it would any runner. Third base coach Whitey Lockman stopped Matty at third, and that's a good thing. I know there is controversy over whether Lockman should have sent Matty home, but he would've been out. To this day I can replay it all in my head, and to this day I still believe Matty would have been out.

I know that Willie Mays, who pulled into second base with a double, was disappointed. But he knows, too, that Matty would not have scored. Whenever we talk about that World Series, Willie tells me, "Chico, if you had been on first base, you would've scored." I believe that, too. I was faster than Matty, and I was taller, with longer strides. And if need be, there was going to be some damage at home plate.

Besides, holding Matty made sense because the next two batters were Willie McCovey and Orlando Cepeda. I can only imagine the uproar if Matty had been thrown out at the plate to end the World Series—with McCovey on deck and Cepeda in the hole.

I mention Cepeda being in the hole because we were convinced that the Yankees, with first base open, were going to intentionally walk McCovey. We couldn't believe it when we saw they were going to pitch to him. On top of that, even though Terry was in trouble, Yankees manager Ralph Houk didn't bring in a reliever. We were looking at each other in the dugout, saying out loud, "Can you believe they are going to pitch to McCovey?" We were *that* surprised.

Years later, when I played for the Yankees, I talked to both Ralph Terry and Ralph Houk. I saw Terry at an old-timers' game, and he told me he felt great all nine innings, that he was really on. He reminded me that the wind was blowing in from center field, which most pitchers like.

Houk brought up the topic of pitching to McCovey unsolicited, telling me how nervous he was. "I knew if he got a hit, I was going to be crucified," he said. "I was begging God that he would make an out." Houk reminded me that Cepeda banged three hits in Game Six, including a double off Whitey Ford. So walking McCovey and pitching to Cepeda with the bases loaded in a 1–0 game wasn't exactly an enviable alternative. I never even thought to ask if he considered bringing in a reliever, given that it was only two years removed from when Terry infamously served up that World Series walk-off home run ball to Bill Mazeroski.

Terry fired an inside fastball to McCovey, and he turned on it like a whip. When we heard the sound of the ball coming off the bat, all of us leaped to our feet. I believe it was the hardest-hit ball I've ever seen. A bullet. Richardson was playing deep at second base, right on the fringe of the outfield grass. I think the ball caught Bobby instead of the other way around. They say baseball is a game of inches, and it was certainly true on that hit. A few inches one way or another, and that ball was going for a hit, and maybe the way it was elevating, it could've been a home run. It was hit *that* hard.

I later thought about how throughout the Series, whenever one of us got on second base, Bobby Richardson would talk to us about Jesus Christ. He even came over to me once when I was on second and acknowledged that I was a believer, all while thumping his glove and readying himself for the next pitch.

After the game Alvin Dark addressed the team, but my mind was elsewhere. I remember hearing the word "proud" a couple of times. It was a hard loss. I still believe that had we won, the celebration and the sensation would not have topped what we felt from beating the Dodgers. But I sure would have liked the opportunity to compare.

The next day I was on a flight home to the Dominican Republic. Again, I wondered how this kid who grew up hitting lemons, limes, and coconuts, who never dreamed of playing baseball professionally, just played in the World Series. I started all seven games, made some solid fielding plays, and got seven hits in twenty-six at-bats. But it's that ninth-inning Game Seven strikeout that still shadows my thoughts.

It didn't occur to me at the time, but I realized later that I became the first man from the Dominican Republic to play in the World Series and the first to get a hit. My brother Matty Alou became the second Dominican to play in the World Series. And Juan Marichal was the third.

It was the twentieth world championship for the Yankees, but it would be another fifteen years before they would win another. For me, I never got back to the World Series—not as a player, coach, or manager.

14

The Alous Said Hello; the Giants Said Goodbye

The message arrived via telegram to my home in the Dominican Republic. I read it, feeling my face flush with anger before I crumpled it in a tight ball and threw it in the trash. Baseball commissioner Ford Frick fined me $250 for having the gall to play baseball games in my home country. I was livid, but not surprised.

There was a lot of post-Trujillo unrest in my country. And with Fidel Castro now in control in Cuba—the roots of communism sinking deeper into its lush soil—the Major League players from there were not only unsettled but exiled from their country, unable to play in Cuba's Winter League. The Dominican Players Association organized a series, pitting a Dominican Republic team against a team of Cuban players who were now living in the United States. It was a demonstration of goodwill and also an opportunity to put a few offseason dollars in our pockets. Frick warned us not to play, intimating that there would be consequences.

My country's leader, Rafael Bonnelly, was probably more outraged than I was, for he stated, "I am the president of the Dominican Republic, and I say it is all right to play." Not that I needed anyone's permission to play baseball, but it was good to know that our president had our backs. Ford Frick did not, and his complete lack of understanding of the situation—both economic and political— was astounding.

I felt for the Cuban players. With Castro in power, not only was access to their home country cut off, but there was no more Cuban Winter League, and there were no more opportunities for them to earn offseason money and—especially for the younger Minor

League players—improve their skills. It showed solidarity with them to play the series in Santo Domingo, something I strongly believed in doing. In fact, to this day I've continued to show my solidarity to my Cuban compadres. Through the years there have been opportunities to go to Cuba—for both baseball and other reasons. But because of the Castro brothers and their communist regime, I have resolutely refused to set foot on Cuban soil. I believe that if Cuban players cannot freely go to their country, then I shouldn't either.

In the 1962 offseason those expatriated Cuban players—guys like Camilo Pascual, Pedro Ramos, Joe Azcue, and Aurelio Monteagudo—wanted to come to my country to play baseball, and I saw no harm in that. Besides, none of us who played in that series were big-money players. All of us needed offseason income.

When I got to spring training in 1963, I complained to Alvin Dark, Chub Feeney, and Horace Stoneham. They all sympathized with me. But the Giants never offered to pay the fine for me, and I wasn't about to ask them. I refused to pay the fine. Maybe they knew who they were dealing with—a guy who flew back to the Dominican Republic with his pregnant wife rather than be sent to the Minor Leagues. So they must have known I wasn't going to pay an unfair fine for playing baseball in my home country. No, no, no. That wasn't going to happen. I later told *Sport* magazine that I paid the fine, just to avoid any further aggravation. I'm pretty sure, though, that the Giants paid it.

One of the things I would have liked is at least an opportunity to discuss the matter with Ford Frick. But to the day he died in 1978 he never once talked to me. You would have thought that perhaps during the season, Frick would have dropped in on me and my brothers—plural—for it was in 1963 that Jesús joined the Giants, and together he, Matty, and I wrote a page or two into the annals of baseball history. Never before or since have three brothers patrolled a Major League outfield together. Not that we thought it was a big deal.

Through the years my brothers and I occasionally discussed the magnitude of it and how improbable such a conflation of events would ever occur again. First of all, you would have to have a large-enough family, which is less the norm these days, to have three boys. All three would have to like baseball and be good enough to make it to the big leagues. They would then have to end up on the same team. They would all have to be outfielders without at least one outfielder standing in their way. It took my brothers and me years to fully appreciate the enormity of what we did, and as more years go by, to me it gets bigger and bigger. I doubt we'll ever see again what we saw a lifetime ago.

But I wonder now if we did it for the wrong team. Not that there was anything wrong with the San Francisco Giants. Certainly not. The organization has meant a lot to my brothers and me. But if we had arrived in the big leagues with an organization without outfielders—and certainly without Mr. Mays—we might've played together in the same outfield for many years instead of a handful of games. After all, it's not like we were bench players. Oh, no. The Alou brothers were everyday players.

Baseball history documents that the Alou brothers first appeared in a game together on September 10, 1963—the day Jesús was called up to the big leagues after hitting .324 for the Tacoma Giants in the Pacific Coast League. Playing the New York Mets in the old Polo Grounds, we batted consecutively in the eighth inning, with Jesús and Matty stepping to the plate before me as pinch hitters. We went 0 for 3 against Mets pitcher Carl Willey—Jesús led off with a ground-out to the shortstop, Matty struck out, and I grounded out back to the pitcher. We were the only three Giants batters that inning. Three Alous up, three Alous down. It is the only time in baseball history that three siblings hit in the same half-inning.

It was five days later, on September 15, 1963, at Pittsburgh's Forbes Field, when the three of us first manned an outfield together. Again, my brothers entered as replacements—this time defensively. We started the game with Willie Mays in center field, Willie McCovey in left field, and me in right field.

After we scored five runs in the top of the seventh inning to take an 8–3 lead, Jesús replaced McCovey, with Dark moving him to right field and me to left field. After we scored four more runs in the top of the eighth inning to take a 12–3 lead, Dark replaced Mays with Matty and moved me to center field. Mays recalls that he told Dark to take him out and put Matty in center field. "It was history," Mays says. "I told him to put Matty in center field because this was history being made by three brothers."

After all the juggling was done, I stood in center field, flanked by Matty Alou in left field and Jesús Alou in right field. That was one athletic outfield. Throughout our careers the Alou brothers collectively averaged only 3.6 errors per season. But that was secondary. What people focused on, and rightfully so, is that this was one outfield manned by three brothers who emerged from a fifteen-by-fifteen-foot shack on a Caribbean island.

People have asked me through the years what I felt. Pride, to some degree. But mostly what I felt was an overwhelming sense of responsibility to look out for my younger brothers. I was more concerned for them than anything. Seeing each other patrolling an outfield together was not a new experience for us. I know everybody else thought it was, but we had been doing it in the Dominican Republic Winter League for the Escogido Lions—including playing for an up-and-coming young manager named Tommy Lasorda. But Winter League baseball is not Major League Baseball. I knew that messing up in the big leagues carried greater consequences than messing up in the Winter League. So I felt a strong sense of duty as the older brother, as the one who had been around longer, to look after them.

Not one ball was hit to my brothers in those final two innings. There was only a ninth-inning single to me in center field. I exhaled with smile.

It wasn't until the media descended on us that we began to realize we had done something special. But even then we were surprised at the reaction and all the fuss.

Two days later the same thing happened. Matty and Jesús entered the game late as replacements, this time in a blowout 11–3 victory against the Milwaukee Braves. Jesús came in as a seventh-inning pinch runner for Harvey Kuenn and then stayed in as a defensive replacement in left field. In the ninth inning Matty replaced Mays, with Dark shuffling us around to create the same outfield configuration— Matty in left, Jesús in right, and me in center. In the eighth inning Eddie Mathews and Joe Torre hit singles to Jesús in right field, and Roy McMillan singled to me in the ninth. Once again it was uneventful. I was more excited about going 3 for 5 with 3 RBI—hitting a home run off Warren Spahn and a double against Wade Blasingame. Jesús also touched Blasingame for a double.

On September 25, four days before the end of the season, we appeared in one last game together, though not simultaneously in the same outfield.

And that was it. For barely more than two weeks we played together eight times. However, contrary to a popular belief, we never started a game together. I was twenty-eight, Matty was twenty-four, and Jesús was twenty-one. You would have thought there would be many more years playing together, but I knew better. I sensed my end with the Giants. There was now a logjam in the outfield, with Willie Mays the only guarantee. Somebody had to go, and I anticipated it would be me.

I knew my fate was sealed when three separate things happened that strained my relationship with MLB and the Giants. You might say that it was strikes one, two, and three.

Strike one: After the season Alvin Dark had one-on-one meetings with the players. I was the last one called in. I guess because he knew I was a leader with the Latino players, he asked me about José Pagán and a female friend of his. "Is she white, black, or Latin?" Dark asked. I felt my anger rising. She was white. I knew it and he knew it. His question was a racist statement rather than an innocent inquiry. "Why do you want to know, and what difference does it make?" I said, my eyes locked on his, challenging him. The conversation didn't go well, and I knew at some point there would be consequences.

Strike two: A few weeks later I was sent a contract for the 1964 season that sliced $3,000 off my salary. After hitting .316 with 25 home runs and 98 RBI in 1962, the Giants deemed that my 1963 campaign with a .281 batting average, 20 home runs, and 82 RBI warranted a pay cut. I knew that wasn't a good sign, either.

Strike three: In November an article I did with *Sport* magazine exploded onto newsstands with a hard-hitting message to Major League Baseball. I knew I would be viewed as militant, though I didn't care.

The genesis of the article came earlier that spring, when I was still seething from Ford Frick's fine. A writer named Arnold Hano approached me about doing a first-person story for *Sport.* The proposal was to communicate the plight of Latino players in Major League Baseball. *Sport* was a national magazine with a stable of top-shelf writers, a monthly periodical that was a rival to the weekly *Sports Illustrated.*

"We can't pay you for the piece," Hano told me up front.

"That's okay," I said. "I would pay to have what I want to write published."

We worked on the article over the course of a week during spring training, with *Sport* holding it until its November issue. It was my manifesto, and it was titled "Latin-American Ballplayers Need a Bill of Rights." The subtitle read, "San Francisco's Star Reveals Some of the Most Shocking, Disgraceful Facts in Sport. His Story Should Be Read Start to Finish. And Something Surely Must Be Done."

And, thus, from start to finish this is exactly what I wrote:

The telegram arrived at my home in Santo Domingo, in the Dominican Republic, on a day in November of last year.

It made me so mad I balled it up and threw it away. It said something like:

"For playing against ineligible players and without permission of this office, you are fined $250, plus whatever money you received in the Cuban series. If you do not pay before the season opens on April 9, you will not be allowed to play baseball in the United States in 1963. Reply requested."

It was signed: *Ford Frick, Commissioner of Baseball.*

The Commissioner's telegram brought to a head the problems facing Latin-American ballplayers in this country. The Latin players need a spokesman to stand up for them. The fine I had to pay was unfair, but there was nobody to explain to the Commissioner, and to the press, and to the public *why* it was unfair. It was not the first hardship done to Latin players in the United States. Unless something is done, unless somebody steps forward and speaks up for these players, it will not be the last hardship.

Let me explain about this "crime" I had committed.

My government, in the Dominican Republic, "asked" me to play in a seven-game series against a team of touring Cubans in November of 1962. In 1962 my country was ruled by a military junta. When the military junta "asked" you to do something, you did it. If I had not played, I would have been called a Communist.

I do not like being called a Communist.

If I had not played, it would have been a slap in the face of the people of my country, who looked forward to this series.

If I—and other major-leaguers, such as Juan Marichal and Julian Javier—had not played in that series, we would have deprived other, less fortunate Class C and Class D ballplayers of a chance to earn badly needed money.

If I had not played, I would have deprived my wife and my children of a few extra dollars.

I weigh all these reasons on one hand. On the other, there is the winter-league rule. The rule says that after a man has played two or more years of major-league baseball, he may not play winter-league ball any place without the Commissioner's consent, except in his own country. Well, winter-league baseball has been suspended in the Dominican Republic for the past two years, because of political unrest. One would think that the Commissioner would grant us Dominicans the right to play in a series of seven games, *in our own country*. Had the regular winter-league been in operation, we would have been permitted to play close to 100 games. So why not seven? It does not make sense. It is not fair. I did right in playing against the touring Cubans. I would do it again.

Perhaps it is because we played "Cubans" that disturbed the Commissioner. Ever since 1920, Cuban teams have visited the Dominican Republic to play baseball. It is an honorable tradition in our countries, and it began long before Fidel Castro took over Cuba, and long before Ford Frick became Commissioner. It is a tradition sports fans in my country cherish, and it is unthinkable to many Dominicans that someone from a foreign country would tell other Dominicans who they can play ball with and who they can't. It would be like a Dominican telling the United States Olympic team it must not compete in the 1964 Olympics, because it will have to face Russian athletes.

Besides, this was a group of anti-Castro Cubans. They flew down from Florida—not Cuba—and they returned to Florida. The money they made did not go back to Cuba.

It turns out now that Cuban ballplayers who are prevented from returning to their country because of Communist control are being prevented from playing in other Latin-American countries by Commissioner Frick.

There is more. In February of 1963, the first *elected* president in over 30 years took over in the Dominican Republic. Before that we had dictators. General Rafael Trujillo ruled my country for 31 years. When he was assassinated in May, 1961, a military *junta* took over. Nobody respected the *junta*, because it was not elected. The people had no say. And the Communists in the Dominican Republic took advantage of all this, just as they always take advantage of situations where there is not much freedom. The Communist Party was very strong. In November, 1962, when the Cuban series was arranged, the Communists screamed. They did not want the Dominicans playing a team of anti-Castro Cubans. But the Communists are very smart. They knew all about the winter-league rule, and the Commissioner's office. The Communists didn't want us to play, and then if we didn't play, the Communists would be able to say, "See, the American imperialists won't let the Dominicans play baseball in their own country."

We had to play that Cuban series.

You have to know all this before you can understand why I was so angered by the action of Mr. Frick. In the United States there is much industry and much employment. If a ballplayer wants to work in the United States in the winter, it is not difficult to find work. If you told a United States ballplayer—you will not be permitted to earn money playing ball in the winter—he would shrug his shoulders. He never has to play baseball in the winter to make money.

In my country there is practically no industry, and very little work. We are ballplayers; it is the only thing we can do. Take away baseball from us in the winter, and you take money away from us.

Not all the Dominicans who played in that Cuban series were major-leaguers. Oh, sure, we had Javier and Olivo and Marichal and myself, and the Cubans had Pascual, Ramos, Pena, Azcue, and one or two others. But many of the players were Class C and Class D players, who earn very little money in the summer. Most of them will never get to the majors. I did not badly need the money. They did. I was to receive $497 for the series. But in order to pay for the transportation of the Cuban players back to Florida, three Dominicans—Diomedes Olivo, Juan Marichal, and myself—agreed to pay $300 each, to charter a plane. That left me with $197 for the series. Out of that $197 I bought bats and other equipment. Maybe I made, all told, $150. The result was I made less money than the Class C and D players who were in the series. But that part is all right. I only mention it to let you know I did not play that seven-game series against the Cubans to make big money. Also I was very tired, and I wanted to rest.

But I *had* to play.

I am proud that I played that series. I am proud the Dominicans won the series, four games to three. I am also proud I was the leading hitter, with 16 hits in 26 at bats, for a .615 average. And when I received the telegram from Ford Frick saying I was fined $250, I could not believe I would have to pay. (Once before in the National League I had been fined. One day in 1959 in Cincinnati, I chatted a few minutes before the game with Cuban player Orlando Pena. League president Warren Giles was in the stands. He said I was "fraternizing," and fined me $10. I said, "Maybe I'll never see Pena again, what with Castro," and I never paid the fine. Maybe the Giants paid it; I don't know.)

Then—two weeks after the first wire—I received a second telegram from Mr. Frick. As I recall, it said, "For not answering me, you must pay the fine before reporting to spring training. If you do not pay, stay home. You will not be allowed to put on a uniform."

I was in a rage. My wife, Maria, was furious. She is the one who saves the money in our family. She saw $250 flying out the window. We have been married four years. We had two children at the time; my wife was pregnant. Now we have three children. I receive a nice salary from the Giants, but I am not rich. I send money home to my mother and father. My father's family is in bad shape. I have uncles, aunts, and cousins who are in terrible shape, out of work, no money. I help. Maybe not as much as I should. But I help. Maria and I need the money I earn. Maria said, "You know you are right. It is your own land where you played. They cannot tell you you can't play."

But right or wrong, there was nothing I could do. I flew to Arizona a day before spring training officially began, and when I went to get my uniform, it was just the way the Commissioner had said. I was automatically suspended until the fine was paid. I spoke with Horace Stoneham, president of the Giants. I spoke with Al Dark. Everybody was very kind, very considerate. But nobody said, "Don't pay." They said, "Pay and forget it. You are right, but pay."

I am sure the Giants would have paid this fine for me, if I had asked. But it was not a question *who* would pay the fine. It was the fine that was wrong. If anyone had to pay, I would pay. And that was what happened. I paid. But I did not forget it.

I guess the Commissioner heard how I felt. It was in the papers. He said he would come to Phoenix, and we would discuss the situation.

I kept waiting and looking, but he never showed up. I'm still waiting. Mr. Ford Frick is the Commissioner of baseball—even in my country, although he has never set foot in my country.

And that is the real problem. We need somebody to represent us who knows what goes on in the Latin-American countries. He does not have to be Latin. He does not have to speak Spanish. He *does* have to see the conditions of these countries, face to face. He has to understand the economic conditions, the poverty. When I was a boy, 13 or 14 years old, I worked on my uncle's farm during the summer recess from school. I got up at midnight. I milked the cows and got the milk ready to be shipped to the city. At four in the morning, I went back to sleep. Then I got up at seven or eight, to begin my regular chores. Maybe I worked 17 or 18 hours a day. I do not think the Commissioner understands about such things: we need somebody to represent us to the Commissioner who does understand. For a while I worked in a concrete factory. I made $3 a day. That was not so bad. Manny Jimenez worked in a Dominican mill for three years, at $1.45 a day, so he could help support nine brothers and sisters. When I was young, my family—mother, father, four boys and two girls—lived in a wooden shack. We had to go a mile to the river for water. We had no car or truck. I carried water on my head and shoulders.

I don't think the Commissioner understands how Latin-American players must make money while we are young enough. If it means playing baseball summer *and* winter, that is how it ought to be. I think I understand why big-league teams do not want their players competing in the winter leagues. They are afraid we will get hurt, or we will burn ourselves out. Well, that is surely *our* problem, even more than it is the team's, or the league's, or the Commissioner's. If we wear ourselves out, we are through. But the Giants will still exist, even without Felipe Alou. The Giants will find more and better players to replace us. As a matter of fact, even if we never play winter ball, if the Giants or any team can find players who are better, they will replace us. It is their business. They must field the best team they can. Otherwise they do not win, and if they do not win they will not make much money. That problem stares all players in the eye. We Latin Americans try to solve this problem by making extra money while we are young and strong, and while our names command some attention.

Nor is that all. Latin-American players who earn money in the United States fall under this country's income-tax law. That is fair enough. But what is not fair—and which I do not understand—is that I, married, and with three children, must pay taxes as a single man. I cannot claim my wife and my children as dependents on my income tax. I bring my wife to this country with me, and my children, and we live in the city of San Francisco, which has just about the highest cost-of-living of any big city in the world. I pay $200 a month rent. We buy food and clothes and everything else, but I am not permitted by law to claim my wife and children as dependents. You know what an enormous difference there is in the tax of a single man, as compared with a married man with four dependents. Yet I cannot take advantage of this difference. You can. I can't. I do not think this is fair, and there is nobody to take this up, either, with the Commissioner or with the government.

People ask me: "Why don't you become an American citizen? Then you can have all the advantage enjoyed by all Americans."

For a while I thought of becoming an American citizen. Under Trujillo, it was very bad in my country. Under the military *junta*, it was a little better, but still bad. The people were unable to speak out. In America, there is freedom. It is a wonderful country. It would have been logical to become an American. But I do not think logic is all that counts. No matter what, I love my country. You have a slogan: "My country, right or wrong." Well, *my* country, right or wrong. I am a Dominican. It is my country. And I love it. Things are a little better now, and I think they will get still better. Our new president is a good man, and he will help the poor people. We live under a democracy. The Communists are now very weak. There is very little for them to yell about. They are very quiet. But I think if things were still terrible, I would remain a Dominican. It is my home.

Citizenship is not the only answer to the problems facing Latin-American ballplayers in the United States. My best friend on the Giants is Jose Pagan. Jose comes from Puerto Rico. Puerto Rico is part of the United States. Jose is an American citizen. Yet he is treated the same way as any Latin who is not an American citizen. This means that the Puerto Ricans find themselves closer to other Latins than to Stateside players. It makes foreigners out of a country's citizens.

This is not to criticize Americans. Latins are different in many ways from Americans. We speak Spanish; you speak English. Some Latin players find it difficult to learn any English. I had a terrible time, and I still speak poorly. Some Latins find it so difficult, they just give up, and speak only Spanish. This creates a barrier.

Perhaps there are a few San Francisco Giants who don't like it when we get together and speak Spanish. They don't know what's going on, and they think we are talking about them. Well, when American players come to my country, or to Venezuela or to Puerto Rico, for winter ball, most of them don't bother to learn any Spanish, and many Latins wonder what *they're* talking about. It works both ways, and I am pleased that many of my teammates on the San Francisco Giants have picked up a little Spanish, just as I have picked up some English. It helps all around.

Not being able to speak English hurts Latin players in advancing their career. Felix Torres came to this country many times to play professional baseball, but each time he became lonely and discouraged because he could not speak English, and there was nobody to speak with. He would go back to Puerto Rico. Now he plays for the Los Angeles Angels, and he is doing very well, but he lost many years because he could not speak English. When Roman Mejias broke into professional baseball in this country, he said, "It is very hard for me. I not expect to be so lonely. I speak no English at all."

But far worse than the language barrier are the insults thrown in the faces of Latin ballplayers. It is said that Latin players "don't care." That Latin players "don't hustle." Latin players "are lazy." Or—this is the worst—Latins have "no guts."

These are insults, and they grow out of ignorance of the Latin temperament. The Latin people laugh more, smile a lot. Does that mean we don't care? We don't go around saying, "I *feel* this defeat very badly." But nobody knows how we take it, inside. Sometimes you laugh *because* you suffer. You laugh, to cover it up.

Roberto Clemente once said:

"In Puerto Rico we like to laugh and talk before a game. Then we go play as hard as we can to win. Afterward, we laugh and talk again. But in America baseball is much more a business. Play well and you get a pat on the back and congratulations. Play bad, no pats, and maybe nobody talks to you."

That is true. In the Dominican Republic if you lose a game, it is still a game, and afterward there is laughing, singing, whistling in the clubhouse. Here, if a man whistles in the Giant clubhouse, Alvin Dark will say, "That man doesn't care, he doesn't really want to win." Even if he got four hits.

But I think a man must not be judged in the clubhouse, but on the playing field. It is said Orlando Cepeda had a bad year in 1962, that he did not come through when it counted. That he did not hustle. That he did not care. That he did not really want to win. The Giants even tried to cut his salary after the season.

I say Orlando Cepeda had a *great* year in 1962. He hit over .300, he had 35 home runs, he drove in 114 runs. He was very tired, but he missed only three games all year. He did all this the same year the Giants won the pennant, so you cannot say it is the case of a man getting four hits and whistling, but the team losing. Cepeda had his bad days, but so did Willie and everyone else. I feel bad when they talk about Cepeda having a bad year. If Cepeda didn't have a good year last year, I'll never have a good year.

But the worst is this business of "no guts." Look at the playoff games against the Dodgers in 1962. That playoff showed if the Latins had guts or not. My brother Matty hit the pinch single that began the ninth-inning rally that won the third playoff game. Orlando Cepeda drove in the tying run in that ninth inning. Pagan had six hits in 13 times at bat. Does that look as if the Latin players folded up, and were cowards when it counted?

I think it is foolish and dangerous to label any people or any nation or any race as having more or less courage, or more or less desire to excel than any other group. They used to say the Giants couldn't win because they had too many Negroes, and that Negroes "choked up." Yet, in the playoff Willie Mays had five hits, including two home runs, in eleven times at bat, plus three walks. It was Willie who made the key hit in the ninth-inning rally.

It just doesn't work. It isn't true. For every Latin who doesn't hustle, I'll show you five who do hustle. For every Negro who doesn't care, I'll show you five who do care.

I hope this labeling is not discrimination. I think it is only misunderstanding. But even if it is misunderstanding, it is about time somebody spoke up and explained the Latin temperament in a way that is not insulting to the Latin.

Not that there isn't some discrimination, as well. When I was signed by the Giants in 1956, I was sent to a Class-D team in Lake Charles,

Louisiana, in the Evangeline League. It was the first time I was in the United States, and I guess I should have learned more about conditions in the South, especially if you have a dark skin. There is discrimination of some sort all over the world. There is a little bit—not much, but some—in my own country. But I was not prepared for what happened in Louisiana.

At Lake Charles, I lived with a ballplayer named Ralph Crosby. Crosby was from Harlem. He and I were the only Negroes on the team. I did not know a single word of English. I followed Crosby all over. We had played five games, when one day they told me I had to leave, and they put me on a Greyhound bus, and shipped me to Cocoa, Florida. Just like that. Without a word. It turned out there'd been a meeting of a representative of each team in the league, with the president of the league. It was decided they didn't want Negroes in the league. Later I heard it was the governor, Earl Long, who sent word down to Lake Charles. "Get them out of here," he said.

Crosby was sent to Visalia in the California League, but pretty soon he quit baseball.

It was better in Cocoa, in the Florida State League. I had a good season. I hit .380. The people in Cocoa treated me very nicely. Some white people invited me to their homes. But it was not perfect. One night the team went to a restaurant in West Palm Beach. All the white players went inside and ate. There were three Negroes—Chuck Howard, who was later released, Jim Miller, who got up to Triple A before he quit, and me. We had to wait outside the restaurant until the white players had finished and brought us our food. A waitress came outside and wanted to help us. She said, "I'll serve you out here." But the owner came out, and he got sore at the waitress, and at us. "You can't eat out here," he said. "You can't wait here in the parking lot. Get out!"

The other two went across the street, to wait there. They wanted me to go with them, but I was tired, and I did not understand what was going on. So I got into the team station wagon in the parking lot, and I figured I would wait there.

Well, the police came, to get me, because I was still in the parking lot. They were going to take me to jail, but the white players came out, and the manager, Buddy Kerr, and he explained that I didn't understand English or the local laws. The white players felt bad and very sorry for us, but that was how things were.

It is not only in the South. One night in 1959, in Pittsburgh, Orlando Cepeda and I went to a downtown restaurant after a game. We were dressed very well, I think. The headwaiter came up and said, "You looking for a job? We have nothing for you." We told him we wanted to eat. He wouldn't let us inside.

These are the things that happen to Latin players in this country. Something should be done about it. But there is nobody to do anything.

It adds up to a feeling I am an outsider. Most Latin players feel they are outsiders. We play ball in this country, we spend the greater part of the year in this country, we have many friends in this country, our names are in the American papers, and we become well known to many Americans, but though we are in this country, we are not part of this country. We are strangers. I need a passport to come here. That makes me an outsider.

But it is not only the American public that does not understand the life of a Latin ballplayer in America. The Latin ballplayer who wants to come to America does not know what is in store for him. If I could give advice to a Dominican boy who wants to enter professional baseball in the United States, I would list five rules.

1. I would tell the boy, "Do not expect a bonus." You read about large bonuses paid to youngsters breaking into organized baseball. If you are a Latin, forget it. Once in a while, there is a big bonus paid to a Latin, but not often. Juan Pizarro got a big bonus. The Dodgers paid Roberto Clemente $10,000. But I got $200. Juan Marichal got $500. Those are typical.

2. In the minor leagues he must outhustle everybody else. Latins are smaller than the average American player, in general. It is unusual to find an Orlando Cepeda, or a Felipe Alou. The shortest San Francisco Giants are two Latins, Matty Alou and Jose Pagan. The roster says they are 5-9, but they are smaller. If you are small, you must make up for it by extra hustle. If you do not hustle more than everybody else, it will be said, "You do not care. You do not have a winning attitude."

3. The Latin player must learn English. When I was in the minor leagues, one of my teammates was Julio Navarro, now pitching with the Los Angeles Angels. He could speak English. I followed him like a puppy dog. He was my interpreter, my teacher. When he wasn't around, I would read the American papers, I would watch television, I would listen to conversations around me.

4. If the Latin is a Negro, he should understand the racial situation in America, and not expect perfection.

5. Do not expect to become rich. Latin players—I think—get less than other players of the same ability. Latins often have and come from large families, and they will be sending money back home, and saving money, out of not-so-big salaries. Matty and I both sent money back when we were in Class D. You will pay large taxes—larger than American players who make the same money. People will tell you: You are lucky. You are lucky to live such a good life. You are lucky to be in the United States. But the truth is: Most Latins leave the game before they make big money, and when they leave they have nothing except a large family, and they are old.

People who read this will say I have resentment. It is not true. I love baseball, as a game. I took up baseball because it was fun. I have learned much, not only about baseball but about life, since I have come to this country. It has been an adventure, an education. I have many wonderful friends in this country. I have met lots of prejudice, but I have also met lots of nice people, great people. It is a beautiful, wonderful country.

But I am not very happy living the life of a professional ballplayer. It is not the kind of life I enjoy. I am not a city boy. I grew up in the country. I love the game, but it is not a natural life. I do not like night games. I like to get up early, and go to bed early. I do not like night life. I do not smoke or drink or enjoy going to nightclubs. I do not even like to watch television at night. I do not like to be on the road, away from my family. I do not like to live in a foreign country, away from my real home.

It may come as a surprise to some people—and as a shock to the San Francisco Giants—but I do not expect to stay in baseball much longer.

Perhaps I will change my mind, but right now I plan to retire before I am 32. Maybe when I am 30. On May 12, 1963, I became 28 years old. I want to own a farm and have some cows. That is the life I want, not playing baseball at night, away from my home and family, in a country where I must resign myself to being an outsider.

I can only imagine, more than a half century later, how those words rocked baseball and the Giants. In his book *Raceball: How the Major Leagues Colonized the Black and Latin Game*, published in 2012, author Rob Ruck said, "Nobody had ever spoken so eloquently or forcefully about Latin ballplayers, much less prescribed how baseball could and should address their unique concerns." Even now, when I read those words that I wrote for *Sport* magazine, I am surprised at how bold I was—surprised and proud.

It was those last several paragraphs the Giants latched on to. I had an active volunteer ministry going. I fell in with a gentleman named Don Rood of the Pocket Testament League. In addition to speaking at churches, I was bringing the Bible's message to jails. We went into some jails in Venezuela that I don't know how God got us out of. In an attempt to explain why they traded me, the Giants told people I was preparing to leave baseball for a Christian ministry. It wasn't true.

Nevertheless, on December 3, only a few weeks after the *Sport* magazine article hit the newsstands, I rose early in the morning at my Dominican home, got into my rowboat, and spent the day fishing, returning home at 5 p.m.

Maria was waiting for me. Before I even entered the house, she called to me, her eyes telegraphing bad news. "They traded you," she said.

The words—just the mere words—rocked me on my heels. It took several seconds before I replied. "To what team?"

"Milwaukee."

It rocked me even further. I disliked the city of Milwaukee more than any other in the league, but I tried to put a positive spin on the situation. "That's not too bad," I said to her, thinking about the prospect of being teammates with great ballplayers like Eddie Mathews, Hank Aaron, Joe Torre, and Warren Spahn.

Then the realization hit me that the Giants had broken up my family—my fleshly family with my brothers Matty and Jesús and my baseball family with my teammates. A fury welled up in me. Then resentment. Finally, as if it were an exclamation point on my range of emotions, one last feeling settled deep within me.

A broken heart.

4

1964–1970s

15

Brave New World

Imagine my reaction when, as the 1964 season approached, I saw that the Milwaukee Braves were scheduled to open their season against the San Francisco Giants—in San Francisco! I went from a broken heart to a heart filled with dread. *Any team but San Francisco.* Sure, I knew I would eventually have to play against the Giants, but not right away, not on Opening Day.

I was still adjusting to the trade, to putting on a different uniform, to a whole new set of teammates. People might not realize or remember, but trades were rarer then than they are today. Plus, there was no free agency. Players tended to stay with a team for most of their careers.

We arrived in San Francisco the day before the game, and Juan Marichal, who years later went on record as saying that trading me "was one of the biggest mistakes the Giants ever made," contacted me. He wanted me to come for breakfast at his place the following morning.

"Juan, aren't you the Opening Day starter?" I asked, more as a matter of statement rather than a query.

"It'll be okay," he said. "I'll pick you up at your hotel."

It was nice for Juan to extend that hand of friendship, but it did little to calm me. I didn't sleep that night. For the first and only time in my life, I was dreading Opening Day.

The following morning, while walking, I somehow ripped the seam in my dress pants. Not a good sign. I changed, and when I got to Juan's home it felt as if I had never been traded. After all, it was only several months earlier when Juan and I roomed together during the World Series, with our families home in the Dominican Republic. His wife, Alma, cooked us a great breakfast of eggs and ham, and then Juan drove me to Candlestick Park, just like old times. From there everything changed. Juan went back to his home to take a pregame nap, and I headed toward the visitors' clubhouse. Because of baseball's silly fraternization policy at the time, I couldn't even hug my brothers or any of my old teammates, much less say hello or even shake their hands. To this day Willie Mays bristles when the topic of the Giants trading me comes up, telling me and anyone within earshot what a bad trade it was.

I thought the Giants made a good trade at the time, but in retrospect I went on to have some great years with the Braves and played ten more years in the big leagues. Meanwhile, in return for me, catcher Ed Bailey, and pitcher Billy Hoeft, the Giants got thirty-four-year-old catcher Del Crandall, who was wrapping up a solid career, along with pitchers Bob Hendley and Bob Shaw. Hendley was 10-11 for the Giants before they traded him to the Chicago Cubs about six weeks into the 1965 season. Shaw went 24-19 before the Giants sold him to the New York Mets less than midway through the 1966 season. I went on to have a seventeen-year MLB career, amassing 2,101 hits, 206 home runs, and a career .286 batting average, making the All-Star Game in 1962, 1966, and 1968, while also finishing in the top ten in MVP voting in 1966 and 1968. I guess Willie Mays might be right.

Of course, looking back with twenty-twenty vision provides perspective, but for the moment I was wearing a Braves uniform and stepping into the batter's box as the Opening Day's lead-off hitter against my good friend Juan Marichal.

The first pitch was a nasty curveball low—a ball. At least that's what I thought, and that's what the umpire called. The next thing I knew Marichal was standing next to me, arguing with the umpire about the called ball. I recognized the look in his eyes. He had his game face on. This wasn't a friendly breakfast of eggs and ham at his kitchen table. This was competition, and this was typical Marichal. He would be so deeply focused on the days he pitched that he rarely even smiled. Not that it would've been much better had I still been wearing a Giants uniform, since our pitcher that day for the Braves was Warren Spahn. I ended the at-bat by popping up to the second baseman, Jim Davenport.

We did nick Marichal for a first-inning run. With two outs Hank Aaron singled to Willie Mays in center field and then stole second. With first base open Marichal pitched around Eddie Mathews, who walked. Joe Torre followed with a single to right, knocking in Aaron. In retrospect, what a group of players occupied that Opening Day game—Marichal, Spahn, Aaron, Mays, Mathews, and Torre, as well as Willie McCovey and Orlando Cepeda. Incredible.

I had no time to think about all that. I was busy battling Juan Marichal, going 1 for 4 with a run scored, while also reaching base on an error by my friend José Pagán at shortstop. Everything seemed so backward, so strange, so surreal. Several times after a third out ended an inning, I found myself running from my center-field position toward the Giants' dugout along the first base line, before realizing my mistake and changing course, hoping no one noticed.

We lost 8–4, thanks to five Giants home runs—two coming off the bat of Willie Mays. We lost 10–8 the next day, when I was 0 for 5, before we headed to Houston for a three-game series. I was never so happy to get out of town. Being there was too emotional. I guess Tony Bennett wasn't the only guy who left his heart in San Francisco.

By the time we got to our home opener in Milwaukee, my worst concerns were confirmed—cold weather. It was so cold that patches of snow dotted the warning track. Worse than that was who we were facing in our home opener—the Giants. And I was facing one of the players the Giants traded for me—Bob Hendley.

People asked me if I wanted to stick it to the Giants. Not in the least. Maybe I wanted to show something to Alvin Dark and the front office. But on the field, what was I going to do? It's not as if I wanted to slide hard into José Pagán to break up a double play. Or wish to see my brothers Matty and Jesús play badly. I think that was the hardest part—playing against my own brothers. When I was traded it demoralized my family. My parents didn't understand.

They didn't understand why three brothers couldn't play on the same team, in the same outfield. They didn't understand the mechanics of baseball. And they didn't understand about Willie Mays.

Mainly because of the family dynamics, it took me a couple of years to get used to playing against the Giants. I don't think there has ever been a trade in Major League Baseball history where someone has had to come back and compete against *two* of his brothers.

History has shown something else, too. My trade turned out *not* to be an anomaly. From a young man's perspective—from *my* perspective—when a team gets you out of college and takes you away from your family, you think you're going to spend the rest of your life with them. But that's not the case. It turns out that all of the great, along with some of the very good, Giants players of that era did not finish their careers in San Francisco. To wit:

Orlando Cepeda was traded to the St. Louis Cardinals in 1966.

Willie McCovey was traded to the San Diego Padres in 1973.

Juan Marichal finished the last few years of his career with the Boston Red Sox and Los Angeles Dodgers.

Gaylord Perry was traded to the Cleveland Indians in 1971.

Matty Alou was traded to the Pittsburgh Pirates in 1965.

Jesús Alou went to the Montreal Expos in the 1968 expansion draft and then was traded three months later to the Houston Astros.

Even Willie Mays didn't finish his career with the Giants. San Francisco traded him to the New York Mets in 1972.

So Felipe Alou was not unique.

What made that first year in Milwaukee even more difficult is that I suffered my first serious injury. Not serious in that it was career threatening, but serious in that on June 26, 1964, in Milwaukee, I underwent knee surgery for a torn meniscus. As I enter my ninth decade of life, I live with almost constant knee pain. The injury happened when I hit a ball into the right-center field gap. Jim Beauchamp, who was learning how to play first base, got in my way as I was rounding first, and I collided with him. It resulted in poor Beauchamp also needing knee surgery.

As it was, I was struggling the first few months of the season. Mostly, I wasn't hitting well. Our manager, Bobby Bragan, tried everything—moving me around the batting order, benching me, playing me again, shifting me from center field to first base. But nothing seemed to work. When I injured my knee, I was batting only .253 with 6 home runs. I was miserable, feeling sorry for myself. But as I convalesced, letters arrived, many of them from parishioners whose churches I had spoken at in the San Francisco Bay Area. Some even came from fellow ballplayers, like Al Worthington and Bobby Richardson. I thought often about Mickey Mantle and the chronic knee problems—and surgeries—he dealt with and found myself feeling sorry for him.

It also turned out to not be such a healthy year for my brothers. On June 2 a pitch thrown by Pittsburgh's Bob Veale struck Matty on his wrist, breaking a bone. And Jesús suffered a spike wound that hampered him much of the season.

The Braves wanted to shut me down for the rest of the season, but I rejected that notion. When the cast came off my leg, it was atrophied. I did my exercises faithfully. I even went to Lake Michigan and ran miles, plodding along in the soft sand. People stared at me, keeping their distance, and I knew why. I was a black man running, so I must have been running from something or someone. Their looks and evasive postures annoyed me more than they angered me, but I didn't allow them to stop me. I was on a mission.

Barely five weeks later I announced myself ready to play. Again I struggled, getting only 1 hit in my first 17 at-bats. My batting average sank, settling at .231 on September 4. That same day New York Mets second baseman Ron Hunt accidentally spiked my brother Jesús during a rundown. Jesús needed ninety-one stitches on his foot, ankle, and calf, which ended his season. Knowing what he was going through made my own woes less painful. It helped that Bobby Bragan stuck with me, and I will always be thankful to him for that. Six days later, on September 10, I hit my first home run since the surgery. Later in that game I hit a ninth-inning RBI double, scoring Denis Menke, to help us beat the Mets 7–6. That was the boost I needed, the spark that not only ignited me for that season but also finally made me feel as if I was a part—an important part—of a new team.

Ten days later I hit a three-run homer against the Chicago Cubs in a game we won 5–2. Momentum was building. I was on my way. I went on a tear, getting 17 hits in my final 44 at-bats to finish with a .253 average, 9 home runs, and 51 RBI. Not great. But given all I had been through, and that I managed 455 plate appearances in spite of knee surgery, I'll take it. Mostly, though, I'll take the fact that I finally felt like I was a Milwaukee Brave, eagerly looking forward to the next Opening Day.

1. The humble home at Kilometer 12 in the Dominican Republic where my father, José Rojas, grew up. From him came five Major League ballplayers—three sons and two grandsons. Courtesy of the Alou family.

2. This is a painting of my parents' home where I and five siblings grew up. It's also at Kilometer 12, about a half mile from my father's boyhood home. Courtesy of the Alou family.

3. With my older sister Maria Magdalena at my Catholic confirmation. I was about ten or eleven years old. Courtesy of the Alou family.

4. My mother, Virginia Alou de Rojas, as a young woman. She gave birth to three Major League ballplayers. Courtesy of the Alou family.

5. My father and my brother Matty sometime in the early 1960s. Every year I'd bring my father a hat from the United States, and he would wear it proudly. Both literally and figuratively, he was a man who wore many hats. Courtesy of Teresa "Tity" Rojas.

6. (*opposite top*) My firstborn daughter, Maria, and my firstborn son, Felipe, who tragically died in a swimming pool accident. I fainted when I was told the horrible news of his death. Courtesy of Maria Rojas.

7. (*opposite bottom*) At my wedding to my first wife, Maria, who is the mother of Moisés Alou. To my right are my parents, José and Virginia Rojas. I entered Major League Baseball as the son of interracial parents almost forty years before Derek Jeter. Courtesy of the Alou family.

8. (*above*) Sitting on Haina Beach, where my friends and I would swim naked when we were boys. Courtesy of the Alou family.

9. Enjoying a special dinner. In the middle is my father. To his right are Matty and his wife, Teresa. Maria and I are to his left. Courtesy of the Alou family.

10. Sitting next to the baby carriage of my firstborn son, Felipe, who died as a teenager. Courtesy of the Alou family.

11. As a proud young player for the
San Francisco Giants. Courtesy of
the San Francisco Giants.

12. The photographer asked Matty and me to jump for this Giants publicity photo. Courtesy of the San Francisco Giants.

13. (*opposite top*) Standing between my friends and former teammates Willie McCovey and Willie Mays. McCovey and I once bought a car together in the Minor Leagues. Courtesy of the San Francisco Giants.

14. (*opposite bottom*) In the clubhouse with Willie Mays and my old roommate Orlando Cepeda, who is threatening to plant a kiss on Mays. Courtesy of the San Francisco Giants.

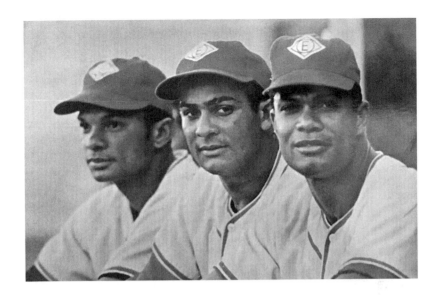

15. (*opposite top*) My brother Jesús played in his first Major League game on September 10 at New York's Shea Stadium. This photo was likely taken the next day, showing the four Dominicans on the Giants' roster—Juan Marichal, me, Matty, and Jesús. Courtesy of the Alou family.

16. (*opposite bottom*) In front of my former teammate José Pagán's 1958 Chevrolet Delray. José taught me how to drive in that car on the streets of San Francisco. Courtesy of the Alou family.

17. (*above*) Well before my brothers and I made history by playing together in the same outfield for the San Francisco Giants, we did so many times with the Escogido Lions in the Dominican Winter League. Some of those games were managed by Hall of Famer Tommy Lasorda. Courtesy of Teresa "Tity" Rojas.

18. It looks like I connected for a home run. The follow-through tells me it was a good, level swing with the catcher, umpire, and myself looking skyward. National Baseball Hall of Fame and Museum, Cooperstown, New York.

19. With my good friends on the Atlanta Braves—Hank Aaron to the far right and my old roommate Joe Torre in the middle. AP Photo.

20. At the May 22, 1992, news conference when the Montreal Expos announced me as their new manager. To my right is former general manager Dan Duquette, and to my left is former president and principal owner Claude Brochu. Courtesy of Gilles Corbeil.

21. Engaging the media after I became the first Dominican to manage in the Major Leagues. Dennis "El Presidente" Martínez pitched us to a victory that night. Courtesy of Gilles Corbeil.

22. (*opposite top*) With a string of trout and three of my Montreal Expos coaches. From left to right are Tim Johnson, Jerry Manuel, me, and Luis Pujols. All three of those coaches became Major League managers. Courtesy of Gilles Corbeil.

23. (*opposite bottom*) Posing with my son Moisés after Topps named him to their 1992 all-rookie team and presented him with this nice trophy. Courtesy of Gilles Corbeil.

24. (*above*) Sitting in the dugout with two of my coaches, Jim Tracy in the middle and Jerry Manuel to the right. Both became Major League managers. Courtesy of Gilles Corbeil.

25. At the 1990 Caribbean Series, I was interviewed at Miami's Orange Bowl by the late Hall of Fame announcer Rafael "Felo" Ramírez. Courtesy of the Alou family.

26. (*oppostie top*) Proudly holding a twenty-two-pound cobia at the pier at Lake Worth, Florida, sometime around 1990. Courtesy of the Alou family.

27. (*oppostie bottom*) Fishing on the pristine Restigouche River in New Brunswick, Canada. Courtesy of the Alou family.

28. The woman who grounded me, Lucie Alou. We married in 1986. Courtesy of Gilles Corbeil.

29. Pointing to the billboard at Montreal's Olympic Stadium after I managed my one thousandth game. Courtesy of Gilles Corbeil.

30. With my brothers Matty (*middle*) and Jesús (*left*). It looks like we're standing in a hotel lobby sometime in the late '80s or early '90s. Courtesy of the Alou family.

31. Sitting in rocking chairs with my beloved mother, Virginia. Her maiden name was Alou. Courtesy of the Alou family.

32. Back to where it all began, only this time I'm managing instead of playing for the San Francisco Giants. Courtesy of the San Francisco Giants.

33. Reunited in San Francisco with my son Moisés. Courtesy of the San Francisco Giants.

34. Standing at the batting cage with Barry Bonds when he was at 713 home runs, one short of the 714 that Babe Ruth hit. AP Photo/Eric Risberg.

35. At a ceremony honoring my brothers and me. Jesús is to the left and Matty in the center. Courtesy of the San Francisco Giants.

36. Standing in front of the Giants' Felipe Alou Baseball Academy in the Dominican Republic. Courtesy of the San Francisco Giants.

16

Settling In

Once I settled into Milwaukee I became fond of the city. I quickly made friends with Lake Michigan, where I would fish for salmon, perch, and walleye. I fell in love with the great cheese, the bratwursts, and the beers—Miller, Pabst Blue Ribbon, Old Milwaukee—which you could find at any tavern, which were seemingly on every corner. And the fans were great. Really nice people. The only thing that wasn't nice was the weather.

But I was there to play baseball, to further my career and become part of something that I hoped would be special. What really makes you feel part of a team is winning and knowing you're contributing to those notches in the W column. What is also meaningful, and what really makes you feel connected, are the friendships. By year two with the Milwaukee Braves I knew I was contributing, and I could see I was fitting in with a great bunch of teammates. As with anything else in life, it's all about relationships.

Our manager, Bobby Bragan, set the tone. As with Alvin Dark, Bragan was from the South, in his case Birmingham, Alabama. But thanks to having been a teammate of Jackie Robinson, an experience he said evaporated any traces of bigotry, Bragan displayed not even a hint of racism. He also played and managed in Cuba, which meant he not only loved Cuban cigars but also understood and appreciated Latino players. Bragan was a character, a funny guy with a big smile that seemed perpetually plastered on his mug. I always thought the face of the Milwaukee Braves' Indian logo looked like him.

Just as important were the relationships with my new teammates, some of whom became lifelong friends. Joe Torre was one of those guys. When I arrived Joe was a Brooklyn boy coming into his own as a young catcher, moving from under the shadow of his older brother, Frank Torre, who had also played for the Braves. You could immediately see Joe could hit, and hit in the clutch, and the combination of the two was going to keep him in the game for a long time. He wasn't the type to hit forty home runs, but he was a pure line-drive hitter with straightaway power. Joe was good-natured and fun-loving, a happy-go-lucky kind of guy, but early on you could also see leadership qualities and his advanced knowledge of the game.

Joe called me F. Even to this day, Joe still calls me F. We later became roommates, and what a great roommate Joe was, mainly because he was single, had friends everywhere, and often left me with our hotel room all for myself. Years later, when Joe got his first managerial job—in 1977 with the New York Mets—we got together during spring training in Florida, and Joe took me to the racetrack. I kiddingly asked him, "So who is going to be your disciplinarian?" It's been wonderful to watch Joe Torre and his career blossom through the years.

Warren Spahn was a talker. He loved to talk, and he usually had insightful things to say. Probably his most famous saying, which really stuck with me, was "Hitting is timing. Pitching is upsetting timing."

Spahny, as we called him, was forty-three, with his career winding down when I became his teammate. I played only one year with him. When we were both slumping, he told me, "Felipe, you and I are still here. The only advantage you have is that you're still young." He was right. That offseason the Braves traded him to the neophyte New York Mets.

Eddie Mathews exuded authority. He was our team captain, and it was obvious that if he wanted to, he could one day manage, which he did. In fact, he was the Atlanta Braves' manager in 1974 when Hank Aaron broke Babe Ruth's all-time home run record. Eddie was a very strong man with a sweet left-handed swing. Although I became a teammate toward the end of his career, when Eddie was losing some of his talent, you could still count on him to hit a big home run and play a good third base.

Eddie was an honest man, and he didn't hide from us that he had a drinking problem, nor did he hide that when he wrote his own autobiography. One time, when we were busing to Shea Stadium in New York City, a few of us got into a debate as to how many games Eddie played the season before. I don't know how we arrived at such a mundane topic, but typical of men the argument turned heated. Eddie was sitting next to me on the bus, hungover and snoring. I woke him up.

"Eddie, we're arguing here about how many games you played last year. How many did you play?"

"Too many," he growled.

Just then we passed a cemetery.

"And you see all those sons of bitches in there?" he barked. "They wish they felt as bad as I do now."

And just like that he went back to sleep, snoring loudly.

Hank Aaron was a complete ballplayer, a fact often overlooked because people think of him as a home run hitter. But Hank was a complete player with all five tools: he could hit, hit for power, run, throw, and play great defense. Although Hank wasn't a speedster, he could steal a base when he needed to. People especially forget that Hank was a really good right fielder with a strong arm. I think the reason his stature as a right fielder gets overlooked is because Hank played at the same time as Roberto Clemente, who might've been the greatest defensive right fielder of all time.

The one player—and the only player in my mind—whom you could compare Hank Aaron to was Willie Mays, and I had the privilege of playing alongside both of them during their primes. There wasn't much difference between the two except for this:

Hank was quietly great.

Willie was spectacularly great.

Other than that they weren't too dissimilar. Hank was a better hitter than Willie, and Willie was a better all-around player. Hank didn't have the benefit of beginning and ending his career in New

York City, with all its media attention, as did Willie. But I'm sure that was fine with him, since Hank was a quiet man and a quiet player. The only thing that wasn't quiet was his swing. When Hank's bat hit the ball the loud *crack!* of that contact could be heard far away. When you heard it, it was unmistakable that Hank Aaron was in the batter's box. He didn't have a long swing like Willie had. Hank had a compact, damaging swing. The only other player with such a short swing who could do big damage was Barry Bonds. It's no wonder why they called Hank the "Hammer" and "Hammerin' Hank."

Conversely, people don't think of Willie Mays first as a home run hitter, even though he hit 660 while missing the 1953 season due to military service. Over the 1954 and 1955 seasons, Mays averaged 46 home runs, so it's not out of the question that he could have finished his career with 700 or more homers if not for that missed season.

Mays and Aaron were both more line-drive hitters, not these long-ball mashers where you stood slack-jawed at the height and distance of their launches. Hank, like Willie, was a pure hitter who prided himself on hitting .300, driving in 100 runs, and stealing bases. A lot of his homers were to right or right-center field, and at old County Stadium in Milwaukee the wind—often a cold wind—blew in from center field. He and Eddie Mathews had to hit some serious line drives to get a home run. When the Braves moved to Fulton County Stadium in Atlanta and Hank saw how the ball carried, he didn't necessarily change his swing, but rather he altered his approach. To my eye he started pulling the ball a little more.

What I most enjoyed about Hank is that he was always a nice guy and a true teammate. He was one of our leaders. A quiet leader. But a leader nonetheless.

I remember one game in particular, which I would like to forget. As I recall, I made two boo-boos. Earlier in the game I caught a long fly ball in center field. Thinking it was the third out, I started jogging in. But it was only the second out, with two runners on base who were now racing around the bases toward home. Suddenly, someone came to my side, reached into my glove, grabbed the ball, and threw it in. That man was the right fielder—Hank Aaron.

Later in the game I hit a triple with nobody out and tried to score an inside-the-park home run. Instead, I was thrown out. It was foolish. With nobody out I should have stayed on third. But I was trying to redeem myself from my earlier gaffe. Instead, I buried myself.

All I wanted to do at that point was crawl into a hole, but the only hole was the dugout. As I sat there, wishing I was invisible, someone came and tapped me on my arm. It was Hank Aaron.

"Felipe," he said, "don't worry about it. Don't worry."

Moments later Hank stepped to the plate and hit a bomb—a home run that helped us win the game. That's what you call a teammate: someone who picks you up when you're down. That was Hank Aaron.

About the only guy I ever saw Hank have a problem with was Rico Carty, one of my fellow countrymen from the Dominican Republic. Rico was easy to have a problem with. He was defiant, belligerent, constantly challenging. During batting practice, when we each got seven swings, Rico would stay in there for eight, nine, maybe ten swings. It was as if he was daring somebody to say something. But nobody would say anything because Rico was a brawny guy who liked to intimidate people.

But one day, standing around the batting cage, waiting our turn, I heard Eddie Mathews say, "I'm going to take care of him." After Rico's seventh pitch, and just as the eighth one was being thrown by the batting-practice pitcher, Eddie lunged in front of the batter's box. While holding his bat in one hand, he caught the pitch barehanded with his other hand. "Get out of here," he told Rico, and Rico did.

It was a ballsy move because Rico was a muscular guy—about six feet three with a chiseled frame. He had a hair-trigger temper, and he used to brag that he had been an amateur boxing champion in the Dominican Republic. I don't know about the latter, but I do know that Rico liked to intimidate people. If you were with him, as I often was because he was a fellow countryman, you ran the risk of getting in a fight somewhere. Rico was a hothead, quick with his mouth.

I first became aware of that my first spring training with Milwaukee. We played the Cincinnati Reds in Tampa, and Rico and I were with Sandy Alomar Sr. and Ozzie Virgil Sr. We asked at our hotel if there were any places that served Latin food, and we were told of a Cuban eatery in nearby Ybor City called the Columbia Restaurant. We were dressed nicely, with coats and ties, and we took an expensive cab ride there to eat. A man who was obviously Latino greeted us.

"You guys want to eat?" he said to us in English.

"Yes, *sí*," Ozzie said.

We could tell right away it was a Cuban place and upscale, a good-looking restaurant. We thought we were home free, in line for a great dinner.

"Look," the man said, "we're not integrated yet. We get Cuban and Puerto Rican ballplayers and other Negroes who come here, and they eat in that room." He pointed to a room at the back of the restaurant, off the kitchen.

Rico was livid. "We're not American Negroes, and we're not Cuban!" he exploded. "The Cubans are running from Fidel Castro! We're from the Dominican Republic!"

Actually, we all were from the Dominican Republic except for Sandy Alomar Sr., who was from Puerto Rico.

The man lowered his voice, hoping Rico would do the same, speaking to us now in Spanish.

"Listen, guys, we have a business," he said. "You only come here during spring training. The white people are here all the time. If we let you eat with them, they'll never come back."

Rico emptied some obscenities on him, but it obviously did no good. We left, getting another cab. A white guy was driving. We told him what happened, and he told us about a barbecue joint in the black section of town that he guaranteed we would love. He took us there, leaving the paved road and driving on dirt and gravel, into the boondocks. The place didn't look like much. It had a dirt floor and picnic-style tables that seated a lot of people. But the barbecue pork chops and ribs were some of the best I've ever eaten. And plentiful.

That there was a lot of food was a good thing because there were some hungry Cincinnati Reds Minor League ballplayers there, Latino guys, including this young Cuban kid, very skinny, with big eyes. Thank goodness the portions were big, I thought, because this kid needs to eat. He was *that* skinny. He hadn't played a Major League game yet, but some of the Reds' Minor Leaguers who knew him were telling me he was going to be a really good player. That was the night I met a future Hall of Famer named Tony Pérez.

So an evening that began with Rico Carty and the rest of us arguing at a restaurant ended rather well. I can't say that about other evenings with Rico.

One year with the Braves we played a Jimmy Fund charity game against the Red Sox in Boston. Leading up to the game, I had been playing every inning of every regular-season game. During the Jimmy Fund charity game, our manager, Bobby Bragan, came to me and Hank Aaron and took us out after five innings. For some reason this rankled Rico Carty.

"You are the bobo of the manager," he barked at me. The implication was that I was some type of teacher's pet who had gotten that way because I brownnosed our skipper. He didn't say anything about Hank—that incident would come later—only me.

I had finally had it. I was tired of Rico trying to intimidate me and others. This time I wasn't going to give in to his tactics. I immediately got in his face. "Listen, I am fed up with you! You've made everybody afraid of you! I'm not afraid! I am from the same place you are from! You are going to have to prove to me that you're a boxer! But I'm telling you right now, you will have to kill me! If you want to fight me, one of us is going to die!"

I watched the rest of the game in the dugout, waiting for Rico to make his move. But he didn't. After the game, nothing. I showered, keeping an eye on him. Still, nothing. On the bus ride to Logan International Airport, Rico started mouthing off again, saying everyone should steer clear of Felipe Alou.

"He has a pistol in his briefcase," he said.

I had a briefcase, but no pistol. I opened it and showed him and anybody else who was curious that there was no pistol inside. Then I gave my briefcase to my roommate, our second baseman Félix

Millán. I was ready to fight. When we got off the bus and ready to board the plane, guys were standing around, watching to see what would happen. But Rico never did anything or said another word.

Many moons later, after both of our playing careers were over, Rico approached me at Juan Marichal Stadium in Santo Domingo. I could see in his eyes that he was carrying a burden and wanted to talk. Rico apologized that day, not only for that incident but for the way he behaved during his playing days.

"I don't know why I was like that," he said, shaking his head. "You never did anything to me."

We hugged like men, and I was really touched by that.

Carty later became mayor of San Pedro de Macorís in our country and managed the Catholic Relief Services, working with children. He is a well-respected man in the Dominican Republic, and I'm happy for that—and for him. He's also become a great mentor for ballplayers in our home country, with Robinson Canó and Alfonso Soriano among his pupils.

I don't know if Hank Aaron ever patched things up with Rico. The difference that erupted between them has been documented, and the date—June 18, 1967—has been dutifully recorded, mainly because we were no-hit that day by Houston Astros pitcher Don Wilson, who also recorded fifteen strikeouts against us. What really has never been told is the backstory of that dustup between Hank and Rico, which I believe I am the only one privy to.

My roommate was Mike de la Hoz. Mike was Cuban, born in Havana, but because of Fidel Castro's regime he hadn't been to his home country in years, with little hope of ever returning. While we were in Houston Mike went for a walk and came back with a bottle of Bacardi rum. That might not seem like a big deal because Bacardi is so prevalent today, as it was back then. But what people might not realize is that while Bacardi is identified today as a Puerto Rican rum, it was originally from Cuba. I don't know how, but Mike came back from his walk with a bottle of Bacardi rum that had been bottled in Cuba. He probably found it on some dusty shelf at an old liquor store, where the bottle had likely been sitting for years. Mike was so proud that he had a bottle of Bacardi directly from Cuba, showing me the proof on the label. It was as if he had found a treasure.

That night we were on a Delta charter flight from Houston to Los Angeles, and the guys at the back of the plane were doing what they normally did—playing cards and drinking, though probably not in that order, since we were still stinging from being no-hit and striking out fifteen times. I was not a card player, but I liked watching. Mike had his prized bottle of Bacardi next to him, drinking a little bit from it here and there.

Without asking, Hank reached over and picked up the Bacardi bottle.

"Hey, hey, don't drink my rum," Mike said.

I think Hank was a little startled.

"How much is the bottle?" he asked.

Hank had no idea it was a treasure to Mike. He didn't know what the big deal was. He was sincerely offering to buy him another bottle of Bacardi. Had he known how special it was to Mike, I know Hank would not have touched the bottle.

It would've ended there, except Rico Carty had to stick his nose where it didn't belong. I think he might've known from Mike that the bottle was from Cuba. "You don't have enough money to pay for it," Rico mouthed off in his typical defiant and belligerent way.

It wasn't the first time Carty's obnoxiousness annoyed Hank. Hank particularly didn't like the way Carty would occasionally loaf; something that also rankled other guys. Joe Torre also recalls that Hank would tense up whenever Rico started getting mouthy. This time, as it was with me at the Jimmy Fund charity game in Boston, Hank apparently had enough. The one thing about Hank is that he hated any kind of racial slur. Knowing that, I marveled years later at how he handled the overt racism he endured when he was breaking Babe Ruth's home run record. But here Carty was, mouthing off in English and Spanish, and for some reason, as Torre recalls, he called Hank "black slick." I don't know what he meant by that, but Hank didn't wait around for an explanation.

In a flash wild punches were flailing. Hank dented the overhead luggage compartment above Carty's head. Both exchanged blows to the face. Guys were soon all over them, rushing from the front of the plane, trying to get in between and separate them. Included in that scrum was our four-foot-two traveling secretary, Donald Davidson. A couple of flight attendants were back there, too, pushing people and yelling. Apparently, the pilots were struggling to right the plane with all the weight concentrated at the aft. Soon everyone was back where they belonged, the pilots got the plane stabilized, and we continued en route to Los Angeles, with tensions as high as our altitude.

I fully expected Carty to be traded the next day—if not, then sometime in the next few days. But he wasn't traded. He spent the rest of that season and five more seasons with the Braves. There were no more problems between Hank and Rico, but they didn't talk much with each other anymore.

It was sad and unnecessary. You would have thought Rico had more important things to be angry about, things related to our home country, which was going through years of turmoil and revolution that claimed thousands of lives.

One of them was almost my brother Juan.

17

Trouble at Home

There have never been four brothers who have all played Major League Baseball in the modern era. In this and the last century there have been other three-brother combinations—such as the DiMaggios, the Boyers, and the Molinas—but never four brothers. I think about that when I think about my brother Juan.

Not many people know there was a fourth Alou brother. Not many people ask. When people do learn there was a fourth Alou brother, the immediate question is, could he play baseball?

Could he play baseball?

Juan Alou had the potential to be the fourth Alou in the big leagues. When I would be home during the offseasons, people were always telling me Juan had solid skills; he could hit like Matty, for a high average, but with power. And he was a switch hitter. Like Matty, Jesús, and myself, Juan possessed a strong arm. But unlike his older brothers, who all broke into the big leagues as outfielders, Juan was an infielder. His body was a solid six feet, barrel-chested, strong, and muscular.

When people hear that about my youngest brother, the next obvious question is, what happened? It's not an easy answer.

To understand what happened you have to understand what happened to my country after Rafael Trujillo was assassinated in 1961. Trujillo's assassination threw the Dominican Republic into years of turmoil and strife, with two factions fighting for power and control. On one side were the remnants of Trujillo's dictatorship, led by his sons and the military who wanted to maintain power, primarily through one of his former right-hand men—Joaquín Balaguer. On the other side were those who resisted and wanted free and fair elections. By the mid-1960s an all-out civil war raged, and it looked like the left-leaning resisters might regain control. That got the United States' attention. Fearing that another Caribbean country would turn to communism—becoming a second Cuba—President Lyndon Johnson declared, "We don't propose to sit here in a rocking chair with our hands folded and let the Communists set up any government in the western hemisphere."

I didn't see it that way, and neither did most of my countrymen. The majority of us—me included—wanted Juan Bosch to rule us. It was only two years earlier, in 1963, when Bosch, a writer, poet, and intellect who headed the Dominican Revolutionary Party, was sworn in after winning our first free presidential election in thirty-plus years. Bosch was a socialist, considered by some a step away from a communist, and that was unacceptable to the United States. Seven months after he took power in 1963, a military junta—remnants of the Trujillo regime—sent him into exile for the second time, plunging our country into two years of abject corruption.

After an uprising early in 1965 pushed back against the corruption, Bosch returned from exile to again run for president. His burgeoning support worried the United States. So on April 28, 1965, an estimated forty-two thousand U.S. troops arrived in the Dominican Republic, occupying our country against our will. It was that quick, that immediate. We woke up one day, and there were tens of thousands of marines, air force personnel, and paratroopers on our island and a navy warship and an aircraft carrier hovering off our coast with thousands more soldiers—all of it to support anti-Bosch forces. The same government that decades earlier helped Trujillo rise to power was now enforcing its will on us again. And it's not like the United States was oblivious to Trujillo's ways and the horrors and atrocities we endured. But Trujillo served the United States' business and political interests, which was all that mattered. It's why President Franklin D. Roosevelt's secretary of state Cordell Hull once infamously said of Trujillo, "He may be a son of a bitch, but he is our son of a bitch."

We didn't want another son of a bitch. While many of us wanted Juan Bosch, we mostly just wanted the opportunity to peacefully elect a new leader. But now, after intervening and occupying our island country from 1916 to 1924, the American military was back again, and it wasn't pretty. There were skirmishes, gunfire, Molotov cocktails, bloodshed, deaths, most of it swept under the rug of U.S. history . . . but not our history.

History, after all, is like a prism. It bends the light of truth into the colors it wants to show. It might be difficult for people in the United States to realize that those colors aren't always red, white, and blue. For instance, ask any school-age child in the United States who discovered their country, and the answer will be Christopher Columbus. Yet the reality is that none of Christopher Columbus's voyages ever set foot on what is now known as the United States. His four voyages to the Americas were all to the Caribbean, and historians document that all four touched Dominican Republic soil, likely more than once right in the area where I grew up. In fact, today there are two sites that claim to have the remains of Christopher Columbus—the Seville Cathedral in Spain and the Columbus Lighthouse at Santo Domingo in the Dominican Republic. Santo Domingo is also the oldest permanent city established by Europeans in the Western Hemisphere.

Obviously, I am proud of my country, as I'm sure most people are proud of theirs. I'm not trying to disparage the United States, but at the same time I don't believe people in the United States fully appreciate what we went through under Trujillo's reign of terror followed by the turmoil that was most of the 1960s. I especially don't believe people in the United States can fully comprehend what it's like to have another country occupying your country, meddling in your affairs without any provocation, dictating what you can and cannot do. But that's what happened to us, to my family and to me. It was demeaning, humiliating, and I'll go to my grave believing it was wrong.

Here is an example of how humiliating it was. One afternoon during that 1965 offseason, I was parked on Avenue Abraham Lincoln, which runs north and south in Santo Domingo, not far from the neighborhood where I grew up. I was waiting for a friend. A U.S. military jeep wheeled in behind me, and out stepped a soldier who looked as if he was a teenager. He was carrying a rifle, while another soldier stayed in the jeep, holding a machine gun.

"You have to get off this road," he ordered.

"Get off this road? Why?"

"This is now a military road," he replied. "No civilians are allowed to stop or park here."

"What do you mean a military road? This is my country. This is my neighborhood. I'm waiting for a friend. I'm not doing anything wrong. You cannot tell me to get off a road in my country."

"If you don't get off the street now, I'm taking you to San Souci."

I learned later that San Souci, which was next to the naval base, was where they sent dissidents—or *desafectos*.

I stared at him, my eyes radiating anger. He was a kid, a punk, a puny little man with a big gun and an even bigger country to back him, telling me what to do in *my* country. Unless you've experienced that, it's hard to describe how demeaning that is.

"Move! Now!" he barked, punctuating his words with jabs of his rifle.

As I listened to the syllables in his syntax, something struck me. I didn't pick up on it at first. But the more he talked, the more I deciphered his accent. It was that same lilt, that same syrupy drawl I heard when I was in Louisiana in 1956—and was told I couldn't play baseball there because of my skin color. Now that same accent was in my country, telling me I couldn't stand on a street in my neighborhood. I left, seething.

There are wounds—not flesh wounds, but something worse—where even a lifetime does not provide enough years to heal.

Historians say the infighting combined with the invasion took an estimated three thousand Dominican lives and the lives of thirty-one U.S. soldiers. And for what? We had done nothing to the United States.

When you have a civil war and another country intervenes, siding with one of the factions, it aggravates and amplifies everything that is so abominable about war. The horrors and heartache increase. Divisions widen. Instead of reducing the magnitude of our civil war, the United States' intervention intensified it. Not only were tens of thousands of U.S. troops occupying our country, but they were also siding with the remnants of Trujillo's regime, and they were killing Dominicans. Our country is a small country. Everybody knows everybody. People don't forget, and neither do future generations of people. Those types of wounds—the wounds of a civil war and an occupation—last a long time. And to think that all we wanted to do was have an opportunity to select and live under the government of our choosing. Instead, gallons of our blood spilled onto our soil.

Thankfully, none of that blood was Alou blood, but there was further humiliation that my family suffered. The United States chose the roof of my parents' home to set up a military post. They didn't ask; they just took. The U.S. military wasn't accustomed to urban warfare, and because of that it was important to establish posts high enough to see what was going on below. It especially gave snipers an edge. Because of the danger inherent in that, my parents were exiled, forced to flee to a relative's home. My brother Juan stayed behind, primarily to keep the home secured and protected from looters.

Imagine my father's anger. Me? I don't have to imagine. One day, when a U.S. helicopter was flying overhead, my father grabbed his shotgun and fired a futile blast as the chopper whirred past, well out of range. It was more of an angry statement of defiance than any real threat.

My brother Juan, a young man who was now attending the university, witnessed much of this. It affected him, as it did most of the young men in the Dominican Republic. Sure, he could play baseball, and who knows what might've happened had he pursued that as his career. But that wasn't what was most important. The future of our country was a consuming concern.

Because of the turmoil there were years when the Winter League seasons were either truncated or eliminated entirely. Scouts were not scouting in the Dominican Republic because the country was too unsafe to visit. Big-league players were going to Puerto Rico and Venezuela to play winter ball. And because Juan was the youngest of the four boys, my parents were trying to hold on to him for as long as they could. My mother especially didn't want to lose him to baseball. And they both wanted at least one of their boys to get a college degree. So even though Juan possessed solid baseball skills, he flew under the radar, as much as someone who carried the name Alou could be under the radar.

Not even the soldiers on the roof of the family house knew who he was. We know that because one of those soldiers came to Juan one day and asked for water. Juan allowed him into the house, and when he did the soldier saw photos on the wall of Matty, Jesús, and me in our big-league uniforms.

"Why do you have pictures of baseball players on the wall?" he asked. "Who are they?"

"Those are my brothers," Juan replied. "The Alou brothers."

Until then the soldier had no clue that he was occupying the roof of a house of the parents of three Major League Baseball players. Incredible. But even more incredible was his next question.

"What country is this?"

Imagine being part of an occupation army, occupying another country, and not even knowing what country that is.

At least after that the soldiers treated Juan in a friendlier manner.

Juan was nineteen at the time, and perhaps under different circumstances he might have signed a professional contract by then and been with a Minor League team somewhere. Based on my success, Matty signed with the Giants when he was seventeen and Jesús when he was fifteen. So it wasn't out of the question. In fact, Horacio "Rabbit" Martínez, who signed my brothers and me, kept asking when Juan was going to sign. But our country's turmoil and my parents' desire for Juan to get an education kept him unsigned, and at home.

Unfortunately, part of the education Juan was getting was in political unrest and civil war. Like the rest of my family and me, Juan sympathized with Juan Bosch's return to power, and he fell in with a group of fellow students who shared the same sentiment. The danger was palpable. People were being detained and often executed.

Juan was detained twice. The first time it was by U.S. soldiers. The second time he was detained Juan was at a bodega with some of his friends when a bomb exploded nearby. He and others were picked up by Dominican soldiers and taken to the depot for military transportation for questioning. Hundreds of other men were being held there, and for three days Juan slept on the floor. He wasn't even fed the first day, and then after that he was given only boiled cornmeal to eat.

One of his friends refused the cornmeal. "I'm not going to eat that," he said.

It elicited a smirking response from one of the soldiers. "I'm sure you'll eat it tomorrow," he said.

The next day when a different soldier again fed him the boiled cornmeal, he ate it.

Fortunately, Juan was released. When my parents learned what happened, they weren't about to take any more chances. Being detained twice was like strike one and strike two, and they were not about to wait to see if strike three would happen. They also didn't like it that the university shut down because of the civil unrest. So they sent Juan to Puerto Rico and ordered him to go to school and blend in. Juan essentially vanished, enrolling at the College of Agriculture and Mechanic Arts in Mayagüez—now the University of Puerto Rico at Mayagüez—which was known as one of the toughest colleges in the Americas. He played a little baseball there, but his real passion was his academics. Juan poured himself into his studies, graduating summa cum laude with a civil engineering degree. He then entered the workforce in Puerto Rico, ironically taking a job with the U.S. government.

And that's what happened to Juan Alou. When I played in the big leagues, people would joke that there was a fourth Alou brother and that, like Baltimore Orioles first baseman Boog Powell, his name was Boog. Boog Alou. Get it? It was supposed to be funny, but I never laughed. I knew the real story of the fourth Alou brother. Instead of baseball, Juan became a highly respected civil engineer in Puerto Rico, where he lives in retirement.

Through the decades I've occasionally come across someone who knows Juan. When I do baseball is never mentioned. Instead, people rave about his brilliant engineering mind. That's nice to hear, and I am proud of Juan, but sometimes I wish he would have become a big-league baseball player. Of course, there is no guarantee that would have happened, even if Juan continued to develop his baseball skills. But the thought of having four brothers in the big leagues, something not done since the 1800s, still intrigues me. Had Juan wanted to pursue baseball, I believe my dad would have been for it. He could see the life baseball was providing for Matty, Jesús, and me. But Juan was the baby, and my mother wanted him to get a university education, and she wanted to hold on to him as long as she could. She didn't quite get to hold on to him the way she wanted, at least not in the Dominican Republic, where his life was in danger. I've always admired Juan's courage, how unafraid he was to step up under all the circumstances he faced.

Instead of possibly becoming the fourth Alou brother in Major League Baseball, Juan became the first and only Alou brother to get a college degree. My sister Virginia also got a college degree and became a veterinarian. That's the way life happens. I've learned that you cannot predict your life. Sometimes you cannot even plan it. History has a way of happening, and sometimes it happens to you.

For me, history brought me to Juan Bosch later in 1965, around the same time that U.S. soldier ordered me off Avenue Abraham Lincoln. Bosch was a man I greatly admired and respected because of his anti-Trujillo stance, which forced him into years of exile. But now, even though he was back in the Dominican Republic, campaigning for president, the U.S. military had him under house arrest because of his left-leaning ideology.

Through a well-known sportswriter named Johnny Naranjo, I learned that Bosch wanted to meet me and the other Major League players from the Dominican Republic. Only three of us summoned enough courage to go. Together with Naranjo and another respected journalist, Tomás Troncoso, we went to meet Bosch.

It was tense. Walking up to Bosch's home was frightening. On one side were the U.S. Green Berets, all of them black soldiers brandishing weapons. On the other side were armed soldiers, fierce-looking Dominican men, bravely ensuring that nothing happened to the man we again wanted to freely elect to be our president.

We were ushered into the house and to Bosch's office, where he was reading a book about the great Major League pitcher Bob Feller. Bosch didn't know much about baseball, and he was reading that book to try to educate himself. Our presence startled him. Then he chuckled as he looked and saw that it was 2 p.m., the scheduled time for our meeting.

"You guys are punctual," he said. Dominicans—then and now—are known to operate on island time.

"That's from baseball," I explained. "When they tell you that you have to be somewhere at 5 p.m., you have to be there at 5 p.m. You have to be punctual if you're going to play professional baseball."

"I'm a Dominican who doesn't know baseball," Bosch said, smiling.

The conversation turned serious as Bosch began appealing to us. I felt for him. Here he was, this tremendous scholar and educator, but history had thrust him into a difficult situation, and now that difficult situation was about to tap me on the shoulder.

"In my own country, I'm a prisoner," Bosch said. "You guys have access to the United States media. When you get back to the U.S., denounce the intervention."

His request rocked me, and it took me several seconds to respond. "Professor," I finally said, "we are really nothing but baseball players. This is not something we should be involved with. If we get involved, we don't know what might happen."

One of the journalists, Tomás Troncoso, spoke up, mentioning the obvious. "You know," he said, "the Yankees don't lose elections in Latin America."

Troncoso wasn't talking about the *New York* Yankees. He was talking about the United States. After suffering that setback in

Cuba, the United States was especially determined to not leave the Dominican Republic until it accomplished what it wanted, in spite of signs that said YANKEE GO HOME! that littered our capital city, Santo Domingo. And what the United States wanted was Joaquín Balaguer in power. The election was a foregone conclusion. Everyone knew it.

I studied Bosch and could see the kindness, the sincerity, in his eyes. This was an intellectual and a philosopher, a poet and a writer. In another time and place his life might've been very different. But not in the time and place we lived in. History had thrust him, and by extension me, into a difficult position.

I knew that what Bosch was asking me to do was too dangerous. I had a wife and three children—my boys, Felipe and José, and my daughter, Maria. My wife was also pregnant with our fourth child—a boy whom we would name Moisés. My parents also relied on me for support.

We respectfully declined Bosch's request. He seemed to understand, as if he knew in advance what our answer would be. He didn't pressure us. The meeting was cordial and brief.

When we left I didn't turn to see if Bosch returned to the book about Bob Feller. I doubt he did. Baseball had not been important to him prior to our meeting, and I doubt it was any more important afterward. I know one thing for sure: it no longer seemed important to me.

18

Hitting the Sweet Spot

You would think I would've been too distracted with the turmoil in my country to accomplish much during the 1966 season. Plus, my fourth child, Moisés, was born in the middle of the season—on July 3. It can be difficult to keep focus when so much is going on—not only back home but in your own home.

But somehow not only did I keep focus, but I also had what many believe was my best big-league season. I still personally point to my 1962 season as my best, though I can certainly see where others can make a strong statistical argument for 1966. That season I led all of Major League Baseball in at-bats (666) and hits (218), tied Frank Robinson for runs scored (122), led the National League in total bases (355), was named the Braves' MVP by the Atlanta writers, finished fifth in the National League for MVP, and made the All-Star team.

Oh, and my .327 batting average was the second best in all of baseball. Second, that is, to my brother Matty.

It was quite a season, which earned the respect and praise of my teammates. "I've never seen anyone stand out head and shoulders the way Felipe did," Joe Torre told *Sport* magazine. "Everything he hit, he hit hard. You can't imagine some of the line drives that were caught." And in the same article, Hank Aaron added, "We think he should have been the league's Most Valuable Player. I've never seen anyone hit so consistently well all season long."

There was one other thing nobody had ever seen—not before or since. For the first and only time in Major League history, two brothers finished first and second in batting average. As proud as I was for the Alou family name, I was also proud for my country.

Not only had two Dominicans finished with the best batting averages in the big leagues, but coming in at third was Rico Carty. Yet another Dominican, Manny Mota, might've been in the mix, too, had he accumulated enough plate appearances. Manny batted .332, but with only 359 plate appearances, which was roughly 143 fewer than what was needed to qualify.

Still, to have three Dominicans finish first, second, and third—Matty with a .342 batting average, me at .327, and Carty at .326—was quite a feat. I believe it also solidified that the Dominicans were here to stay in Major League Baseball. Not only were players from my country making our mark only eight years after I entered the league as the first to go from Dominican soil to the big leagues, but more elite players were coming. The pipeline was open, and it wouldn't be too long before the trickle turned into a flood.

That season was Matty's first in Pittsburgh. The Giants traded him on December 1, 1965, to the Pirates for pitcher Joe Gibbon and our friend catcher-outfielder Ozzie Virgil Sr. I guess I can't blame the Giants. After all, Matty batted .264 and .231 the previous two seasons as a part-time player. But in retrospect, Gibbon went only 12-13 for the Giants over the next three-plus seasons, while Virgil batted .213 in 1966, before being sent to the Minor Leagues. He finished with only one more big-league at-bat, in 1969.

Meanwhile, Matty became one of baseball's best hitters. After leading the Major Leagues in hitting in 1966, he went on to bat .338, .332, and .331 over the next three seasons and finished with a .307 career batting average. Matty was a good all-around athlete, with great reflexes and hand-eye coordination. He even pitched the final two innings in an August 26, 1965, mop-up game that the Giants lost 8–0 to the Pirates at Pittsburgh's Forbes Field. He gave up three hits but didn't surrender a run and also struck out three—including Hall of Famer Willie Stargell, twice.

But Matty wasn't in the big leagues to pitch. He was there to hit. And it was during that spring training in 1966 when Roberto Clemente and Pirates manager Harry Walker turned Matty from a pull hitter into a line-drive hitter. The transformation was dramatic.

I can't say I was surprised. From the time we were kids, I always knew Matty was a hitter. We used to play with little coconuts and a makeshift bat, and no matter how hard I tried I could never get him to swing and miss because of that incredible hand-eye coordination he possessed. Plus, even though Matty was generously listed at five foot nine, he was fearless. So tough. One time, during a Winter League game, Matty and Rico Carty ran into each other chasing a fly ball in the outfield. It was a horrific collision, and as both men lay on the ground, I thought Matty was dead. But it was Matty who got up and Carty who was carried off the field on a stretcher, muttering, "Now I know for sure that the Alous are witches." No, not witches. But strong. Matty had our father's height and build. He was barrel-chested with Popeye forearms.

When I saw Matty during that 1966 season, I noticed he had developed a beautiful left-handed swing. Of course, beauty is in the eye of the beholder. Hall of Fame pitcher Steve Carlton once called Matty "the worst .300 hitter I've ever seen." But as I've always believed, everyone has their own hitting style, unique to them, like a fingerprint. Another Hall of Famer, Ted Williams, once told *The Sporting News* that Matty "violates every hitting principle I ever taught." Yet he was a career .307 hitter who could hit gap-to-gap line drives and also bunt and run. The tools were all there, and Matty was maximizing them.

I would be lying if I said I wasn't aware that my brother and I were battling for the batting crown. I would also be lying if I said I was rooting against Matty. I was enormously proud of my little brother and was, in fact, rooting *for* him. When a writer from *The Sporting News* asked me about the batting race between my brother and me, I told him, "It would be a wonderful thing for Matty to win it. Wonderful for the Alous, and wonderful for baseball in the Dominican Republic. We always sort of took care of Matty because he was so small. Now look at him, leading all of us in hitting."

At the same time, I purposely stayed away from checking the newspapers to see what the latest statistics were. I was more aware of what Rico Carty was doing because we were teammates, and as such I was also rooting for him. Although Rico wasn't always a pleasure to be around, he was a joy to watch at the plate. He was one of the best right-handed hitters I ever saw and hands down the best two-strike hitter I ever saw. If not for injuries and also that Rico contracted tuberculosis during the prime of his career, there is no telling what kind of numbers he might have amassed. He was some kind of special talent with a bat in his hands.

The media took note that two Alou brothers and three Dominicans were battling for the batting title, but this was really nothing new for us. In the Winter League—Matty, myself, Carty, my other brother Jesús, and Manny Mota—we were always the best hitters. The only difference is that now it was translating to the Major Leagues.

But here is the crazy part. I saw Matty during the season when the Pirates were in Atlanta. I ran into him during batting practices, and we stopped and chatted briefly, just a few pleasantries. The next day both of us received telegrams from Major League Baseball, telling us we were each fined for fraternizing. Back then they would situate an umpire behind home plate during pregame to see if opposing players would talk to each other. It was beyond silly, and at some point over the past fifty years baseball stopped doing that. Just watch players today, hugging before games when they see each other, chatting and laughing. To tell me I couldn't exchange a few sentences with my own brother was ridiculous. I could not believe it. The very definition of fraternizing is to *associate as brothers*. Well, this *was* my brother. Flesh and blood. And now we were being fined for doing what brothers should do, which is to behave like brothers. Incredible. Instead of using the opportunity to promote that two brothers were the two best hitters in the game, Major League Baseball chose to fine us. I still cannot believe it.

Toward the end of the season, people were noting that Matty's batting average was higher based on fewer at-bats—and presenting that as a negative. To me that put more pressure on Matty. An 0-for-4 day would damage his batting average more than it would mine. So I rejected the notion that it was easier for him because he finished with 131 fewer at-bats. I also bristled when people said he was a slap hitter and a bunter. Matty had nine triples that year. You don't reach third base that many times slapping at the ball or by bunting.

All in all, it was a fun year. I was in a good groove. Sandy Koufax won the Cy Young Award and finished second in the MVP voting, thanks to his 27-9 record with a 1.73 earned run average. Yet that year I hit three home runs off Koufax, two of them coming in one game.

It was my best statistical season, but it ended on an ominous tone. A Sammy Ellis pitch when we played the Cincinnati Reds on September 18 caught me inside, hitting my left hand and breaking a small bone near the first knuckle on my index finger. I missed six days and returned just in time to face Juan Marichal and the Giants. I didn't miss a beat, going 2 for 4 against Juan. But missing those *6* games meant that I finished with *666* at-bats during the '*66* season. I'm really not superstitious, but I am a believer in the Bible, and that's too many number 6's for me.

For whatever reason, I could feel my body starting to rebel against me after that. In the seasons that followed I started to understand how, when I was a younger player, I would see veterans spending extra time in the whirlpool and seeking the trainer's hands more. Now that was me.

I had abused my body. Baseball will take its toll. But the main abuse came from how I grew up in the Dominican Republic. It was time to pay the dues for the hard work I did in my father's blacksmith shop and especially the grueling work I used to do in a rock mine. I worked the mines during the summers when I was fourteen, fifteen, and sixteen, and to this day it is the hardest work I've ever done. It also permanently damaged me.

The work wasn't only hard; it was relentless. I would work eight hours straight, from 10 p.m. to 6 a.m., picking up boulders with my friend Carlos Rojas and throwing them into an automated crusher. It helped that Rojas was left-handed and I was right-handed. We would bend over, pick up those boulders, and toss them into a crusher we called Korea because of how relentless and unyielding it was. That machine never seemed to get enough boulders to crush, and we were constantly struggling to keep up. There were no breaks, either, other than maybe a quick gulp of water out of a dusty tin cup. Trucks were constantly arriving from the quarry with more boulders. Three shifts worked around the clock, with fifteen men to a shift. At the end of the week the shift that did the most work got a bonus of 10 pesos, which we never saw. Instead, it went to the man in charge of that shift.

It was the kind of work an animal would do, and I hated it. But I was the oldest child, and I had to help feed the family. The work did two things. It earned me $16 a week, which would go straight to my dad, who was a foreman at the rock mine. And it also permanently wrecked my right arm.

Nobody knew it, but when I entered professional baseball, my right arm was damaged goods, thanks to the rock mine and working with my father in his blacksmith and carpentry shop. Then I jammed my arm sliding headfirst during the 1962 World Series. After that I noticed I couldn't totally extend my arm—a condition I kept quiet. To this day my right arm remains crooked. If I want to get a nice suit, I have to get it tailored to accommodate the difference in length between my right and left arms. And it hurts. It always hurts. To this day there is a dull pain at my right elbow, especially if I touch it.

Toward the end of the 1967 season I started to feel numbness in my throwing hand, particularly at my pinkie, and it was causing me trouble to hold and throw a baseball. Gripping a bat was even more difficult, much less swinging it with any authority. They discovered twenty-six bone chips and a damaged ulnar nerve, and subsequent surgery shelved me for the last month of the season.

I rebounded in 1968, leading Major League Baseball in plate appearances (718) and at-bats (662) and tying Pete Rose for the lead in hits (210). I also batted .317, an MLB third-best behind Rose and—who else?—my brother Matty. Batting over .300 that season was no small feat, given that the NL average dipped to .243 and only six hitters in all of baseball batted better than .300. After that 1968 season, which was known as the year of the pitcher, the mound was lowered from fifteen inches to ten inches and the size of the strike zone reduced.

Although it was a nice comeback season for me, the aches and pains were getting worse, and my recovery time was taking longer. I could sense the end approaching, and I guess so did the Braves. After batting over .300 the first couple of months in 1969, I suffered a broken finger when St. Louis Cardinals right-hander Chuck Taylor hit me with a pitch. To fill my spot the Braves acquired left-handed hitting Tony González from the San Diego Padres. When I returned the Braves platooned Tony and me in the outfield, which sent me a big signal.

The next signal came in the divisional series, the first ever in Major League Baseball. As the NL West champs, we went against the 1969 Miracle Mets from the NL East—and were swept three straight games in a five-game series. I appeared only as a pinch hitter in the eighth inning of the final game, ripping a line drive off Nolan Ryan right into the glove of shortstop Bud Harrelson for an out.

During the 1969 offseason what seemed inevitable happened. The Braves traded me on December 3 to the Oakland A's, beginning what would be a five-year final stretch where I played for four different teams.

I could see the finish line to my playing career. But that wasn't the only thing coming to an end. So had my marriage to Maria.

19

Family Matters

Baseball is hard on families; there is no getting around it. A man is on the road a lot, away from his wife and kids, in an environment fraught with temptations. There are always women hanging around baseball clubs. Beautiful women. At the ballparks, at hotels, at restaurants, on the street, everywhere. And the last thing on their mind is your family.

My family was always on my mind. I remember a night game on July 2, 1966, when all I could think about prior to it was my wife, Maria. The Atlanta Braves were in San Francisco for the third of a four-game series against the Giants. It also was the third day of what would be an eleven-game road trip. But my mind was in Atlanta, where Maria was pregnant with our fourth child. I flew my mother and sister Virginia in to help her, but there were still so many details I needed to tend to, and I didn't like being away.

I called Maria before the game. She was having a difficult time with this pregnancy, but she assured me all was fine. Comforted with that report, I went 4 for 5 that night, with three singles and a two-run home run, to help lead my team to a 3–1 victory against the Giants.

What I learned later was that Maria was not fine. She had not been feeling well, but she did not want to burden me with any concerns. Later that night, right about the time I was hitting that two-run homer, Maria was en route to the hospital. The next morning she gave birth to our third son, Moisés. Later that same day, on July 3, 1966, after I learned the news of our new family addition, we exploded for twenty hits and seventeen runs against the Giants. Our pitcher that day, Tony Cloninger, made history. Cloninger became the first National League player, and to this day the only pitcher ever, to hit two grand-slam home runs in one game. Tony drove in nine of our seventeen runs in addition to pitching a complete game in a 17–3 cakewalk victory. Every starter in our lineup had either a hit or a run scored—or both—except for one player: Felipe Alou.

Sometimes when a ballplayer is having a bad day, or a bad stretch, the public isn't aware of what is going on behind the scenes. Is he distracted with domestic concerns? Are there problems at home? Is one of the children sick? Did he and his girlfriend just break up? Is there an aged parent or a grandparent in failing health?

In my case I went from a 4-for-5 day where I got almost half of my team's 9 hits and accounted for all 3 of our runs by way of 2 RBI and 1 run scored, to an 0-for-3 game with no runs scored on a day when our team pounded out 20 hits and scored 17 runs. What changed?

The birth of my third son and fourth child while I was playing baseball on the opposite end of the country—that's what changed. The box score can tell a lot, but it cannot tell the whole story. It cannot tell you what is going on in life.

By the mid-1960s societal mores were rapidly changing—especially sexual mores. The freedom of sex blew wide open during that decade. Add to that the reality that when you're young and successful in sports, the temptations can be overwhelming. I admit they were for me. It wasn't uncommon for us as ballplayers to check into our hotel on the road, and waiting for us would be three or four messages from women we didn't even know. How does a man in his twenties or thirties resist that again and again? But that's the baseball culture. Marriages can be difficult enough without those types of extra challenges.

Of course, nobody goes into a marriage thinking it's not going to last. I've been married four times. Only one has lasted—my current marriage to Lucie, which is now thirty-two years strong. We have two children together—Valerie and Felipe Jr. (a name we had to quickly give him because we were told we were having another girl). I'm not going to blame baseball for what happened to my three other marriages. I blame myself. But baseball didn't help. I wasn't immune to the evils of a traveling ballplayer. Even still, as a believer it pains me to know that I gave in to temptation. For that I accept my responsibility before God. He knows everything—all my steps, my thoughts, my weaknesses, my failures. Instead of honoring God, as I was told to do in the Bible, I listened to the offers of Satan. Once you become a believer, you become a bigger target to sin. And I was vulnerable to sin. I had a weakness with women, which Satan attacked. Alcohol and drugs were never a temptation for me. I was spared from that, for which I thank God. But with women it was different. Sin humbles a man. I thought I was invincible. But no man is. The minute we get careless with God . . . well, it doesn't take much.

There were many times when, with God's help, I fought back, when I resisted temptation. But temptation was always there. One time, when I was in a hospital bed in Houston, recovering from surgery, I awoke to discover that the nurse had climbed into my bed with me. I stopped that before it went any further. Another time I was invited to an evening party by some Venezuelan guys. When I got there everybody was naked, swimming, standing around. Beer, wine, and liquor were everywhere. It was early in the evening and things had not yet gotten too wild, but I could tell it was about to. Somebody told me where I could go take off my clothes and join the party. Instead, I left. Another time I was invited to a house party, only to be greeted by the overwhelming scent of marijuana smoke as I walked through the front door. There were women everywhere, and not one of them had a stitch of clothing on. I saw people having sex. I turned and left.

So I fought it. I fought the temptation. Yes, there were too many times when I failed, but there were also many times when I succeeded in honoring God.

Those failures took their toll on my failed marriages. I admit that. But I will also say this: it takes two to tango. I do not believe that it is all one person's fault when a marriage fails. With Maria I take most of the blame. We married young. She was my first love.

We were from the same hometown. Not only was it a marriage I thought would last, but for years after we divorced in 1968 I had it in the back of my head that we would get back together. We never did. But in our ten years of marriage we did have four children together—Felipe, Maria, José, and Moisés.

In the late '60s I met a woman in Atlanta, Beverly Martin, who in 1969 became my second wife. She was American, college educated. The home I still have in the Dominican Republic I built for her and the three beautiful daughters we had together—Christia, Cheri, and Jennifer. But Beverly would openly complain, in front of other people, that there was no way her children were going to live in the Dominican Republic, that it was no place to live. This was at the time when my career was winding down, which meant that our home in the Dominican wasn't going to be for the offseason. It was going to be our permanent home. Now, from the distance of time, I can see Beverly's fears. It was a nice house, but many times the electricity could go out and not come back for several days. Sometimes you could lose water for a week and would have to rely on truckloads to come by and provide water that was good enough only for the toilet. Beverly's concerns were valid. But at the same time, if you are demeaning my country, you are demeaning me. Both happened too often, and our marriage lasted only five years.

Without a woman who wanted to live in the Dominican Republic, I then chose to marry a Dominican. In this case it was my third wife, Elsa Brens. We had two boys—Felipe José and Luis Emilio. Elsa worked as a secretary for the owners of the new Dominican summer league, so she was aware of the culture. Maybe it was because of that, knowing how ballplayers could be, that she was always suspicious of me, always accusing me of infidelity. One day I was served divorce papers, and that was the end of our marriage.

The ones who suffer the most from failed marriages are the children. You go from being in their lives, under the same roof, to snapshots of time with them. It's difficult. I'm proud that all of my eleven children were the products of a marriage, and depending on where they were born—in America, Canada, or the Dominican Republic—

they came into the world with either Alou or Rojas as their surname. But no matter where they were born, none of my children was born in the street, and all of them have become outstanding adults. Not one of them has ever done anything to disrespect the family name, something I preached from the time they were old enough to understand. Though I'm not proud that I've been married four times, I am proud that my children are products of those marriages and not of affairs. That's not me. I'm not a man who likes to be unmarried. I like having a wife. And I like having children.

When my children with Maria were young, it was the best feeling. You remember the little things. Sweet memories. Innocent pleasures. Those tender young children would try their hardest to wait up for me at night to come home from the ballpark. I would bring them bubble gum from the clubhouse, and they would be thrilled. You miss simple moments like that.

You also miss big moments, too. Thank goodness I was still married to Maria when Moisés was two years old and we were at the beach together in the Dominican Republic. Moisés was out of my eyesight for what seemed like a second, when I saw him facedown in a small puddle of water, no more than five inches deep, his belly bloated and his body turning blue. I lunged into action. I believe I must have helped little Moisés vomit a gallon of water. It was scary. Moisés didn't leave my eyesight after that, and what I noticed fifteen minutes later was that he went straight back to the same spot where he almost drowned. As a parent you file away those moments, moments you might miss if there is a divorce. When Moisés was only two years old I could already see that he was like Uncle Matty. Fearless.

Other stories you're not there for. Instead, you hear about them from a distance, from what is now talking to your ex-wife on the telephone, often over the static of an international connection. Like the time when Moisés was seven, playing with matches underneath his bed, setting a fire ablaze. Thankfully, his sister, Maria, acted fast enough and called the fire department before it raged out of control. Then there was also the time when Moisés was nine and dislocated his thumb playing with firecrackers. And another time, when Moisés was eleven, he hopped a neighbor's fence to retrieve a rubber ball, only to have a German shepherd maul him so viciously that to this day he still has scars on his chest.

The biggest event I missed, the one that haunts me, arrived on March 26, 1976. I say event, but it was really a tragedy, the biggest tragedy of my life. My playing career was over, and I was invited to be a spring training instructor for the Montreal Expos. We were playing a Grapefruit League game against the Minnesota Twins at Tinker Field in Orlando. I was coaching third base that night when I heard my name over the loudspeaker.

"Mr. Alou, please come to the Twins' office!"

A few moments later the same message again boomed across the loudspeaker: "Mr. Alou, please come to the Twins' office!"

My heart raced. My parents were up in years, and I thought something happened to one of them. I came off the field and, still in uniform, went to the Twins' office. Calvin Griffith, the Twins' owner and general manager, was there, and I could see in his eyes that I was about to hear something dreadful.

"I have bad news," he said. "Your son died in a swimming pool accident."

I fainted. Mr. Griffith caught me before I hit the ground.

How long I remained passed out, I don't know. What I do know is that I probably didn't sleep for days. I had a home for Maria and our children in the best neighborhood in Santo Domingo. Felipe, my firstborn, was sixteen at the time—a good-looking boy, a good athlete, an aspiring ballplayer, with so much life ahead of him. He was with his friends when they came across a swimming pool that was under construction. Thinking that the water was deep, Felipe dove in. The water was shallow. He broke his neck and died in that pool.

Our trainer drove me to our spring training camp in Daytona Beach so I could get my passport and other documents I needed, and then to Miami, where I was to catch a Dominicana Airlines flight. Tears streamed down my cheeks much of the way. I made the flight, but we sat on the plane outside the terminal for one hour, then two hours, then three hours. I lost it, especially when I learned that the delay was because of a late flight coming in from New Orleans that had a Dominican Republic general on it. They were delaying an entire flight just to accommodate him. I started yelling at the cockpit, uncontrollable. It was horrible. Only a parent who has lost a child can possibly understand.

When I got home and to the funeral home, I saw my firstborn son's body lying in an open casket, wearing a gray-and-white-checkered suit. Family, friends, and relatives were there, crying and wailing. I was crying. I noticed that the only one not crying was my youngest son, Moisés. Nine years old and his face was like steel, defiant at death. He sat there in a chair as if he were guarding his big brother, as if he were ensuring that nothing more was going to happen to him. My tears fell heavier when I saw that. I will never forget the look on Moisés's face. He pulsated anger, anger at the fate of his big brother. Moisés hated what happened. Hated death.

I felt the same anger, along with despair. I was afraid of sharks, but I found myself snorkeling alone, descending deeper into the dark depths of the Caribbean Sea than I had ever done before, holding my breath for so long I wondered if I would make it to the surface in time. As for sharks, I yearned for one to confront me.

I had a round-trip ticket to go back to the United States, but I never used it. I truly believed I was done with baseball, done with life. I wanted to retreat into the Dominican, deep into my sorrow. That might sound dramatic, but for the next decade I drifted. People sometimes ask me why it took so long before I got a Major League managerial job. There were a lot of factors, one of them being the obvious reason that field-managing jobs were slow to come to Latinos. But I have to be honest in saying that for many years baseball and life didn't seem that important. I was haunted. I had nightmares. Many times I wanted to be left alone. For about a dozen years I couldn't even talk about my son's death. And then one night, while I was sleeping, I swear I felt Felipe's hand on my head—a brief reassuring touch. It was only after that when I believed I could move on with my life.

But you never really move on.

20

Winding Down

A ballplayer's career ends in two ways—gradually and suddenly. It happens to everyone who has ever played this game. You might be able to outrun a baseball, but you won't be able to outrun baseball itself. The game catches up with you. It catches up with everyone.

You start to notice little things. Things that fans don't see. Things that the box score doesn't record. They say numbers don't lie, but sometimes they don't tell the whole story. You notice that going from first to third on a single to right is no longer a guarantee. I could sense that I had lost a step or two, or maybe three, which can make all the difference on a baseball field.

In 1968, my penultimate season with the Atlanta Braves, I put up good numbers. But I was thirty-three years old, and I could tell my strength was declining. Two seasons earlier, in 1966, I had hit a career-high 31 home runs. But even with all the good numbers I posted in that '68 season, I hit only 11 homers. Those numbers weren't lying.

Players will do just about anything to stay on the field and also to get an edge—or to at least maintain the edge they once had. By the late '60s amphetamines had flooded into the game—uppers as well as downers. It wasn't uncommon to see trays with different colored pills in the clubhouse—like jellybeans. Mostly it was green amphetamine pills, or what came to be called greenies. Players were also drinking something called red juice. Wild Turkey bourbon whiskey was the liquor of choice to relax. Traveling through time zones, and the daily grind of games can wear you down—and at the same time it can make it difficult to relax and sleep. I was never much for liquor, and I never had a problem with energy, not to the point where I felt like I needed to take any pills. I took a couple of B-12 shots late in my career, and that was it.

Years later, when steroids overtook the game, I told a reporter that ballplayers will do anything to get an edge, and I used the example of amphetamines in my day. That comment came back to haunt me in 2006, when I was called to testify all day for former senator George Mitchell's investigation into steroid use in baseball—or what came to be known as the Mitchell Report.

But no matter what you do, or don't do, your body is going to eventually let you know that your time has come and gone. The game will let you know, too. After 1968 I played for five teams over the next six seasons. That's an obvious indicator to let you know your career is winding down. It's also a good opportunity to see how different organizations do things and also to make a few more lifelong friends and connections.

The second time you're traded is not as traumatic as the first time. But it's still not easy. I played six years for the Braves, the same number of years I played for the Giants, so it felt like my second home in the big leagues. But the Braves traded me to the Oakland A's on December 3, 1969, for pitcher Jim Nash, who played only three more seasons in the big leagues, going 23-25. So it was back to the Bay Area for me. Only this time it was on the other side of the bay. I would look across the water at the San Francisco skyline, and I realized that I missed it terribly.

The 1970s Oakland A's had a young team with a lot of talent, and they were looking for a veteran presence. You stick around in baseball long enough, and that's what you become—a veteran presence.

One of the young talents was a kid coming off a 47 home run, 118 RBI season. His name was Reggie Jackson. His middle name was Martinez, which was the first name of his father, who was half Puerto Rican. Reggie was proud of his Hispanic roots, and he was always close to the Latinos, always trying to talk with us in Spanish. Broken Spanish. But Spanish nonetheless. Reggie was cocky, but he was cocky because he was good. We could all see that. His power was obvious. But what people tended to overlook is that Reggie had a tremendous arm in right field. He could have been a pitcher; his arm was that good. His only flaw is that he didn't have a quick release. Reggie would wind up before he threw. But what an arm! And he could run, too.

The other talents on that A's squad were guys who would go on to form the nucleus of three straight World Series championship teams in 1972, 1973, and 1974—Sal Bando, Bert Campaneris, Joe Rudi, and Gene Tenace. And the young pitching was outstanding—Jim "Catfish" Hunter, John "Blue Moon" Odom, Vida Blue, and Rollie Fingers.

I believe your leaders are not always your best players, or even your starters. You need both. That A's team I joined had leadership in the everyday lineup and on the bench. Three of us went on to become Major League managers—myself, Marcel Lachemann, and an intelligent twenty-five-year-old middle infielder who didn't play very much but who was passionate about the game, always paying attention, always keenly observing, analyzing, asking questions.

One day I went up to him and did something I never did before or since. I told him he should think about getting into coaching. He laughed, and I'm sure he thought I was being a smart aleck or disrespectful. But I was serious. To my eye I was looking at a future big-league manager.

Forty-four years later that young kid was inducted into the Hall of Fame . . . as a manager. His name? Tony La Russa. Tony managed for three different big-league teams—the Chicago White Sox, the Oakland A's, and the St. Louis Cardinals. He won three World Series titles and six pennants. At his side as his pitching coach for all that success was one of our teammates on that 1970 A's team—backup catcher Dave Duncan. Like La Russa, Duncan was an intelligent guy. It wasn't surprising to me that he became one of the game's premier pitching coaches.

People remember all the personalities around those Oakland A's of the early '70s, mainly because of the way the owner, Charlie Finley, marketed the team with the nicknames, the white shoes, the sleeveless uniforms, and the mustaches. He gave us $300 to grow mustaches, which a lot of us, including me, did. I still wear a mustache to this day. Charlie got Major League Baseball to adopt the designated hitter. He even got them to experiment with an orange baseball, which didn't catch on.

To me one of the oddest things about playing for the A's was that our mascot was a mule. A real mule! I would be taking batting practice and would look over and see a mule eating hay. I thought maybe I was back in the Dominican Republic.

Unfortunately, I played barely more than a year for Oakland and thus never got to enjoy playing for those three World Championships teams. I also didn't get to enjoy playing together again in the Bay Area with my brothers Matty and Jesús. Matty played for Oakland in 1972 and Jesús in 1973, each of them earning the World Series ring I never got as a player.

Just three games into the 1971 season, on April 9, A's manager Dick Williams called me into his office and told me they were going with Joe Rudi as their regular left fielder and they were trading me to the New York Yankees. In return, the A's got a couple of journeyman pitchers who won a combined total of twenty-two Major League games in their careers—Rob Gardner and Ron Klimkowski. Nothing against Gardner and Klimkowski, but this was yet another indicator that my playing career was winding down. I was essentially unloaded.

Although I was going to the most iconic franchise in all of sports, these weren't the Yankees of my youth or even the Yankees I played against in the 1962 World Series. These Yankees were on a steady decline since their last World Series appearance in 1964. Starting in 1965 the Yankees finished sixth, tenth (last place), ninth, fifth, and fifth (second to last since MLB went to the division format in 1969). In 1970, perhaps as a harbinger, they finished second, mainly on the strength of their Rookie of the Year catcher, Thurman Munson.

Three years later things really moved forward when a shipbuilder from Ohio named George Steinbrenner purchased the franchise, becoming its principal owner.

Because of the abruptness of the trade at the start of the season, the Yankees were kind enough to allow me to drive across the country rather than catching a flight and reporting right away. I hadn't even found an apartment yet in Oakland, and my family still hadn't arrived, although all our belongings had been shipped to me. I had an Oldsmobile 88, and I loaded it with bats, duffel bags, gloves, pots, pans, my clothes, my wife's clothes, children's clothes . . . and on Easter weekend I headed on the highway. My car was so packed I barely had enough room to move. I first had to drive south and then head east on 1-40. Somewhere on the outskirts of Kingman, Arizona, on a stretch of open road that sloped downward, I was cruising at 100 mph. In my rearview mirror, far back in the distance, I saw a car, and I could tell that it, too, was moving at a pretty good clip. It got closer, closer, closer . . . then lights started flashing. It was an unmarked police car.

All the normal questions followed. It quickly became apparent to the officer, which was confirmed by my driver's license, who I was and why I was heading to New York with a car full of belongings.

"I'm going to give you a break," he said as his eyes scanned the backseat of my car. "But can you spare one of those bats?"

"Sure," I said, grabbing a bat and handing it to him.

"Thank you," he said.

"No, no. Thank you."

I slept one night at a Holiday Inn in Memphis, but only for a few hours. The sounds of people having sex in the room both to the right and to the left prevented me from getting any rest. So I got back on the road and kept driving hour after hour. At 2 p.m. on April 14, I rolled into the parking lot at Yankee Stadium. It must have seemed to the parking attendants like Jed Clampett from *The Beverly Hillbillies* television show had arrived. I met Yankees manager Ralph Houk, who was happy to see me.

"Are you able to play tonight?" he asked.

The Yankees were facing the Detroit Tigers and their tough left-handed pitcher Mickey Lolich that night.

"Sure," I replied.

In my second at-bat, leading off the bottom of the fourth inning, I hit a fly ball that smacked the foul pole for a home run. It helped us and our starting pitcher, Fritz Peterson, get an 8–4 victory. The next day I hit another home run. In doing so I became the first New York Yankee in history to hit a home run in each of his first two games. Since then only five other Yankees have accomplished that feat—Graig Nettles (1973), Dave Kingman (1977), Joe Lefebvre (1980), Aaron Judge (2016), and Ji-Man Choi (2017).

I could see the makings of why the Yankees were back on the rise and also the remnants of why they had so many down years. I batted second in the lineup, between Horace Clark and Thurman Munson. Roy White, a real gentleman, batted cleanup. Danny Cater batted in the five hole, followed by John Ellis, Bobby Murcer (who would bat .331 that season), and our smart shortstop, Gene "Stick" Michael.

The other thing I immediately saw with this team is they partied more than any team I had ever been on. That became apparent a couple of days after I arrived, when we were in Baltimore for a three-game series. I knew there had been some partying going on at the hotel that Saturday night—you couldn't help but hear it—but I still wasn't prepared for what I saw the following morning. The door to the hotel room Murcer and Cater roomed in together was off the hinges and leaning against the wall inside the room, and their TV set had been thrown out the window onto the street below.

I fell in with a young third baseman named Jerry Kenney, and he quickly told me who was who and what was what. All the guys were great teammates, but when you were with a bunch of wild partyers, you needed to be cautious with whom you hung around.

"Be careful of going out with John Ellis," Kenney said. "He likes to fight."

I filed that bit of information away.

The following spring training in Florida, on our first road trip, we bused to St. Petersburg from Fort Lauderdale. After we checked into our hotel, Kenney and I went to a sports bar. John Ellis was already there with a couple of other teammates. All of a sudden I heard guys yelling and a *boom! boom!* Ellis had knocked two guys to the floor with a couple of punches. It was that quick. I looked at Kenney, and he gave me an I-told-you-so nod.

This was also relief pitcher Sparky Lyle's first season with the Yankees, having come over from the Boston Red Sox in a 1972 spring training trade for Danny Cater and Mario Guerrero, a fellow Dominican who was a Minor League middle infielder. The craziness really ratcheted up with Sparky in the mix. Once, when we left Yankee Stadium on a bus, heading to the airport, a car full of young women followed us. Sparky went to the back of the bus and, bending over, pulled down his pants, exposing his bare ass and more. The first opportunity those women had to get off the road, they did.

Without a doubt, though, the craziest thing that happened occurred during spring training in 1973. Two of our starting pitchers, Fritz Peterson and Mike Kekich, announced that several months earlier they swapped wives and kids. They even traded their pet dogs. It made national news. To say we were shocked was an understatement. That team had a lot of sin, but two players trading wives and kids? Unbelievable. It became a distraction, not only for the team, but I'm sure for Peterson and Kekich.

Kekich's roommate was Celerino Sánchez, a third baseman from Mexico. Celerino would tell me how at night Kekich was inconsolable, crying and yelling that he wanted his wife and family back. Instead, Kekich was traded on June 12 to the Cleveland Indians, who released him the following spring. He was never the same pitcher again. He and the former Marilyn Peterson didn't last. Fritz Peterson was traded the next season, also to Cleveland, in a trade that brought the Yankees two key players who helped them win championships—Chris Chambliss and Dick Tidrow. Fritz and the former Susanne Kekich ended up marrying and are still married to this day.

That unconventional family story overshadowed a more conventional family story. Two of the Alou brothers were reunited—Matty and me. On November 24, 1972, the Yankees swung another trade with the Oakland A's, with whom Matty had just won a World Series, bringing him to New York for the 1973 season. It was wonderful to be reunited with Matty, especially now, at the end of our careers. Matty and I roomed together, and it struck me that I could finally fraternize with my brother without worrying that we would be fined. Matty became buddies with Munson, who used to kiddingly call him "Topo Gigio" after the children's puppet character.

Even with all that news going on, without a doubt the biggest news to hit the Yankees in 1973—even bigger than two players trading families—was George Steinbrenner becoming the franchise's principal owner. His presence was felt immediately. I had gotten close to our manager, Ralph Houk. Or maybe I should say that Houk had gotten close to me. He saw in me my future, telling me I had the makings of a field manager. During two offseasons the Yankees even asked me to join our third base coach, Dick Howser, and work with young players in the Instructional League, which I was happy to do.

One day during the 1973 season Houk called me into his office. "Felipe," he said, "I'm going to be leaving. I want you to know that wherever I go, I'm going to try to get you there with me."

I didn't know what he meant at first, but then he explained how Steinbrenner was driving him crazy, calling him at 4 a.m. and asking him stupid questions, meddling with the way he managed the team. Houk wasn't going to be badgered or pushed around. This was a former player who had won two World Series titles managing the Yankees—one of them the 1962 team that beat the San Francisco Giants team I played on. Houk also fought in the army during World War II and was one of the soldiers who landed on Omaha Beach in Normandy a few days after D-Day. He was greeted with a bullet that pierced his helmet and almost penetrated his skull. He later fought in the Battle of the Bulge. After the war ended he was awarded the Bronze Star, the Silver Star, and the Purple Heart and earned the rank of major, which became his nickname—the Major. And now some shipbuilder who put enough money together to buy a baseball team was going to tell him how to manage men? No way.

"I don't need that," Houk groused as I sat with him in his office. "I'm not getting any younger."

True to his word, Houk resigned as the Yankees' manager on the final day of the 1973 season, after we finished in fourth place with an 80-82 record. Two weeks later he was introduced as the new manager of the Detroit Tigers.

I wasn't with the Yankees at the end of the 1973 season. On September 6 the club put me on waivers, and the Montreal Expos claimed me. On the same day the Yankees sold my brother Matty to the St. Louis Cardinals. I could see that I was following the natural progression of a long baseball career. You go from being traded for frontline players to being traded for journeymen to being claimed off the waiver wire.

I finished the season in Montreal and waited to see what would happen in the offseason. On December 7, 1973, the new Major League franchise in Milwaukee, the Brewers, purchased my contract. Their general manager, Jim Wilson, called and told me they had a team with some up-and-coming talent—young guys like Robin Yount, Darrell Porter, Gorman Thomas, and Sixto Lezcano. He said I wouldn't play much but that he wanted me as a veteran leadership presence. He told me that not only would the Brewers match my 1973 salary of $58,500, but that I also was guaranteed to make the team.

That spring training I played mostly in B-squad games, but I recall playing well, hitting six home runs in thirteen games. On the last day of spring training I was summoned into an organizational meeting. As I entered the room I heard a little bit of a commotion, and then it got quiet.

"Felipe, we want you to know you made the team," said the manager, Del Crandall.

I didn't know what to say. Before I even came to spring training I was told not to worry, that I had made the team. But after that comment from Crandall, and hearing that little bit of commotion, I didn't feel comfortable. True to the general manager's words, I didn't get much playing time. I got three pinch-hit appearances in the team's first sixteen games, which resulted in a strikeout looking against Boston's Diego Segui on April 5, a fly out to center field against Baltimore's Bob Reynolds on April 12, and a strikeout swinging against Chicago's Terry Forster on April 24.

We had an off day in Milwaukee on April 29, which I learned later was a deadline a team didn't want to pass if they didn't want to pay a player his full salary. A lot of players and coaches still hadn't secured a place to live yet, so many of us were staying at the Schroeder Hotel, which is where we had a team rate. I was at the hotel restaurant, eating breakfast and reading the newspaper. We were supposed to have a team workout that day, but it was one of those tough Milwaukee days, cold, with a threat of snow, so the workout was called off. Del Crandall came into the restaurant and saw me sitting there.

"Hey, Felipe, where did you get the newspaper?" he asked.

I told him the restaurant was out but that there was a rack on the street corner. Crandall went and got a newspaper, and when he came back he sat down with me.

"Oh, Felipe," he said. "I forgot to tell you. We're going to release you today. We wouldn't be able to use you much."

Just like that my playing career was over.

Seventeen years, 2,101 base hits, 206 home runs, and a .286 career batting average—and it all ended with a few flip words, as if it was an afterthought.

I soon found myself back in the Dominican Republic, contemplating my future, knowing that I was going to have to get used to the life of a man who can't play baseball. Or maybe not.

Ralph Houk called to see if I was interested in coming to Detroit and playing for him there. The Philadelphia Phillies, who needed a first baseman after Greg Luzinski went down with a knee injury, also inquired. I looked at the mountain of suitcases and duffel bags stacked in my home, emblazoned with a hodgepodge of logos from the different teams I had played with. I was tired. Tired especially of the travel. I also turned forty, and too many parts of my body ached. I thanked Ralph Houk and told him I wasn't interested. Same with the Philadelphia Phillies.

I was done.

5

1975–Today

21

The Transition

When your baseball career ends, so does your income. And my income when I was playing wasn't like today's salaries. The most I ever made was $58,500. Although that was a good income for the early 1970s, it wasn't quite as good as it might seem. When I paid taxes during most of my career, I couldn't claim my Dominican-born wife and children as dependents. It was as if they didn't exist. I often had to pay city, state, and federal taxes, too. I was also helping family and relatives to financially survive in the Dominican Republic. Divide my baseball salary in half, and that usually was what my take-home pay was.

Most every Major League player of my era had to get offseason jobs to make ends meet. A lot of guys worked in sporting goods stores, in insurance, at factories. I knew ballplayers who worked as postmen in the offseason—and not the kind of postmen who today drive from house to house in vehicles. They carried satchels and walked up and down streets. Imagine that today. Imagine Alex Rodriguez, Derek Jeter, Mike Trout, or Clayton Kershaw in the offseason, delivering mail by foot in order to make ends meet. But those are the things ballplayers from my era did to support ourselves. All those years that I and other guys played winter ball, it wasn't because we didn't get enough baseball during the Major League season. No, no, no. It was mainly to make ends meet.

I struggled to make ends meet during my career and especially after my career ended. There was no income. Very little savings. Mouths to feed. What was I going to do?

In 1975 I and some other ballplayers partnered with a group of investors and in the Dominican Republic started what we called the Summer League of Professional Baseball. Julián Javier was one of those other ballplayers involved, but Javier broke away and formed a rival summer league to the north. The league I was involved in was to the south, primarily in Santo Domingo.

Our intent was to develop players—young guys about eighteen to twenty-one years old who had been released in the United States and now had nowhere to go. A lot of those guys were still growing, still improving, still had a future in baseball—if only someone gave them a second chance and some more instruction. That's where we stepped in, and we had our share of success stories. Pascual Pérez and Nelson Norman both got their start in that summer league. Pérez pitched eleven years in Major League Baseball, and Norman, a shortstop, had a six-year MLB career.

I was the president of our league, and I also played on one of our teams—the Capital Beasts. I led the league in hitting that inaugural season. I also lost $6,000. The former did little to assuage the latter. Losing that kind of money when I had very little money to begin with hurt. The league to the south lasted two years and the one to the north a little longer. But I don't consider them failures because with the help and vision of a superscout named Rafael Avila, those leagues evolved into the highly respected baseball academies that now dot the Dominican Republic.

Today, every Major League Baseball team has an academy in the Dominican, developing players and playing league-format games against each other. Japan and baseball leagues from countries other than the United States also have academies there. In fact, Alfonso Soriano, who hit 412 home runs in sixteen solid Major League seasons, came out of a Japanese academy and started his pro career in Japan before coming to the United States and the New York Yankees.

It's a nice legacy to know that all the academies in my country today grew out of those summer leagues. I'm proud of that. But in 1975 my immediate concern was that I had just lost $6,000 on top of not bringing in any income, which put me in a deeper financial hole.

One of my other occupations after I retired was raising goats. At one point I must have had forty. I made the mistake one day of saying in front of my brother Matty that I had too many goats. Later that day—that *same* day—I'm sitting on my porch, and I see Matty walking by with a rope around a goat, leading it away. It wasn't just any goat, either. It was my best goat. Matty didn't waste any time. I said in the morning that I had too many goats, and that afternoon he had my best goat.

"Hey, what are you doing?" I shouted.

"You have one less goat to worry about," Matty shouted back, as he kept walking.

I wanted to kill him.

I tried my hand in broadcasting. I joined my old journalist friend Tomás Troncoso, a radio talk show host, and we broadcast a radio show together every weekday at noon. I also scraped enough money together to buy some expensive broadcasting equipment for television. I was my own cameraman, too. My equipment was cutting edge at the time, the first of its kind in the Dominican Republic that could broadcast remotely for sports. When the Miss Universe pageant broadcast from the Dominican Republic in 1977, they came to me and rented my equipment for $500. Together with another old journalist friend, Johnny Naranjo, we started a sports T V show that aired Monday through Friday. We discussed and covered all sports, not only baseball.

When there was a tennis tournament in the Dominican Republic that featured a teen sensation from Sweden who won the French Open the year before in 1974, I secured an interview with him. They brought the young man to our studio so I could interview him through an interpreter. I didn't know anything about tennis, but I still couldn't believe this kid was a tennis phenom. He was nineteen, with a mop of blond hair, but he didn't look more than twelve. His name was Björn Borg.

I also flew to Puerto Rico in February 1976 and met with Muhammad Ali at the Roberto Clemente Coliseum in San Juan, where Ali was training to fight a Belgian boxer named Jean-Pierre Coopman. I was pleasantly pleased that Ali knew who I was.

After that visit with Ali in Puerto Rico, I headed to the United States to work as a special spring training instructor for the Montreal Expos. It was while I was there when my firstborn son, Felipe, died in that horrible swimming pool accident. When I returned home I went into a hole that was deep and dark. The Expos called a few times, trying to get me to come back, but I turned them down. As the months passed I found myself sinking deeper into that hole, a hole that was both financial and emotional. Especially emotional. I couldn't sleep, haunted by what had happened. Being out of money only compounded my feelings of despair. Here I was, a former Major League player, with no money, struggling to make a living, trying to cope with the death of a child. Those were dark days, the darkest I've ever been through.

Although I never thought I would go back to baseball, it was baseball that eventually saved me. I always prided myself on being a provider, going back to when I was a boy and I worked with my father in his blacksmith shop and the grueling work I did in the rock mine, with my paycheck always going straight to the family. But how was I going to provide now?

It didn't take me long to realize I wasn't a journalist. I wasn't a color commentator. That was not my vocation. That was not what I was born to do. I was a baseball man. During those tough days the realization came to me that I still had a place in baseball. More than that, I knew baseball was the only way out of the hole I was in.

All I needed was an opportunity.

22

The Road Back

The months after my son died in the spring of 1976 are a blur. I was sleeping in restless fits filled with nightmares. I felt as if I was drifting, and I knew the one anchor I could rely on was baseball.

It was either that December or maybe in January 1977 when I picked up the phone and called the Montreal Expos. The Expos' president, John McHale, and their vice president in charge of player development, Jim Fanning, knew me well. They were part of the front office that brought me to the Milwaukee Braves from the San Francisco Giants and later to the Expos from the New York Yankees.

I got Fanning on the phone. "Mr. Fanning," I said, "I need a job. I want to get back in the game. I really want to manage."

I thought for sure I could manage Class Double-A ball or higher. That wasn't being presumptuous. I always knew I had leadership skills, going back to when I was a boy and was the ringleader that led to hacking down a coconut tree so we could have an unobstructed field to play baseball. But it wasn't only boyhood leadership. I first managed in the Dominican Winter League when I was twenty-four and again when I was twenty-eight. Both times I played while also managing, and both times managing seemed to come easily for me. The words of Ralph Houk, my manager with the Yankees, were ringing true in my ears.

"Felipe," Houk told me, "I believe you're going to wind up managing."

Fanning was interested, but he didn't have much left to offer me. "The only opening I have is in Class A ball," he said.

"Okay, thanks," I said. "If you don't mind, I'm going to call some other people."

I never did. A few days later I called Fanning back and asked him about the Class A job. He told me it was still available if I wanted it and that it was in West Palm Beach. When I heard West Palm Beach, I perked up. I always liked West Palm Beach. It was close to the ocean, where I could fish, and the weather reminded me of the Dominican Republic.

"I'll take it," I said.

I didn't even have a car, so I moved into a tough, low-income neighborhood known as the Tamarind section of West Palm Beach, which was walking distance to the stadium. It was probably good that I didn't have a car, because it seemed as if cars in my neighborhood were broken into on a weekly basis. Thinking that I was now making big money because I was back in pro baseball, my ex-wife Beverly took me to court, demanding more child support. In the courtroom I saw the female judge's eyes widen when she looked at my pay stub. I was making a mere $14,000 a year. My apartment was so dank and dingy it felt like a cave, with the toilet right next to the kitchen. My son Moisés will tell you that he grew up without a bicycle because the money was so tight. Those were some tough times financially. But I was back in baseball, and for that I was happy and thankful.

I knew now that managing was my next career. I also knew that with the meager paycheck I was earning, I was managing essentially to eat. I didn't have any dreams or visions of going far in the game as a manager. In many ways it felt like it did when I was a kid playing baseball in the Dominican Republic, when blacks had not even broken the color barrier in Major League Baseball, much less any Latinos.

By 1977, my first year managing the West Palm Beach Expos, there had been only one black manager in Major League Baseball—Frank Robinson, whom the Cleveland Indians hired before the 1975 season and fired barely two months into the 1977 season. So by that summer of '77 there were no black managers in the Major Leagues and hardly any Latino coaches. The only Latino who managed full-time in the big leagues was Preston Gómez, a white Cuban who managed the San Diego Padres from 1969 to 1972 and the Houston Astros from 1974 to 1975. Although he would have a short stint managing the Chicago Cubs in 1980, Gómez wasn't managing in 1977. So I didn't hold out hope of one day managing in the big leagues. I was just content to have a job in baseball.

Right away I started learning the game on a different level and in a different way. In the Minor Leagues, and especially in Class A ball, there are prospects, and then there are guys on the roster who are there to fill spots around the prospects. But what you soon discern as a manager is that some of the players aren't as good as the organization thinks they are, and some of the players aren't as bad as the organization thinks they are. You're forever juggling what the organization sees and what your own eyes see.

One of those guys was Bobby Ramos, a Cuban catcher the Expos weren't promoting. He went from the rookie Gulf Coast League to two straight years at Class A West Palm Beach. Now he was being asked to come back to West Palm Beach for a third year, which coincided with my first year managing there. He refused, requesting a trade.

I got his phone number and called him in Miami, where he lived. I told Bobby he had a Latino manager, and I was going to give him a fair shake. He reported, and right away I saw that he had Major League potential. He wasn't a good receiver behind the plate. The only tool he had was a good arm. But he developed, eventually making it to the Major Leagues. He played for six years, mostly backing up Hall of Fame catcher Gary Carter for the Montreal Expos. Bobby later became a coach and a player-development coordinator—paying it forward, I'm sure.

I wasn't one to play baseball games just to develop players. I believe if you play, you play to win. You're not only teaching young men the game of baseball, but also teaching players how to win. I also believe a field manager shouldn't teach only players; he should teach the coaches how to teach—teach the teachers. Not that I had a staff of coaches during those early years. I had a pitching coach, and that was it. I managed, threw batting practice, warmed up pitchers, and coached third base. Bernie Allen, who played twelve years in the big leagues as an infielder, was working at a local sporting goods store, which was owned by the owner of the team. He filled in part-time as a first base coach for our home games. Otherwise, a position player who was not in the lineup that day manned the first base coaching box.

I guided my team to a 77-55 record that 1977 season, and we easily won the Florida State League's South Division. The North Division was won by the Lakeland Tigers, managed by a man who would become a lifelong friend—Jim Leyland.

I guess because of my success the Expos promoted me to the Class Double-A Memphis Chicks in the Southern League for the 1978 season. We finished second in the West Division to a very good Knoxville Sox team with a very good young manager whom I knew well. It was the teammate I had with the Oakland A's eight years earlier, the one I said had a future in the coaching profession— Tony La Russa.

I guess the success I had at the Class Double-A level with the Memphis Chicks also got me promoted to the Major Leagues for the 1979 season, where I joined my old Oakland A's manager, Dick Williams, becoming his third base coach.

I was glad to be out of the Southern League, where the bus rides were brutally long. When we left after a night game in Memphis, we arrived in Jacksonville, Florida, just in time to go to the ballpark and get ready to play that night. A few days later when we left Jacksonville for Knoxville, we were halfway between Macon and Atlanta when a highway patrolman closed in behind us at 3 a.m., flashing his lights. Suddenly, the officer's voice boomed over his speaker system, imploring us to pull over because the bus was on fire. It's a good thing he got to us when he did, because when we did pull over we saw flames spewing from underneath the bus. Several fire trucks rushed to the scene. We were all safe, although several uniforms were burned and we had to wait for another bus, which put us way behind schedule. La Russa agreed to wait for us, and we rolled into the Knoxville stadium at 8:30 p.m. for a 7:05 p.m. game. That's the Minor Leagues.

But I still liked managing in the Minor Leagues better than being a coach in the Major Leagues. After two years coaching first and third bases for the Expos, I asked to go back to the Minor Leagues so I could manage again.

The Expos sent me to the Class Triple-A American Association in 1981, where I managed the Denver Bears and where I also got a visit during the season from the entire Expos coaching staff, including Dick Williams. The reason the Expos sent them to Denver was because of the Major League Baseball strike that lasted about seven weeks that summer. Williams and the staff would be out on the field pregame, hitting fungoes, working with the team. But once the game started they couldn't be on the field. So they would retreat to the clubhouse and mainly into my office, where I was well stocked with a regional beer that was gaining national prominence. They must have liked that beer, because by the time the game was over, my office was littered with empty Coors bottles and cans.

I managed the Denver Bears to a 76-60 record and a second-place finish in the West Division, three games behind the Omaha Royals. Across the way the East Division champions were the Evansville Triplets, who were in their third year being managed by Jim Leyland. We beat Leyland's team in the playoffs and then swept Omaha, 4–0, to win the American Association championship. I knew by now Leyland was really good, but it was the Omaha manager, Joe Sparks, who caught my attention.

Through the years, with all the success I had managing in the Minor Leagues and all the players I believe I helped to develop, people would tell me I wasn't getting a chance to manage in the big leagues because I was both black and Latino. While I don't doubt it held me back, I would still always point to Joe Sparks. Here was a blond-haired white man who was an excellent manager. Sparks had a lot of success managing a lot of different teams in the Minor Leagues, winning championships. He also coached for the Chicago White Sox, Cincinnati Reds, Montreal Expos, and New York Yankees. Yet he never got a shot at managing in the big leagues. There were a lot of Joe Sparks in the Minor Leagues—good guys, good teachers, and good managers who were perennial Minor League skippers. So when people played the racism card with me, my response was, "What about Joe Sparks?" Not that I'm naive. Even today there is a noticeable dearth of black and Latino managers in Major League Baseball. But to attribute that entirely to racism is unfair.

After my year in Denver I managed two more seasons in the American Association, with the Wichita Aeros, when the big club called again before the 1984 season. This time the Expos wanted me to be manager Bill Virdon's first base coach, mainly because they wanted me with a Latino player I managed in the Minor Leagues—Venezuelan shortstop Ángel Salazar. They were expecting big things from Salazar, but once he got to the Major Leagues he wasn't the same player. That happens. Some guys get to the big leagues and then fall apart.

There was also the possibility that another Venezuelan, first baseman Andrés Galarraga, would get called up to the big leagues, and the Expos were well aware of my relationship with him.

In 1977, after my first year managing in the Minor Leagues, I managed the Caracas Lions in the Venezuelan Winter League. One day the general manager came to me with a request. "I know this fat kid, sixteen years old, who can hit the ball nine miles," he said. "Can I bring him in so you can look at him?"

What was I going to tell the general manager—no? Of course not. He brought the kid in, and he was right. The boy must have weighed 280 pounds. We didn't even have a uniform that could fit him. He stood there in the batting cage wearing khaki pants and just mashed pitches. The kid could hit. The only two players on my team who could hit the ball farther were two Major Leaguers—Tony Armas and Bo Díaz. That was my introduction to Andrés Galarraga.

I told the Expos that I thought this Andrés Galarraga kid was a prospect. But when I inquired with Galarraga's family as to how much it would take to sign him, they said $10,000. There was no way back then that a Latino player was going to get a $10,000 signing bonus.

Over the weeks Galarraga continued to work out and hit with the team, always raking line drives all over the field and launching bombs into the bleachers. He was losing some weight, too. Finally, his family agreed to cut their demand in half, asking for a $5,000 signing bonus. I told the front office he was worth it, and we signed Galarraga to a contract. As he worked his way to the Major Leagues, Galarraga lost his baby fat, slimming down to about 235 pounds over a six-foot-three frame, becoming known as "el Gran Gato"—or the Big Cat. Before his career was over Galarraga played nineteen years, recording 2,333 hits, 399 home runs, and a .288 batting average. He won the National League batting title in 1993 with a .370 average, which was also tops in MLB. He also earned more than $55 million for himself and his family.

Galarraga, however, didn't get called up to the big leagues when I was there in 1984. He was still a year away. By then I had put in a year in Montreal, helping Ángel Salazar transition to the big leagues, and I didn't want to stay any longer. I didn't want to coach, and I didn't think managing in the Major Leagues was in my future. I was turning fifty, and I thought the confluence of being black, Latino, and getting older meant my chance to manage in the big leagues had passed me by. But I still wanted to manage somewhere. During the offseason I asked to go back to the Minor Leagues. I specifically asked to go back to West Palm Beach, where the weather and fishing were good. If I was going to be a Minor League manager, I was going to do it where I enjoyed living.

There also were other reasons I wanted to leave. A lot of people were asking, "Do you think the Expos will ever name you manager? Why do you think you haven't been given an opportunity yet?" It was getting to be annoying, and I was tired of it. I thought A ball was a good place to hide, a good place to get away from all the questions. After all, they don't normally promote Class A managers to the big-league managing job.

But the Expos' front office didn't want to accommodate me. Not that they balked at my managing again in the Minor Leagues. They just worried how it would look sending a minority coach who managed in Class Triple-A ball back to Class A. So they sent me to the American Association for the 1985 season, where I managed the

Class Triple-A Indianapolis Indians. After that they sent me back to West Palm Beach and the Florida State League, where I managed Class A ball for the next six years.

Although my one year coaching for Bill Virdon in Montreal wasn't what I really wanted to do, it did result in something special. During that 1984 season I met a heavy-set, good-natured Dominican man who years earlier had been one of the drivers for the dictator, Rafael Trujillo. He was living in Montreal and driving for various people there. I used him on occasion for trips to the airport and such. One day I left him a ticket to a game at Olympic Stadium. When I saw him sitting at his seat pregame, I gave him a big wave.

Sitting near him was a pretty, young French Canadian woman who thought I was waving at her. She waved back, but I never noticed her. Thinking I was interested, she gave a note to one of our coaches who later gave it to me. I discarded it. She was undaunted, though. She showed up on photo day with her parents and struck up a conversation with me. She also worked in the immigration office, and one time, when she knew the Expos were returning from the United States, she showed up in uniform on her day off, just so we could cross paths again. Those few little meetings led to a dinner date and more dates over the next year. When I got back to West Palm Beach, managing Class A ball again, I asked her to marry me. I knew it was love when she said yes.

The reasons I knew it was love were obvious to me. Here I was, a man twenty-three years older than her, married three times with eight kids, and making next to nothing managing in the Minor Leagues. She took a chance with me, this man with little money but with a pocketful of kids. I didn't represent any future for her. At that time in my life I felt the only thing I was famous for were marriages and divorces. After a pastor friend of mine met Lucie, he told me, "This woman is a gift from God for you. This is a blessing. Don't lose it." I haven't. Thirty-two years later, the former Lucie Gagnon and I are still happily married, with two wonderful children of our own. More than any other woman, Lucie stabilized my life.

23

Big Time Again in the Big Leagues

I managed 1,636 games in the Minor Leagues and countless more in the winter leagues of the Dominican Republic, Puerto Rico, Venezuela, and Mexico. I knew I could develop players, and I knew I could manage. By the early 1990s I saw guys I managed against—friends of mine like Tony La Russa and Jim Leyland—managing in the Major Leagues and having success. But with every passing year I was getting older and further away. I lost hope that I would ever manage in the big leagues.

Although there were times when I was frustrated, I was still very content to continue in the Minor Leagues, developing players and men, teaching them the game of baseball and how to win. Besides it wasn't about me. I've always believed that if a manager is trying to make it to the Major Leagues ahead of his players, then he's not doing his job. A manager's job is to develop players to the Major Leagues. Players first. Organization first. I would sometimes hear Minor League managers complaining, saying how they had won pennants and weren't getting promoted. What they didn't realize is that it wasn't about them. It's always about the players.

The same goes for general managers and other front-office people. When Dave Dombrowski joined the Expos in 1987 as the director of player development, he impressed me right away. It wasn't about him. It was about the organization and the players. Dombrowski came to West Palm Beach, where I was managing Class A ball, and sat with me and talked. "You guys are grossly underpaid," he said. Soon enough he increased the salaries of everyone in the Expos' Minor League organization.

But it was more than that. Dombrowski shared with me that he wasn't much of a baseball player in school. He told me he played a little bit of college football, but it wasn't what he wanted to do. "I have a passion for baseball," he told me, and his passion came through louder than his words. I saw potential in him. He was a people person who had time for everyone. And he wanted to learn. He was incredibly committed to the job and to the organization. He wasn't a know-it-all. He took a bus ride with me and asked a lot of questions. You appreciate that. He was player and organization first, and it's not surprising to me that Dave Dombrowski has become such a successful MLB executive.

In the Minor Leagues, and especially in Class A ball, you are a father figure. I took that seriously. I saw too many promising careers ambushed by immaturity. In 1977 the Expos drafted both Scott Sanderson and Bill Gullickson—two good-looking kids and pitchers who would go on to have solid Major League careers. At that level it's like a college team, with players behaving as though they're living in a frat house. For many kids it's their first time on their own.

Gullickson's parents came to me before he was assigned to West Palm Beach and expressed a desire that their boy would be with me. When he finally did get to me, I could see he was a talent. Right out of high school he pitched five shutout innings in his first game as a pro. About half of the team was staying in an apartment complex across the street from the stadium. One day the landlord came to me and complained about some things that were going on, that some of the players were flashing, or what they call mooning, other tenants from their apartment window. It was stupid stuff, kid stuff. I called a team meeting and discerned it was Gullickson and a couple of other guys. I talked to the three of them together, but later I called only Gullickson into my office. I told him I expected more from him, that I knew he was of good character and came from good parents. I also told him his parents hoped he would be entrusted in my care.

"Listen, we're going to leave it this way," I said. "Everything starts right now. I don't want to hear anything new. If I do, I'm going to have to contact your parents."

Nothing ever happened again. Gullickson kept his nose clean, and he kept progressing, pitching fourteen years in the Major Leagues, winning 162 games.

In 1986 I had a tall left-handed pitcher who could really bring it with an abusive fastball that instilled fear in hitters. But he was a bit wild—on and off the field. One night the team was in Daytona Beach during spring break, so there was a lot going on in the way of partying. At 2 a.m. I awoke to a phone call in my hotel room.

"Is this Mr. Alou?"

"Yes."

The voice on the other end of the phone informed me that he was a police officer in Ormond Beach, a town just north of Daytona Beach.

"I have one of your players here," he said.

"What's his name?"

"Randall David Johnson."

"You mean Randy Johnson?!"

Randy was driving a scooter on the street with a suspended California license. He had also blown past our 11 p.m. curfew, which I wasn't happy about. I had to take a cab to the police station and dig into my wallet for $100 to bail him out.

I can only imagine what it must have looked like to have seen a six-foot-ten Randy Johnson riding a little scooter. But that was Randy. He had a girlfriend who had a convertible he would drive around West Palm Beach, with his head jutting above the windshield. I would laugh every time I saw him in that car.

But I wasn't laughing now. Randy was scheduled to pitch later that same day, and he assured me he would be okay. But he wasn't. In the first inning he airmailed several pitches over the catcher's outstretched glove, all the way to the backstop screen, and also walked about six guys. He didn't last an inning. But he was a good kid after that. I never had any more problems with him. I think Randy learned a lesson that served him well during a twenty-two-year Major League career that saw him garner five Cy Young Awards and a 2015 first-ballot induction into the Hall of Fame.

You see a lot of young talent and a lot of crazy things in the Minor Leagues. I remember one game that merged the two. We were playing the Cocoa Astros in 1977, back in the same town where I started my playing career in 1956 with the Cocoa Indians. All those swarming mosquitoes that were always there when I was a player must have been waiting to reconnect with me, because they were swarming around me again. My players were making fun of the Astros' catcher because of his large head, which I didn't appreciate their doing. The Astros, meanwhile, were getting the last laugh because their pitcher, Dave Smith, was not only throwing a no-hitter against us but also pitching a perfect game.

With two outs in the ninth inning, our catcher, Bobby Ramos, was walking from the on-deck circle to home plate for our last chance. I don't know why, but I turned and looked down our dugout and saw one of our infielders, Godfrey Evans, holding a bat in his hands.

"Hold on, hold on!" I shouted to the umpire. "I'm going to pinch-hit." Turning to Evans, I said, "You're going to hit."

I thought he was going to crap his pants. Dave Smith had been unhittable, nasty, throwing heat. Evans took so long getting to home plate that the umpire had to shout at our dugout to get a batter up.

The first pitch was a sizzling fastball inside. Strike one. The next pitch was a curveball that Evans waived at. Strike two. Smith decided to waste one with his third pitch, throwing a fastball up and in. Evans took an awkward tomahawk swing and somehow connected. The ball blooped over the first baseman's head for a single . . . and there went the perfect game.

Dave Smith went on to play thirteen years in the big leagues, saving 216 games with a 2.67 earned run average, primarily as a closer. Unfortunately, he died young, at fifty-three, from a heart attack.

As for the Cocoa Astros' catcher with the large head—he went on to win three World Series championships managing the San Francisco Giants. In fact, he succeeded me in managing the team. And someday soon, Bruce Bochy's plaque will also grace the Hall of Fame. Bruce has become a good friend, and he and I still laugh about that game.

As for Godfrey Evans, he played two more years in the Minor Leagues before he was released. I have no idea where he is today.

I was fifty-six years old in 1991, finishing my sixth consecutive season managing the West Palm Beach Expos. I expected to finish my career managing there, when the big-league club came calling again. Dan Duquette had taken over for Dave Dombrowski as president and general manager, after Dombrowski left to become the first general manager of the expansion Florida Marlins.

Dombrowski fired Buck Rodgers forty-nine games into the 1991 season and promoted the third base coach, Tom Runnells, to manage the club, even though Runnells was only thirty-six years old, making him the youngest manager in the Major Leagues. Rodgers had a laid-back style, and Dombrowski wanted someone who was more of a disciplinarian. Runnells, who managed the Class Triple-A Indianapolis Indians to the 1989 American Association championship, had that reputation. But Runnells's record for the remainder of the 1991 season (51-61) wasn't any better than Rodgers's record (20-29).

That offseason, after Duquette took over for Dombrowski, he told me he needed a veteran man to help Runnells, and he wanted me to be the bench coach. I told Duquette I didn't want to do it and to find someone else. I didn't want to go back to the big leagues. At fifty-six I was getting older, and like a lot of older people I was enjoying life in Florida. I also had a home there, and I knew all of the local fishermen. I was happy. A few days later Duquette called to tell me he hadn't found anybody else—in reality he never even looked—and that I was the bench coach.

"Okay," I said. "I guess I'm the bench coach."

Although I didn't want to go, there were some side benefits. After coming up in the Pittsburgh Pirates organization, my son Moisés was now with the Expos. So was my nephew Mel Rojas, my father's grandson from the woman he had been with before marrying my mother. It felt good to be with family, but that 1992 season didn't start off well, even though we had some good talent. In addition to Moisés and Mel, we had Dennis Martínez, Ken Hill, John Wetteland, Marquis Grissom, Larry Walker, Delino DeShields, Brian

Barnes, and Spike Owen. We also had some solid veteran players—guys like Tim Wallach and Gary Carter—in the last years of their careers. This was a good team, but we weren't winning.

The team was tight, too tense, probably because of the way Runnells tried to enforce so many rules and regulations. Runnells liked his reputation as a disciplinarian, even going so far—as a joke—to show up on the first day of spring training wearing army fatigues and brandishing a bullhorn. It didn't go over well with the media, who skewered him. Serge Touchette, a sportswriter for *Le Journal de Montréal*, nicknamed Runnells "T-Ball," because he thought what he did was a Little League move.

We were in San Diego when the Rodney King riots erupted in Los Angeles, and our four-game series against the Dodgers was canceled. Runnells ordered the team to San Diego's Jack Murphy Stadium for an early morning workout before our coast-to-coast flight later that day to Montreal. That rankled some players, especially the veterans.

In spite of Runnells's efforts to impose himself as the authority figure, my son Moisés came to me one day when we were standing around pregame on the field. It was a father-son talk in Spanish.

"You know, Papá, to all of the guys *you* look like the manger," he said. "The guys keep telling me that you look like the leader."

I certainly wasn't trying to present myself ahead of Tom Runnells, but I understood what Moisés was telling me. There was a twenty-year age difference between Runnells and myself, and you couldn't deny the way that looked. I was also probably carrying myself like a manager because I felt like a manager. Not *the* manager. But I was *a* manager. After all, I managed at all levels in the Minor Leagues and in Venezuela, Mexico, Puerto Rico, and the Dominican Republic. I couldn't simply hide my experience. I couldn't change my countenance. If you're around a trade long enough, you carry the air of someone who knows what they're doing. My job, though, was to help Tom Runnells, and I was 100 percent committed to doing that.

It puzzled me, then, when Duquette pulled me into his hotel room when we were on the road in St. Louis. He wanted to talk.

The team was 7-11, not playing to its potential. "Are you helping Tom?" Duquette asked.

I didn't know what he was getting at. Did he think I wasn't doing my job? I wasn't sure. "I'm trying to help him," I said, "but he's the manager."

A short while later we were home playing San Francisco. Clinging to a 3–2 lead in the ninth inning, Runnells summoned our closer John Wetteland. What he didn't do, though, is shift our fielders to protect the lines against an extra-base hit.

"Are we going to protect the line?" I asked, loud enough so that those in the dugout could hear. I was trying to get Runnells's attention. He heard me. But he didn't do anything. He didn't believe in protecting the line, which I know is the philosophy of some managers.

"I'd like to see this guy pull a 98-mile-an-hour fastball," Runnells said.

Sure enough, batting left-handed, the Giants' Kevin Bass pulled a pitch, hitting a three-hop grounder between our first baseman, Tim Wallach, and the bag that slowly rolled into the right-field corner. Bass raced to a triple, and one out later he scored the tying run on a Matt Williams single.

Two innings later the switch-hitting Bass came to the plate again. This time he was batting right-handed against our left-handed reliever Bill Landrum. He pulled the ball down the line between our third baseman, Archi Cianfrocco, and the bag. It led to an explosion of five Giants runs in that eleventh inning, and we lost 8–3. Had we followed basic baseball strategy, we probably would have won that game. Those things don't go unnoticed to general managers.

We struggled to a 5-4 record over the next nine games before we had an off day on May 21. I went fishing with a group of Expos people, and we were spread out over three boats on Lake Saint Pierre, about an hour northeast of Montreal. I was in the boat with one of the Expos' French broadcasters, Jacques Doucet, when another boat approached us from the marina and told me that Dan Duquette called and wanted me at Olympic Stadium. I went straight from the lake to Duquette's office. I was still in my fishing clothes, smelling of fish, smelling awful.

"We're going to make a managerial change," Duquette said. "I'm going to fire Tom Runnells. I want to name you the manager."

His words stung me. If Runnells was failing, then I was failing. I was hired to help him, and now they wanted to fire him. I took it personally.

"I don't want the job," I said. "I feel too bad. I feel like I didn't do enough to help TR. Why don't you give him more time to get things together? The team is young. And so is TR."

We argued and debated for what seemed like hours.

"We are making a move," Duquette finally said. "I've already decided. Do you want the job or not? If you're not interested, I'm going to offer the job to Kevin Kennedy."

Kennedy was a career Minor League catcher who had worked his way up managing in the Minors and was now the Expos' Minor League coordinator. I knew him to be a good guy, but good guy or not, if the Expos were going to hire a new manager and the job was being offered to me first, I was going to take it. And I did.

Still, there was one hang-up. Duquette wanted to fire the entire coaching staff. I didn't want that. "If you're going to fire all the coaches, then go ahead and name Kennedy the manager," I said. "Those guys have been with me in the Minor Leagues, and they're not going to be with me now? No, no, no. Go ahead and fire all of us together and name Kennedy the manager."

Duquette gave in, and I agreed to manage the team the rest of the season for $160,000, which at the time was the most money I had ever made in baseball. Two of those coaches who didn't get fired—Joe Kerrigan and Jerry Manuel—later became Major League managers.

It didn't hit me at first that I had become the first manager in Major League Baseball from the Dominican Republic. I thought about it later. I also thought later about how Montreal, this wonderful and diverse city, the city that paved the way for both Jackie Robinson and my friend Roberto Clemente to play Major League Baseball, was about to be a part of history again.

I had more pressing concerns, though, the first of which was my introductory press conference on May 22, 1992, and then taking over the helm and managing my first big-league game.

I knew there were sportswriters wondering why it took the organization so long to name me manager. Since I had twenty more years of experience over a thirty-six-year-old Tom Runnells, there was the feeling I should have initially been offered the job over him. Now there were questions as to why I was named an interim manager instead of the permanent skipper. Also, because Duquette named Kevin Kennedy my bench coach, there were already rumors that my interim status was so Kennedy could learn from me and then take over the job the following season.

Serge Touchette, the sportswriter from *Le Journal de Montréal* who had lambasted Runnells for showing up on the first day of spring training wearing army fatigues and holding a bullhorn, was now challenging Duquette.

Touchette asked why I had been given the job only on an interim basis. He pointed out my experience and history with the Expos organization. It also wasn't any secret, especially to the media, that over the years, the Expos had passed me over five times for managerial jobs. So why the interim title?

"We are going to evaluate him at the end of the season," Duquette said, with the clear implication that my job status going forward hinged on that evaluation.

I felt a surge of indignation. Maybe it was too much pride. I felt the same way when, after I had played baseball in America, I returned home and told my father I was going to be in the game for a long time. I now knew my level of talent as a player, and I knew I belonged. Now here I was, a fifty-seven-year-old man who had managed thousands of games and won championships in the Minor Leagues, as well as in the Dominican Republic, Venezuela, Puerto Rico, and Mexico. I knew I could manage, and I knew I could manage at the Major League level.

When it was my turn to talk I looked straight at Dan Duquette and said, "If an evaluation at the end of the season is going to determine if I'm going to continue to do this, then I am going to be doing this for a long time."

Little did I know how true those words would prove to be. I would go on to win 1,033 games as a Major League manager, 691 of those with the Montreal Expos, more than any other manager in the franchise's history.

Years later, in 1995, Dave Dombrowski told *Sports Illustrated* writer Michael Farber that he regretted how long it took the Expos to name me their manager. Said Dombrowski: "The biggest mistake I've made in my career was not recognizing his ability to be a terrific major league manager. He's one of the best in the game."

Those were nice words, which I've always appreciated. And I'll also always be grateful to Dan Duquette for being the man who gave me my opportunity. But even with my strong words to him and everyone else at my introductory news conference, I knew they were only that—words.

All I had in front of me was an opportunity.

Now it was time to deliver.

24

A New Beginning

Sitting at my desk as the new manager of the Montreal Expos, I opened one of the drawers and was startled at what I saw—check after check written by players, plus envelopes stuffed with cash. I realized it was money Tom Runnells collected from fining players for violating one of his many rules—including frequent bed checks on the road—which many of the players chafed at. It was a lot of money, more than what would normally be collected six weeks into a baseball season.

When I held my introductory team meeting with the players on May 22, 1992, I went to a chalkboard and drew a small circle. "You guys have been operating inside this circle, this tight little circle, and it looks like you couldn't live inside this one," I said. "You guys had a problem complying with the rules."

Then I drew a circle about three times the size of the first one. "This is my circle," I said. "I only have three things I demand of you—be on time, make curfew, and keep your appointments with the trainers. That's it. But I am telling you right now, if you cannot live inside *this* circle, then you are going to find out that the fine is as big as this circle." I also told them I was giving them their money back.

That night veteran Dennis Martínez, who just turned thirty-eight, was the pitcher for my first game. A Nicaraguan, Martínez had a commanding presence, which contributed to his nickname—El Presidente. He was his own man, and I respected that. But what I didn't like is what I saw a couple of times that season. When Runnells went to the pitcher's mound to relieve Martínez, El Presidente was reluctant to give his manager the ball.

I pulled Martínez aside before the game. "Listen," I said, "I know you've been pitching a long time. But when I go to the mound, I want the baseball."

He didn't say anything. He simply pitched a gem against the Atlanta Braves, and their excellent pitcher Tom Glavine. Martínez went the distance, hurling a two-hitter in a 7–1 victory.

After the game the coaches and I were celebrating in my office, drinking wine. Late in the evening, well after the other players left, Martínez appeared at my office door. I knew something was up.

"Hey, *jefe*," he said, which is Spanish for "chief" or "boss." "I understand you've been around the game a long time, but there are times when I feel I can get the next guy out or finish a game."

"I know that," I said. "But I still want you to know that when I go to the mound, I am coming for the ball. I have already signaled the bullpen."

We locked eyes for a second, and then Martínez gave me a hug. He also gave me something else—the ball. He gave me the game ball from that win, my first as a big-league manager. Those two years I had Martínez in Montreal, El Presidente never once challenged me when I came for the ball.

The next day after my debut I heard from some of my fellow managers, buddies of mine who were happy for me.

Jim Leyland, who was managing the Pittsburgh Pirates, called. "Congratulations, Felipe," he said. "You're finally going to be able to buy a decent fishing boat."

Detroit manager Sparky Anderson, whom I played Winter League ball with, also called. "Felipe," he said, "go to the mirror and see how many black hairs you have. And then after the season, go and see how many gray hairs you have."

After Dennis Martínez pitched us to a victory in my managerial debut, we lost eight of our next twelve games. I never for a moment lost hope, though. I never lost confidence. Not hardly. I knew there was talent on that roster, and I knew I could manage.

Sure enough, the team took off and won thirty-one of our next fifty games. We went from a 23-28 record on June 5 to a 54-48 record on July 30 and a tie for first place. We maintained our momentum the rest of the way, and in my first—albeit partial—season managing in the Major Leagues I notched a 70-55 record. Add that to the 17-20 mark from the start of the season under Tom Runnells, and the Expos finished 87-75, which was quite an improvement over the 71-90 record and last-place finish in the National League East the year before. In fact, that 1992 record was good for second place in the NL East, nine games behind the Barry Bonds–led Pittsburgh Pirates.

Bonds, who turned twenty-eight that summer, was hitting his prime. He made the All-Star team that season, won the Silver Slugger and Gold Glove Awards, and was named the NL's Most Valuable Player for the second time in three years. I recall thinking that he would be some type of player to manage. Little did I know . . .

Our finishing with a winning record in 1992 really got the fans going. In the two games before I was named manager, our attendance was 8,760 and 9,651. By mid-July, when we returned home from a two-week road trip that saw us climb to a .500 record, we drew an average of 30,026 fans for a four-game series against the San Diego Padres. Several days later we pulled in crowds of 41,935 and 46,620 fans for two weekend games against the Los Angeles Dodgers.

Where the fans go, the media are sure to follow, and one of the story lines the media were all over was the father-son angle. It seemed as if everywhere we went, reporters wanted to know what it was like managing my son and, from my son Moisés's perspective, what it was like playing for his father. I still get asked that today, and I'm sure Moisés does, too.

In retrospect, I was probably a little too tough on Moisés. But I will say this: it seemed to turn out well. When you're managing a team and your son is one of the players, you obviously think about the perception people might have. You're extra cautious to not present even a hint of favoritism. I was also aware that every one of my players was a son to somebody, that I was dealing with the sons of other fathers. I took that responsibility seriously. So with Moisés I overcompensated. But again, it seems to have turned out well.

It sure helped that Moisés had a lot of talent—all five tools. When

Moisés was coming up in the Pirates organization, Leyland was the first person to tell me my son was going to be a good player. That was a solid endorsement as far as I was concerned. Still, I didn't know how good Moisés was until I got him in Montreal. I never saw Moisés play baseball when he was growing up because Moisés didn't play baseball. Basketball was his sport. It wasn't until his mother took him to play in the Manny Mota Baseball League in the Dominican Republic, when Moisés was a teenager, that he began to show an interest in baseball.

I knew Moisés was a tough kid. I knew that from various experiences when he was growing up. Toughness is in his DNA. I also believe the divorce of his parents and tragically losing his oldest brother added to his inherent resolve. But it's when I saw Moisés's toughness on the baseball field that I really came to fully appreciate it.

In a September 16, 1993, game at St. Louis, at a time when Moisés had established himself as our left fielder and a middle-of-the-order bat, he got a base hit against Cardinals pitcher Lee Guetterman. It was his second hit of the game, and it was one of those hits where Moisés thought about going for two. But after making a wide turn around first base, Moisés decided better. When he put on the brakes to retreat to first base, his cleats caught on the artificial turf, and his lower left leg snapped and his left ankle dislocated. People still call it one of the most gruesome injuries to occur on a baseball field. As Moisés held his leg up, it grotesquely dangled from the middle of his shin, his bone protruding from the skin. It was difficult to look at, and some chose not to. Second base umpire Bill Hohn turned away and covered his face with his hands.

I didn't run to where Moisés was. I walked. I dreaded what I would encounter. The year before, Moisés finished second to Los Angeles Dodgers first baseman Eric Karros in the National League Rookie of the Year voting. But now I thought for sure his career was over. At that moment I was both a father and a manager—and probably in that order. My heart hurt. When I got to Moisés he was sitting between first and second base with several players hovering around, including St. Louis third baseman Todd Zeile.

When Zeile's gaze caught mine, I saw tears in his eyes. I looked at Moisés, and the expression on his face was as if nothing had happened, as if it was somebody else who had broken their leg. That was Moisés. Tough. When he was in the hospital having surgery, which included inserting a pin, Jim Leyland sent a fruit basket and a nice card. You don't forget gestures like that, especially when it comes to your son.

Even with that season-ending injury, Moisés hit .286 with 18 home runs and 85 runs batted in.

Baseball is not a contact sport, but awful injuries do happen. Moisés's injury prompted me to think back to 1969, when my brother Jesús was playing left field for the Houston Astros in a June 10 game against the Pittsburgh Pirates and our brother Matty. In the third inning Al Oliver hit a pop fly between shortstop and left field. Jesús ran in, and shortstop Héctor Torres ran out. The collision was horrendous. Torres's forehead smashed into Jesús's face so violently that it caused Jesús to swallow his tongue. As Jesús lay unconscious, Pirates trainer Tony Bartirome rushed to the scene and probably saved my brother's life. Bartirome pried open Jesús's mouth, inserted a rubber tube, and breathed into it. Doing that opened an air passage enough so Jesús could breathe again. Both players were carted off the field on stretchers and whisked to a hospital. In addition to almost dying, Jesús suffered a fractured jaw, and he and Torres both incurred concussions. Jesús missed six weeks and finished that season with one of his lowest batting averages in the big leagues—.248. But he bounced back in 1970 to hit .306.

I didn't know if Moisés would bounce back.

That offseason I would go fishing in my aluminum boat. Moisés would grab his crutches and come with me, dangling his injured leg off the side of the boat, letting the saltwater wash over it. I looked at the leg, still discolored and with all the zippered scars from surgical incisions. I couldn't see how he could come back and have a career.

But that following spring Moisés was ready to go. He batted .339, became an All-Star for the first time, won a Silver Slugger Award, and finished third in the MVP voting. He proved to be a fast healer. I think he got that from his old man.

The one thing Moisés didn't get from his old man—and I do want to be clear about this—is this ritual he had of peeing on his hands to supposedly toughen them up. Moisés was known for never wearing batting gloves, which I don't know why should be a big deal. In my generation hardly any of us wore batting gloves. We worked calluses into our hands during spring training, and that's how we toughened our hands. If you find an old picture of me wearing a batting glove, it's only because I was protecting a hand injury. Moisés, on the other hand—no pun intended—would pee on his hands, convinced it was toughening his skin. Don't ask me. And I never asked Moisés about it, either. I do know this: baseball players will invent crazy rituals that defy logic.

When I became Montreal's manager early in 1992, Moisés was coming off shoulder surgery that caused him to miss the entire 1991 season. When the 1992 season started, the doctors and trainers wanted to bring him along slowly. But Moisés wanted to go full speed. A couple of times he came into my office with a question on his lips.

"I want to know why I'm not playing," he said. "I deserve to play." At that point he was one of my players and then my son—in that order.

"You're going to play," I said. Then I explained to him what the doctor's orders were, that he was gradually recuperating, and he would therefore gradually return to the lineup as an everyday player.

"I'm healthy now," he insisted.

"Well, you're going to have to be patient," I said. "You'll get your chance."

Moisés was like that TV soap opera—young and restless.

But isn't that how all of us start—young and restless? Time catches up with everyone, though. It caught up to Gary Carter that year, the man they called "the Kid"—even when he was no longer one. The Expos plucked Carter off waivers on November 15, 1991, which meant I had him my first season managing the team in 1992. Carter came up through the Expos organization and was an icon in Montreal, beloved by the fans. He was also thirty-eight, and the game and the surgeries and all the wear and tear that go with the catching position had beaten his body down.

I always liked Carter, going back to when I was the first base coach on the 1984 Expos team. Carter batted .294 that season and tied Philadelphia third baseman Mike Schmidt with 106 RBI to lead the National League. In addition to being a fan favorite, he was the team's best and highest-paid player. It was only two years earlier, in 1982, when Montreal signed him to a seven-year $14 million contract. But because of being a small-market team, I could sense the Expos' front office was having buyer's remorse. One September day during the 1984 season, when Lucie and I were dating, I went to her parents' home and repaired their fence. It was more work than I thought it would be, and I got to the ballpark at 3:30 p.m., about ninety minutes late. When I walked into the coaches' room, it was empty. I could see street clothes hanging in lockers, but none of my fellow coaches were anywhere to be seen.

One of the clubhouse attendants appeared at my side. "Felipe, they're waiting for you upstairs," he said. "They're having a meeting in Mr. Bronfman's office."

Bronfman was Charles Bronfman, the team owner, so I knew it was serious. Still in my street clothes, I hustled to his office. When I walked in I saw Bronfman with our manager, coaches, and other front-office personnel. Someone was collecting pieces of paper.

When general manager John McHale saw me, he said, "Felipe, we're having a vote. Should we trade Gary Carter? It's only yes or no."

I was handed a piece of paper, and I wrote NO.

A little while later I was back in the clubhouse and about to change into my uniform when the clubbie appeared again.

"Felipe," he said, "they want you back in Mr. Bronfman's office."

I thought maybe I was in trouble for being late.

When I got to Bronfman's office, it was just him, McHale, and me. Bronfman spoke to me, saying, "Felipe, you're the only person who said don't trade Gary Carter. Why?"

I was stunned. Relieved that I wasn't in trouble for being late, I was stunned that I was the only one who thought trading Gary Carter, a future Hall of Famer, was a bad idea.

"Charles," I said, knowing that Bronfman preferred being called by his first name, "you have told me many times, and I have read many times, that you don't want to get out of this game until you get to the World Series. I believe good teams start with good catchers, with good leaders behind the plate."

"Well," he said, "I've heard that Gary has problems with the black players."

I knew that wasn't true. I knew this was strictly a financial decision, and it bothered me that any kind of negative innuendo was attached to Gary's name. I also knew there were guys who didn't like Carter's squeaky-clean image. Finally, I knew human nature, and human nature is such that when somebody lives their life in a way that makes someone else feel guilty about the way they're living their lives, the tendency is to tear down that person. That's what I believed was going on with Gary and some of his teammates.

"Gary Carter is a clean player," I told Bronfman. "But there are rumors that some of the players are using drugs, and I can tell you that Gary Carter isn't one of them."

What I said didn't matter, though. That offseason—on December 10, 1984—Montreal traded Gary Carter in what I believe was one of the biggest mistakes the franchise ever made. They sent Carter to the New York Mets in a four-for-one trade that brought Hubie Brooks, Mike Fitzgerald, Herm Winningham, and Floyd Youmans to the Expos. Two years later the 1986 Mets won the World Series with Gary Carter behind the plate.

So when Gary returned to us in 1992 for a final hurrah, I wanted to give him a proper send-off. Our last home game that season was September 27 against the Chicago Cubs. I put Gary in the lineup, at catcher. In the seventh inning, with two outs and Larry Walker on first base, Gary came to the plate against Cubs pitcher Mike Morgan. Morgan, no doubt knowing this would be Carter's final career at-bat, grooved a couple of fastballs. They weren't exactly batting-practice pitches, but they were right there for Gary to hit. Gary fouled them both and was now in an 0-2 hole. The third pitch came in, another grooved fastball, and Gary connected slightly late on it, sending the ball deep to right field, just over the outstretched glove of Cubs right fielder Andre Dawson.

Montreal fans were ticked at Dawson, a former Expo, for going all out for the ball and almost catching it. Thankfully, it fell in for a double, a one-hopper off the wall that scored Walker in what proved to be a 1–0 victory for us. I substituted a pinch runner for Gary, allowing him to bask in the love of the Montreal crowd as he came off the field, waving his helmet and pumping his fists in the air, smiling that big Gary Carter smile that could light up a room. To this day people say they never heard Olympic Stadium thunder with so much applause and cheering as it did at that moment.

A year later, during the offseason, I was sitting at home in South Florida when my phone rang. It was Gary Carter.

"Hey, skip," he said, "I feel good. I had knee surgery, and I feel better right now than I did the last three, four years when I was playing. I want your advice. Do you think I should make a comeback?"

I knew where Gary was coming from. Every retired ballplayer goes through the same things—the same thoughts and emotions. I know I did. I missed playing when I retired. I still miss playing. To this day I have dreams that I'm still playing. Sometimes I have nightmares, like Mickey Mantle and other ballplayers have had, where I'm late for a game or I've missed a team bus to the ballpark. It's unfortunate that there is often a perception that ballplayers are in it only for the money, because I've had retired players tell me they would pay to be able to play the game again.

I paused for a second before I tried to let Gary down gently. Firmly, but gently. When a guy like that loses it, it's visible from every form and angle. You lose something in your body. You cannot compete with that baseball anymore—that white rabbit. You lose your timing. When I retired I was still strong enough to pick up a desk and throw it across the street, but I could not time a fastball anymore. It happens to everybody. You reach a point with that white ball where you cannot time it to hit it and you cannot time it to catch it. But then you get away from the game for a few months, a year, and you forget that. You believe you can come back and help a team, but it never happens that way.

"You're retired," I told Gary. "You are retired."

"Okay, skip," he said. "I'm retired."

He never called me again, and he didn't attempt a comeback.

The game is hard. It's hard on both players and managers. Managing takes its toll. You're always thinking about the game. There is always an urgency to come up with the right solutions. There are losing streaks to contend with. Dealing with the general manager. Meeting with the media at least twice a day. Sending players down. And at least for me I always felt something more, an extra responsibility. When I started managing in Montreal, I believed I was representing a city, an organization, and also two countries—Canada and the Dominican Republic. And perhaps most important, I was representing my family's name.

I knew I had a lot of managing left in me. But after the 1993 season ended I looked in the mirror one day and immediately thought of Sparky Anderson's words when I took over the team early in the 1992 season. For the first time in my life I had more gray hairs than black hairs.

25

1994

A lot was lost because of the baseball strike of 1994 that stretched all the way into 1995. The game lost an immeasurable number of fans who never returned. Owners and players lost a lot of money—an estimated $580 million for the owners and $230 million for the players. People whose livelihoods depended on Major League Baseball lost vital income. Baseball forever lost 948 games that were canceled, which led to losing the World Series—marking the first time since 1904 that it wasn't played.

Nobody, though, lost more than Montreal. The city lost the best shot it ever had at winning a World Series title. Because of that Montreal lost any hope of getting a new stadium, which resulted in the city losing the Expos.

If you look at Major League Baseball in the decade of the '90s, this is what you'll see:

The 1998 New York Yankees, managed by my friend and old roommate Joe Torre, finished with the decade's best winning percentage: .704.

The 1995 Cleveland Indians finished with the decade's second-best winning percentage: .694.

The 1998 Atlanta Braves finished with the decade's third-best winning percentage: .654.

And then there was us, the 1994 Montreal Expos, who finished with the fourth-best winning percentage: .649.

The only difference with us is that while we finished with a .649

winning percentage, we didn't have an opportunity to finish the season. The 1998 Yankees did, and they won the World Series. The 1995 Indians did, and they won the American League pennant for the first time since 1954. The 1998 Braves did, and they won the National League East.

Not once in the twenty-five years since the Expos became a franchise in 1969 had they ever finished in first place. But baseball lost its season, people lost money, many fans lost interest in the game, and we lost our one chance to finish first for the first time. Those were a lot of losses for one summer.

For me, though, the worst loss was losing my father.

As irony—or maybe fate—would have it, my father was born in 1905, the year that began eighty-nine years of continuous World Series play. Eighty-nine was also my father's age when he died. My father, José Rojas, had a full life, and he made the most of the opportunities he had in his lifetime.

The 1994 Expos were a young, vibrant team, but they were denied the opportunity of a lifetime.

I knew we were going to be a great team. I knew it toward the end of the 1993 season, then in the offseason, when we acquired a young Pedro Martínez from the Los Angeles Dodgers, and finally in spring training, when I could see this team coming together with the kind of chemistry that gives a team a single heartbeat.

We had it all—pitching, bullpen, speed, power, defense, base running, bench players, grinders, energy, hunger, cohesiveness, confidence. This was not only a team built to win the World Series, but a team built to last, a dynasty in its infancy.

Because of being a small-market franchise, the Expos historically had to be smart in finding and developing talent. We had great guys with great eyes for that—hardworking scouts and talent evaluators like Gary Hughes, Jim Fleming, and Fred "the Shark" Ferreira, who tirelessly ran our Latin American operations. We also knew the young talent in other organizations, because if you're the Expos, you're often trading an established player who is reaching his prime earning years for prospects.

In November 1993 our general manager, Dan Duquette, approached me about a one-on-one trade. The Dodgers wanted our second baseman Delino DeShields, and they were offering us a twenty-two-year-old pitcher whom they hadn't figured out yet— Pedro Martínez.

"Do it," I told Duquette. "That's a no-brainer. Make the trade."

I liked DeShields. But I knew we had Mike Lansing coming up as a second baseman. I also knew we were letting Dennis Martínez leave as a free agent, and we were going to need another starter. Replacing one Martínez for another seemed like a good idea. Most important, I knew Pedro Martínez, a fellow Dominican country-man, and I knew he was going to be special. I managed Pedro a year earlier in the Caribbean Series, when I would kid him about his dad, with whom I played amateur baseball many moons earlier. I would needle Pedro that his dad threw harder than him. But in reality nobody threw like Pedro. Not even his older brother Ramón, who by 1993 was an established big leaguer who had gone 20-6 in 1990. When I was managing the West Palm Beach Expos, Ramón told me before a Minor League game in Vero Beach, Florida, that he had a kid brother who was going to be better than him. He was right.

"Make the trade," I implored Duquette, and he did. On November 19, 1993, we exchanged Delino DeShields for a future three-time Cy Young Award winner and Hall of Famer.

The question mark the Dodgers had with Pedro was whether he was a starter or reliever, but I knew he was a starter with ace poten-tial. Since we were so good going into 1994, I tabbed Pedro as a back-of-the-rotation starter, which is what I told him the first day of spring when I called him into my office.

"You're my number-four starter," I said, as Pedro stood there wide-eyed. "But I want you to know that you're my number one when-ever you take the ball."

I could see it gave him confidence, which Pedro needed. I could also see he was going to be a handful. Pedro was headstrong. We had a very good pitching coach in Joe Kerrigan, but I also knew Joe was hard on pitchers. I should have anticipated that a hardheaded pitcher and a pitching coach who was hard on pitchers were not going to be a good combination. Sure enough, almost from the first day, the two did not get along.

Pedro was still learning how to command the inside fastball, which fed into his reputation as a headhunter. To help him learn to pitch inside without hitting so many guys, Kerrigan got a mannequin-type of dummy and propped it up in our bullpen. He stationed it at home plate, mimicking a batter. Pedro zeroed in on its head and destroyed the mannequin with a pitch. Actually, it was probably more than one pitch. Kerrigan thought Pedro did it on purpose, using the mannequin for target practice, and I didn't disagree with him. I saw it all unfold from a distance, as I sat in the dugout. Suddenly, I saw Kerrigan storming toward me. Arriving in the dugout, he angrily tossed some paperwork at where I was sitting.

"I'm done with him!" he barked. "He won't listen! He's all yours!"

That was Pedro—he could aggravate you. But I was sure happy to have him on our side, and I'm sure Kerrigan was, too. He was such a talent.

In his first regular-season start for us, Pedro pitched six strong innings, striking out 8 while surrendering only 3 hits, 1 walk, and 1 earned run. But we didn't hit that game, and we lost 4–0. In fact, we lost 9 of our first 13 games. It's curious how that sometimes happens. In 1998, when the Yankees won 114 regular-season games, they started the season 1-4 before taking off. After our slow start we also took off, winning 11 of our next 12 games.

We had some hiccups after that, but as the season progressed we accelerated, gaining momentum and getting better. This was a young team with an average age of 26.2, so some setbacks were to be expected. Among our everyday position players, our oldest starter was our 28-year-old third baseman, Sean Berry, who was in only his second season as an everyday player.

Not only was our outfield young, but I also believe it was the best outfield in baseball that season. Marquis Grissom, 27, manned center field, hitting .288, with 36 stolen bases. In right field was Larry Walker, 27, a native Canadian, who had freakish hand-eye coordination. Walker hit .322 that season. And in left field was my son Moisés, 27, who rebounded from his horrific leg injury to hit .339 with 22 home runs.

Our rotation was solid, with Ken Hill, 28; Jeff Fassero, 31; Kirk Rueter, 23; Pedro Martínez, 22; and Butch Henry, 25. In reality, because our bullpen was so good, my starters needed to give us only six innings. John Wetteland was our lockdown closer, and my nephew Mel Rojas was our eighth-inning arm who could also close games when we needed him to. Jeff Shaw, who later became the Dodgers' closer, could shut teams down in the seventh inning. Then there was Tim "Country" Scott, who could come in and throw 100 mph heat and throw multiple innings, too. All four were only 27 years old, and all four helped turn nine-inning games into five-inning games.

We had a 21-year-old Cliff Floyd and a 22-year-old Wil Cordero playing first base and shortstop, respectively.

Off the bench were guys like Rondell White, 22, and Lou Frazier, 29, who stole 20 bases as a part-time player in a truncated season. Our old veteran, 32-year-old Randy Milligan, was the kind of bench player who was always encouraging, patting guys on the back, keeping things fun and loose and upbeat in the dugout and clubhouse.

Everything clicked. Even when things went wrong, they went right.

Once, with Moisés at the plate and Grissom on third, I signaled for a squeeze play. Moisés missed the bunt, and I thought Grissom would be dead at home. But he jumped over the tag and scored, essentially stealing home. You know things are going your way when sure disaster turns into triumph.

In his book *Up, Up, & Away*, author and Montreal native Jonah Keri quoted Cliff Floyd saying this about that team: "We were a one-heartbeat type team. We stood up for one another. Our energy level was high. There was no thinking that we were going to lose. We knew we were going to win every night. We knew no one could beat us. If we lost tonight we knew we were going to win tomorrow night."

And from Larry Walker: "Most of my career, you'd go to the park that night, and hope you were going to win it. In '94, we pretty much knew we were going to win it. Losing wasn't part of the equation."

One day a sportswriter asked me, "Who's the toughest team?" He wanted to know who I thought our stiffest competition was. My answer surprised him.

"The Expos," I said. "The only team that can beat us is ourselves."

Even I, someone who had been in the game so long, was amazed at how that group of men performed together. It was incredible. Everybody on that team was a contributor.

Five of our players made the All-Star Game that season—Ken Hill, Wil Cordero, Marquis Grissom, Moisés Alou, and our catcher Darrin Fletcher. But for whatever reason, immediately after the All-Star break, we came out of the second-half gate losing four straight at home to the San Francisco Giants. After that fourth loss I gathered the team together in the clubhouse for a quick comment. "Guys, this is nothing," I said. "We can lose ten straight and still win this. We are going to kick some ass."

And we did. We went on a tear, winning fourteen of our next fifteen games. On August 3, on the last day of that streak, with the Montreal Expos holding the best record in Major League Baseball, I got a phone call from my brother Jesús in the Dominican Republic.

"Papá died," he said.

My father had gone to bed the night before, and he didn't wake up the next morning, his body cold when they checked on him. I took a flight home for the funeral, but I wouldn't allow Moisés to go.

"The Expos can get by without one Alou," I told the media, "but not two."

I felt the same way about my father's other grandson Mel Rojas, and I also told Mel to stay with the team.

I flew from Montreal to Newark to Santo Domingo, and just as when my son died twenty-eight years earlier I went straight from the airport to the funeral home. The whole town, hundreds of people, gathered for my father's funeral. To the day he died people called my dad Don Abundio. In Spanish *Don* is an honorific title, and *Abundio* means "abundance." That was my dad. He was an honorable man who in so many ways lived an abundant life. He was also a humble man. José Rojas—this *Don Abundio*—never came to the

United States to see either his three sons or two grandsons play, but he would listen to our games on a transistor radio.

After burying my father and being gone for two days, I returned to an Expos team that did not miss a beat. Winning fourteen of fifteen was just a precursor. The guys quickly stretched that streak to twenty wins in twenty-three games. By then not only was our 74-40 record and .649 winning percentage the best in baseball, but we also were the hottest team.

Hot? We were *en fuego*.

But the threatening storm clouds of a work stoppage that had hovered over the 1994 season not only rained on our potential parade but also produced the worst rainout in MLB history. Unable to reach a new collective-bargaining agreement, which had expired on December 31, the players walked out. The strike lasted from August 12, 1994, to April 2, 1995, making it the longest and most devastating work stoppage in MLB history.

I think the only people happy about the strike was our ownership group, led by Claude Brochu. I believe Brochu was afraid of that 1994 Expos team. Had we gone to the World Series, and especially if we won it, there was going to be tremendous pressure to keep this young team intact and pay some big salaries. I don't believe ownership wanted that, especially Brochu, who I suspected was already working behind the scenes to line up replacement players for the 1995 season. Brochu was heavily involved in the negotiations from the ownership side, and I never felt he had the Expos' best interest at heart. I believe Brochu was hell-bent on beating the Players Association. Had he checked the history of these strikes and lockouts, he would have learned it never happens that way. The Players Association always wins.

No matter how cheap the Expos could be, it always seemed as though they were looking for new ways to be cheaper. As it was, that 1994 Expos team—the team with the *best* record in baseball—had the *second-lowest* payroll. Ownership was paying our roster $18.8 million. Only the Pittsburgh Pirates, with a 53-61 record, had a smaller payroll, at $13.5 million.

There was some hope during the early days of the strike that a new collective-bargaining agreement could be ironed out and the season salvaged. But on September 14 MLB commissioner Bud Selig pulled the plug, canceling the rest of the regular season, the postseason, and the World Series.

I learned of the devastating news from Dan Duquette. It hurt. The only thing that could've possibly hurt more is if I committed a mistake—a managerial blunder—that prevented the team from getting to the World Series. Now *that* would be painful. I truly believe only an outside force, or a managerial mistake, could stop that 1994 team from winning the World Series. If we had maintained our 74-40 pace for the rest of the season, we would have won 105 games, the most since the 1986 World Series champion Mets. In fact, only two teams logged more single-season victories in the decade of the '90s—the 1998 Yankees (114) and Braves (106). It's why I felt so bad for the players. Fans were always giving me credit for how we were winning, and I would tell them no, no, no—it's this team. Those guys were so talented. They could make so many plays and win in so many different ways—an inside-the-park home run, stealing home, striking out the side with the bases loaded, clutch home runs, diving catches, double steals, grinding at-bats.

The media, the fans, the players . . . they've never forgotten that team. Not a week goes by when I'm not asked about the 1994 Montreal Expos. It still hurts. I hurt for the fans who were packing Olympic Stadium and turning it into a madhouse. And I hurt for the players who deserved a better outcome. I was named NL Manager of the Year after the season, but to me it never felt legitimate. Why should I win something when the players didn't have a chance to win anything?

The day after the season was canceled I was home in South Florida. I stopped by our spring training facility in West Palm Beach, where I had stored some things. Atlanta shared the same complex, and as I was leaving I ran into Braves pitcher Tom Glavine in the parking lot.

When the season ended the Braves were in second place, six games behind us in the NL East standings. Nobody else was even close.

The New York Mets were in third place, eighteen and a half games behind; the Philadelphia Phillies in fourth place, twenty and a half games behind; and the Florida Marlins were in last, trailing us by twenty-three and a half games.

The six-game lead we had over the Braves felt like a wider margin to us, and evidently it also did to Glavine. "I really feel bad for you guys, Felipe," Glavine said, and I could read the sincerity in his eyes. "You have some kind of team."

And then, knowing there was still some hope the season would resume, Glavine, who was one of the main player reps, said something I've never forgotten and have always appreciated. "I don't think we can overtake you," he said. "Not with the team you have. It's going to be tough for us. You guys have our number."

I believe he was right. But we'll never know. The season that could have been never was. That 1994 MLB season lives in infamy. But the 1994 Montreal Expos achieved a measure of fame.

We're the most famous team that didn't get to the World Series. Famous for being denied.

26

The Demise of the Expos and Me

What's worse—a slow death or an abrupt execution? Over my next seven years managing the Montreal Expos, I experienced both. There was the slow death of the franchise and my sudden execution as the manager.

Being fired I could deal with and move on from. It's the disappointment and sadness I feel for the people of Montreal that still linger with me.

It's been said that Major League Baseball was never the same after the 1994 strike. Neither were the Montreal Expos. The difference is that Major League Baseball is still around. The Montreal Expos are not.

I saw the demise—the slow death—coming. I believed the only chance Montreal had to keep the Expos was to build a stadium. Not a *new* stadium, because to build a new stadium you have to have built an old stadium. Montreal never built a stadium for the Expos. The franchise originally played its first eight seasons in Jarry Park, which existed before the Expos came into existence. Then, after the 1976 Montreal Olympics, the Expos moved into Olympic Stadium. It was time for Montreal to finally build the Expos a stadium, and I believed for that to happen it was imperative that the 1994 team get to the World Series. When the latter did not happen, neither did the former.

It would have helped if there were owners who wanted to keep the Expos in Montreal. But I don't believe Claude Brochu and later Jeffrey Loria had that in mind. Especially Loria.

With Brochu it wasn't that I was suspicious of his motives. It was more that I was dubious of his judgment. As for Loria it didn't take long after he became the Expos' managing general partner in 1999 for me to see that he had no interest in keeping the franchise in Montreal. To borrow a French phrase—*au contraire.*

The Expos' slow decline started after the strike ended in the spring of 1995, when the organization did not even offer pending free agent Larry Walker arbitration. It dismayed and disappointed me. In addition to being our best player, Walker was at the time the greatest everyday player to come out of Canada. He still might be the best ever, although some could now make a strong argument for Joey Votto.

Walker loved playing in Montreal. Had Brochu offered Walker arbitration and Walker refused and opted for free agency, we could at least have gotten a first-round compensation pick in the amateur draft. But I'm convinced Brochu didn't do that because he was afraid Walker would accept and he would have to pay him for a one-year contract, as if that would have been so terrible. I did not understand that logic, that judgment. Normal teams with normal owners would have jumped at the chance to keep their best player for a relatively cheap one-year contract. But relatively cheap never seemed to be cheap enough for the Expos. Brochu let Walker walk, without getting anything in return. Walker has gone on record as saying the Expos never even contacted him after the 1994 season ended.

Sadly, Walker wasn't the only star player we lost from that 1994 team. Immediately after the strike was over, Brochu butchered the team, gutting it of three star players.

What set everything in motion was a March 31, 1995, ruling from a district court judge named Sonia Sotomayor, who would later become a U.S. Supreme Court justice. Sotomayor issued an injunction against MLB's owners, barring them from using replacement players in regular-season games. It effectively ended the strike. It also began the fire sale.

With the strike over Brochu ordered our new general manager, Kevin Malone, to trade away the heart of our team. And just like that, on April 5 and 6, we dealt our staff ace Ken Hill to the St.

Louis Cardinals, our closer John Wetteland to the New York Yankees, and our center fielder Marquis Grissom to the Atlanta Braves. The dust hadn't even settled when, on April 8, Larry Walker signed as an unrestricted free agent with the Colorado Rockies.

The effect on us was immediately detrimental. Just look at what Grissom, Wetteland, and Walker went on to accomplish:

> That year Grissom batted .524 in the National League Division Series and .360 in the World Series to help the Braves win their first championship in Atlanta.
>
> In 1996 Wetteland led the American League in saves and won the Rolaids Relief Man Award. He was also named the World Series MVP when he helped the Yankees win their first championship in eighteen years (over Grissom's Braves, despite Marquis hitting .444).
>
> In 1997 Walker was the NL MVP, and in 1998, 1999, and 2001 he also won the NL's batting titles, hitting .363, .379, and .350.

As for us, in return for trading Hill, Wetteland, and Grissom we received Kirk Bullinger, Bryan Eversgerd, DaRond Stovall, Fernando Seguignol, Roberto Kelly, Tony Tarasco, Esteban Yan, and a toe tag for the franchise. I don't mean to disparage those players, but it's safe to say we woefully got the short end of the stick on every trade.

At the very least, Brochu should have kept the team intact until the midseason trade deadline, giving the new GM, Malone, some time to assess the landscape and deal those players for Minor League prospects and young MLB players who could help us restock. Instead, Brochu ordered him to gut the team within hours of the strike ending. Everyone knew we were unloading, so everyone took advantage of us.

The other option was to keep the team intact and see if we could again have the best record in baseball by the trade deadline. If anything, we proved in 1994 that our brand of baseball captured the attention of the city. Night after night we were packing Olympic Stadium with delirious fans. But Brochu was always overly conservative. Rather than spend money to make money, Brochu chose to save money. But in saving money the eventual result is Montreal lost the Expos.

They've had reunions for the 1994 team. At one of those reunions Cliff Floyd told Jonah Keri for his book *Up, Up, & Away* that he "ran into Claude Brochu" and that Brochu "brought up everything that happened. You just look at him, and you go, 'You could have had a dynasty. You could have hung your hat on this team for all time.'"

Instead, we went from being baseball's best team in 1994 to finishing last in the NL East in 1995, twenty-four games behind an Atlanta Braves team—with Grissom—that pitcher Tom Glavine told me several months earlier wasn't as good as we were.

Our farm system gave us an influx of young talent—players like Mark Grudzielanek—and our GM, Malone, made some shrewd trades, especially acquiring Henry Rodríguez from the Dodgers, that helped us finish second in the NL East in 1996.

But year after year it was the same old story. We would develop players from our farm system, or prospects we acquired from another team, only to trade them away before we could fully benefit from them. Sometimes I sit back and think about all the talent that passed through the Expos organization in the franchise's history: Gary Carter, Andre Dawson, Tim Raines, Randy Johnson, Pedro Martínez, Dennis Martínez, Vladimir Guerrero, Larry Walker, Marquis Grissom, Andrés Galarraga, Moisés Alou, Mel Rojas, Ellis Valentine, Wil Cordero, Steve Kline, Ugueth Urbina, Warren Cromartie, John Wetteland, Larry Parrish, Rusty Staub, Tim Wallach, Steve Rogers, Jeff Reardon, Cliff Floyd, Steve Rogers, Bill Gullickson, Scott Sanderson, Jeff Shaw, Ken Singleton, Jeff Fassero, Bryn Smith, Ken Hill, José Vidro, Orlando Cabrera, Bob Bailey, Javier Vázquez, Tim Burke, Tim Foli, and on and on and on.

Four of those guys were developed through the system and became Hall of Famers—Carter, Dawson, Raines, and Johnson—but none of them spent their entire careers in Montreal. Part of me also wants to put another Hall of Famer, Pedro Martínez, in that group, because although Pedro came to us from the Dodgers, he developed into a great pitcher with the Expos.

Not to make it sound like sour grapes, but during my eight years managing the Expos these were some of the players traded or allowed to leave as free agents: Dennis Martínez, Pedro Martínez, Ken Hill, Larry Walker, Marquis Grissom, John Wetteland, Cliff Lloyd, Mel Rojas, Jeff Fassero, Jeff Shaw, Rondell White, David Segui, Mike Lansing, and my son Moisés. Just to name a handful.

In 1998, after failing to get the Expos a stadium, Brochu agreed to sell his ownership shares to New York art dealer Jeffrey Loria. Initially, I was impressed with Loria. He spent two days asking me questions about the franchise, our attendance, the team. A lot of his questions were intelligent. But I soon found out that some weren't.

Loria cornered me one day pregame in the Milwaukee Brewers' visiting dugout. "How come you put the lineup card here?" he asked, pointing to where it was on the dugout wall.

At first, I did not know if he was joking. He wasn't. "I put it here because this is where the bat rack is," I said. "This way a player, when he's getting his bat, can see if I've made any changes."

"You should switch it up," Loria said. "You're too routine. Move it around to different spots, especially when the team is on a losing streak."

Once again I wondered if Loria was joking. He wasn't. I showed him the tape residue from where every manager put their lineup cards in the exact same spot. I don't think I convinced him.

At the same time, it didn't take me long to be convinced that Loria was conning people into believing he had Montreal's best interest at heart. Little by little, Loria took financial control of the Expos from the other partners. I could see what he was doing: he was maneuvering things to take the team out of Canada.

By December 1999 the takeover by Loria and his stepson, David Samson, was complete. The following May I pulled *Montreal Gazette* sportswriter Jack Todd into the visiting manager's office in San Francisco and shut the door. Todd was a journalist I trusted and respected. I warned him that Loria could not be trusted and that he had no intention of keeping the Expos in Montreal. This was at a time when a lot of people were still fooled by Loria, thinking he would be the savior for the Expos in Montreal. Todd never forgot that conversation and wrote about it years later when my prediction came to fruition.

I, on the other hand, wanted to stay in Montreal and even turned down an opportunity to leave after the 1998 season, which was another rough year when we had too little talent to contend with. Following Brochu's orders, Jim Beattie, who was yet another new general manager, flew to St. Louis to deliver some news. After a tough loss to the Cardinals, Beattie came to my office and told me another team was interested in my services, doing so within earshot of some of the media. It seemed bizarre but also obvious. Brochu wanted me to leave.

I know Brochu to this day says that wasn't the intent. But he sure seemed to be in a hurry to tell me another team was interested in me, sending his GM halfway across the country to do so. Couldn't he wait until I got back to Montreal? And did I have to be informed after a tough loss?

I knew what was going on. I was too popular and too powerful in Montreal. I had embraced the city, and the city had embraced me. I was also married to a French Canadian woman and made an effort to learn the language. All of that—and what I always considered to be a good working relationship with the media—put ownership in a bind. I was the last impediment standing in the way of moving the team. Firing me would be a public relations nightmare. Having me leave on my own volition would better serve their purposes.

I soon learned it was the Los Angeles Dodgers who were interested in me, which didn't surprise me, since our old general manager Kevin Malone was now the Dodgers' general manager. With permission granted, Malone and Dodgers team president and chief operating officer Bob Graziano came to my South Florida home that offseason. They didn't come to interview me. They came with a contract in hand and with plane tickets for Lucie and me to fly to Los Angeles for the press conference.

The contract sat on our coffee table, which included buying me a home in Southern California. I was about to sign it when it was suggested we hold off and instead sign the contract in Los Angeles during the formal press conference introducing me. We all agreed it seemed like a good idea.

Working in the background, though, were some of the Expos' minority owners who wanted me to stay. Leading that brigade was Mark Routtenberg, who was the president of Guess Jeans in Canada. I had a solid relationship with Routtenberg, who was not only a smart businessman but also a passionate baseball fan who desperately wanted the Expos to stay in Montreal. Routtenberg saw my value to the franchise, and he once made me promise that if I ever thought of leaving the Expos, I would at least give him a chance to have a face-to-face discussion with him.

Well, when Routtenberg heard the Dodgers were after me, he called my home and, with Malone and Graziano sitting in my living room, reminded me of my promise. He also told me he was in South Florida with the GM, Jim Beattie, and one of the team's other minority owners, Jacques Ménard.

"Can Jim Beattie and I come by and talk?" he asked.

I knew I owed them at least the courtesy of a conversation. Malone and Graziano understood. They told me they were going to get a bite for lunch and would return a little later.

When Routtenberg and Beattie came to my door, I greeted them with a smile. "You know," I said, "my blood is already Dodger blue."

Routtenberg gave me a pained look as the color drained from his face, and I felt sorry I greeted him that way. We went to the living room and sat down, and Routtenberg got straight to the point. "If you leave now, the team is doomed to failure," he said. "You're the last source of credibility we have left."

As we chatted more, Routtenberg told me a new ownership group was coming in and Brochu would be gone. He promised me that with this change in ownership, a stadium was also coming. Routtenberg was so confident Brochu was going to be gone and a new owner coming in that he disregarded something Brochu told him when he granted Routtenberg permission to talk with me. Brochu told him he could attempt to convince me to stay, but he was not to negotiate with me. But negotiate he did.

"What are the Dodgers offering?" Routtenberg asked.

When I told him, his response was immediate. "We'll match it."

And they did. Aside from offering me a house in Montreal, which I really didn't need, they matched everything.

The phone rang. It was Jean-Claude Turcotte, a cardinal and the archbishop of Montreal's Roman Catholic archdiocese. Ménard had arranged for the phone call. Turcotte pleaded with me to stay, telling me the city and the Expos needed me, that it was the only hope of keeping the Expos in Montreal. "Please don't leave," he kept saying, adding that he was praying for me to stay.

When I got off the phone with him, the phone rang again. It was Jacques Demers, the former head coach of the National Hockey League's Montreal Canadians. It was Routtenberg who arranged for Demers to call, and his message was the same: please consider staying.

I was overwhelmed. I could also feel my blood returning to Expos blue from Dodgers blue.

My mind rewound through my postplaying career. I had been with the Expos organization during that entire time, some twenty-five years. My roots, in more ways than one, were in Montreal. Not only was my wife French Canadian, but we lived with her parents in Laval, a city just north of Montreal. When the Expos hired me to manage the team, one of the newspaper headlines blared: "Expos Hire Laval Man." Our oldest child, Valerie, was born in Canada. There were so many things that tied me to Montreal and to the franchise. I felt an overwhelming sense of loyalty.

Naively, I thought I might be able to save the franchise. Maybe with a new owner things would change. Little did I know, though, that the next owner would be Jeffrey Loria and that he would be the worst thing to ever happen to baseball in Montreal.

I told Routtenberg and Beattie I would stay. Later that day Ménard, who was at his South Florida home monitoring events, came by with a contract, which I signed.

When Malone and Graziano returned and I told them I had changed my mind, they were devastated. I'll never forget the looks on their faces. Total shock and disbelief. I felt terrible. I had given those two men my word, and now I had gone back on it. In the months that followed I had a hard time sleeping. Going back on my word weighed heavily on me then, and it still does to this day.

Years later Brochu wrote a book, *My Turn at Bat*, which I understand was so popular it sold about fifty copies. It's mostly Brochu's revisionist history, his version of events in defense of himself. Regarding the meeting Routtenberg and Malone had with me, he wrote: "I didn't for an instant imagine they intended to negotiate with him."

Brochu also wrote that, because the Expos were 80 percent financed by MLB's other clubs, Commissioner Bud Selig was livid and wanted to know why the franchise was paying me so much. Brochu said he didn't learn about my new contract until after Selig called him and demanded: "What the hell is going on?"

Brochu then slammed Ménard and Routtenberg in his book, calling what they did a blunder. Yes, a *blunder*.

He's entitled to his opinion, but now I'm entitled to mine. I think about all my years with the Expos organization, all the years before Brochu even arrived on the scene with the franchise, and how I had always been the loyal company man. When I think about my history and dedication to the Montreal Expos, and then Brochu's, these questions come to mind.

Where was Claude Brochu all those years I making $14,000 managing in the Minor Leagues?

Where was Claude Brochu when I rode for hours and hours on buses?

Where was Claude Brochu when I needed elbow surgery because of the thousands of batting-practice pitches I threw?

Where was Claude Brochu when I was wearing a Montreal Expos uniform and heard the news that my firstborn son was killed in a swimming pool accident?

I paid my dues. I worked hard. I found talent, developed talent, and sacrificed some of the best years of my life for the Montreal Expos. But now paying me the same salary that another franchise thought I was worth was a blunder? It was, and still is, insulting.

But Brochu wasn't done in his book. He also wrote, "Ménard and Routtenberg would come off as champion negotiators. They had managed to keep Alou, the media would proclaim. But at what cost? And on what conditions? Obviously, Ménard and Routtenberg didn't live on the same planet as the other Major League Baseball executives."

To me, that doesn't sound like somebody who wanted me to stay.

And then it all got worse with Jeffrey Loria. Like Brochu before him, I became convinced Loria wanted me to leave. What especially convinced me was a move he made midway through the 2000 season, a move that made his bad intentions blatantly obvious. We were preparing to play a July 20 afternoon getaway game at Olympic Stadium when I was summoned to the front office. Waiting for me were Loria, Samson, and Beattie. Loria didn't waste any time.

"We're releasing two of your coaches," he said, meaning they were firing two of my guys.

I tried to keep my composure. "Who are the two coaches?" I asked.

"Bobby Cuellar and Luis Pujols."

It hit me immediately. Loria was firing my only two Latino coaches—Cuellar of Mexican descent and Pujols, a Dominican. Now I was angry, which is what Loria wanted. He wanted me to be so angry I would quit. But I wouldn't give in to his scheme.

"I understand what you're doing," I said. "If you believe I'm going to quit because you're firing my two Latino coaches, you're wrong. I am going to stay, and you are going to have to pay me the last cent of my salary. When you're done paying me my last cent, I'm going to get another job."

I stormed out and found Cuellar, who was my pitching coach, and Pujols, who was my bench coach and like a son to me. It was tough to tell Bobby and Luis what Loria had done. Both their families were there. I saw their wives crying, just devastated, their children, too. In front of everybody workers had to pull their luggage off the truck that was to take all our equipment and luggage to the airport after the game. It was humiliating. Just awful.

The following season, in 2001, I was dogged with rumors of my impending dismissal. It got so bad that Loria came into the clubhouse before a game in Montreal and called a team meeting. Putting his right hand on my shoulder, he said, "Guys, there is no way I'm ever going to fire Felipe Alou. Felipe is an icon."

The players believed him. But the coaches didn't. And neither did I.

Barely more than a week later we were flying home from Atlanta on May 30 when pitcher Javier Vázquez came to where I was sitting. Vázquez, who had been my starting pitcher in a 4–3 victory against the Braves earlier that day, had been surfing the Internet. "Felipe, do you know you've been fired?" he asked.

I didn't say much. When we landed I went to my in-laws' house and went to sleep. At 7 a.m. Lucie's mother knocked on our door. "Felipe, it's all over TV that you've been fired," she said.

I still hadn't heard a word from the Expos. I went back to sleep.

At 9 a.m. there was a commotion outside. TV trucks were parked in front of my in-laws' house, and people were gathering in the street to protest my dismissal.

Finally, a phone call came from Jim Beattie, who was assigned to do Loria's dirty work. I felt sorry for him. Beattie was a good guy who wound up quitting at the end of that season. He used to tell me I was the only one who could handle Loria.

"We want you to come into the office," he said.

"I already know what you're going to do," I said. "What's the point of me coming in? I'm not the manager of the Montreal Expos anymore."

I didn't go in.

Instead, I went home to South Florida and went fishing. After more than a quarter of a century with the organization, my execution was that swift.

As for the Expos their agonizing demise lasted three more years, which is such a shame considering the rich history of baseball in

Montreal. Save for a few years during World War I, Montreal fielded a professional baseball team from 1897 to 1960, when the city's distance from Los Angeles became too great to be the Dodgers' Class Triple-A affiliate. By the end of the decade, though, Major League Baseball expanded, and in 1969 the Expos came into existence. They lasted only thirty-seven years, about the age when a good veteran ballplayer retires. After the 2005 season MLB uprooted the Expos from Montreal and relocated them to Washington DC, where they became the Nationals.

Baseball was done with Montreal.

Felipe Alou, though, wasn't done with baseball.

27

It Ain't Over till You're Done

I was sixty-six years old when the calendar flipped the page to 2002—an age when most people retire and men like me rarely get an opportunity to manage in the big leagues. I didn't believe I was done. I believed I had something to offer to a team and an organization. But the rumors were that I had no interest in managing again. I don't know how rumors like that start, but they were out there.

When spring training arrived and I wasn't in a Major League camp, it felt strange. A few days turned into a few weeks, and the thought occurred to me that maybe I *was* done.

One night, sitting in my South Florida home, the phone rang. I looked at the clock. It was 10 p.m. When you have ten kids and an elderly mother, phone calls that late at night send your mind racing in all the wrong directions.

"Hello?"

"Hello. Is this Felipe?"

"Yes."

"Felipe, this is Mike Port . . ."

And so began a conversation with the new general manager of the Boston Red Sox.

In a convoluted, backdoor way that still smells of suspicion, Jeffrey Loria somehow parlayed owning the Montreal Expos into ownership of the Florida Marlins. John Henry, now the former Marlins owner, took over ownership of the Red Sox. And MLB assumed ownership of the Expos, which they tried to dissolve but instead moved the franchise to Washington DC.

In the first few months after purchasing the Red Sox, Henry and his ownership group fired two former Expos—Dan Duquette, the general manager who hired me and was their GM, and Joe Kerrigan, my old pitching coach who was their manager. But now, oddly, Henry and the Red Sox were interested in another ex-Expo—me.

"We'd like to interview you for our managerial job," Port said. "Would you be interested?

Of course I was.

"Could you be here at 8 o'clock tomorrow morning?"

Wow, I thought. They're moving quick.

The following morning I rose before the sun, tanked up my gas-guzzling Toyota Sequoia, and drove the lonely back roads across the state from my home in South Florida to the Red Sox spring training facility in Fort Myers. When I pulled into the parking lot at City of Palms Park at 8 a.m., nobody was there. I got out, looked around . . . nothing. Doors were locked, and the facility was empty except for workers tending the grounds.

Eventually, a van pulled into the parking lot, and out stepped my brother Jesús and a gaggle of Latino players. Jesús was John Henry's director of the Dominican operations when Henry owned the Marlins, and he brought Jesús to the Red Sox in the same capacity.

My brother was surprised to see me. "What are you doing here?" he asked.

"I'm here to interview for the manager's job."

We chatted for a few minutes before Jesús had to start working with the Latino players.

"I hope you get the job," he said.

I hoped so, too.

But nobody showed up. The clock went from 8 a.m. to 9 a.m., and the office doors opened. I went inside and asked the receptionist for Mike Port.

"And who are you?" she asked.

"I'm Felipe Alou."

"Does he know why you're here?"

"He should," I said. "I'm here for an interview."

But Port wasn't there yet.

I went into the stands and sat there, watching the players work out. Sometime around 10 a.m. Port found me.

"Hey, Felipe, sorry to keep you waiting," he said. "The interview has been pushed back to noon. Is that okay?"

What was I going to do but wait?

At noon Port showed up again. "It's been pushed back again to 3 p.m.," he said.

At 3 p.m. Port got me and said we were going to drive to a local marina where we would board Henry's yacht, have dinner, and then conduct the interview.

The yacht was spectacular, with workers scurrying around taking care of things. I met John Henry, and we engaged in some small talk. I found him to be a very polite person. He told me how he liked my brother Jesús so much that he brought Jesús with him from the Marlins to run the Red Sox's Dominican operations. We were waiting for team president Larry Lucchino, and eventually he arrived and we sat down to a great dinner of salmon, soup, and salad. Finally, after dinner, we started the interview. By now it was dark.

I knew the Red Sox organization well enough that I could answer questions with specifics instead of generalities. We talked and talked and talked . . . for at least three hours, well into the night. When we were done there was no feedback, just a perfunctory, "Okay, we'll let you know." There was also no offer to reimburse me for my travel costs, much less an offer to put me up for the night. Not that a couple of tanks of gas or a hotel night was a big deal, but the whole thing seemed rushed and ill-planned, as if they couldn't wait to get me in and out.

I got to my Toyota Sequoia and in the middle of the night drove across Florida's back roads again, getting home at about 2 a.m. Lucie was awake, waiting for me. "How did it go?" she asked.

"I did what they wanted me to do," I told her. "I got there at 8 in the morning, and the interview did not start until dark. I answered all their questions. There were times I could tell they were surprised at how well I knew their organization. It seemed like it went well."

Later that day Mike Port called. "We're going to hire Grady Little," he said, thanking me for my time.

When I hung up the phone it hit me. A last-minute phone call at 10 p.m. A hastily and poorly arranged interview. A quick decision less than twenty-four hours later. Had I just been used? Was I called in to check off a box so they could say they interviewed a minority candidate?

My phone rang. It was a sportswriter from the *Boston Globe*. He knew I had interviewed with the Red Sox, and he told me the word from Larry Lucchino was that I didn't show enough interest.

"You have to be kidding me," I exclaimed.

I went into detail how everything went down—about the phone call, driving across the state the following morning before the sun rose, spending all day and night in Fort Myers, answering all their questions, and then driving home in the middle of the night.

"I wish somebody would explain to me how that is not showing enough interest," I said.

Years later, in the summer of 2015, the Red Sox held a ceremony for Pedro Martínez to retire his number 45 jersey. Pedro asked me to be at the ceremony. At one point on the field at Fenway Park, I saw John Henry and shook his hand. He held my hand for a second or two longer than a normal handshake, what I would describe as an honest man's handshake. I learned that same day that Henry had wanted to hire me to manage the team, but because the Red Sox operate as a democracy he was outvoted.

It was good for me to hear that. Even if I was brought in only to satisfy a requirement to interview a minority, at least I impressed the owner enough to have elevated myself to a legitimate candidate.

But in the spring of 2002, not getting the Red Sox managerial job wasn't my most pressing concern. Rather, it was simply having a job. Any job.

For a few days that spring I thought I might even be headed back to Montreal. Omar Minaya, a Dominican whom the now MLB-owned Expos appointed as the new vice president and general manager, called to tell me he wanted me as his assistant. Since I was leaving for the Dominican Republic and wouldn't be back for several days, we decided to talk when I returned. A few days after I was back in the United States, Minaya called and told me he couldn't get the position he wanted for me approved. All he could offer me was a job as a scout. I told him thanks, but no thanks.

Weeks passed and the phone didn't ring. The regular season started, and for the first time since 1975, I wasn't a part of it.

But that changed quickly. Only six games into the season, the 0-6 Detroit Tigers fired their manager, Phil Garner, and their general manager, Randy Smith. It was a bold move by the franchise's new president, who happened to be an old friend—Dave Dombrowski. After firing Garner and Smith, Dombrowski assumed the GM role and named the team's bench coach the interim manager, who also happened to be another friend—Luis Pujols.

Almost immediately after those events transpired, my phone rang. It was Dombrowski. He and Pujols both wanted me to be their bench coach. I needed a few days to think about it. A reporter called, and I told him this: "It's fifty-fifty. Luis is my friend, almost like a son. And I've known the GM since we rode buses together in the Minor Leagues. I just don't know what I want to do, and I don't know when I will decide what I'm going to do."

When I saw Pujols lose his first couple of games, I knew I needed to help him. I called Dombrowski and accepted the job. By the time I joined the team in Minneapolis and got settled in, the Tigers were 0-8, en route to an 0-11 start. It was a tough situation to walk into, but I was happy to be there, and they were happy to have me.

"I'm thrilled that he accepted," Dombrowski told the media. "It's tremendous for the organization to have somebody with Felipe's knowledge, background, and experience. I don't think you could describe a better fit right now."

Pujols, who was smiling from ear to ear when I took the job, chimed in with these words: "It would take a book to describe everything I've learned from Felipe."

As for me, when I walked into the visitors' clubhouse at the Metrodome and realized I was back in the game of baseball, I told the media, "It's nice to be home. Once I got to the ballpark, I realized this is home for me."

It was not a very good Tigers team, though. There were too many bloated salaries that didn't translate to talent on the field. After that 0-11 start, the team went 55-95 the rest of the way.

There was, however, one bright spot to the season. The Tigers and Royals made history on June 25, 2002, when they faced each other at Kansas City's Kauffman Stadium. With Luis Pujols managing the Tigers and Tony Peña managing the Royals, it was the first time two Dominican-born managers opposed each other in a Major League game. It was a proud moment for me and my country.

But because of all the losing and the fact that Tigers owner Mike Ilitch wanted to bring in favorite son and former franchise shortstop Alan Trammell to manage the team, Pujols was let go after the season. Dombrowski wanted me to move into a front-office role. As I considered doing that, I also knew I wasn't ready to take off my uniform.

In early November 2002 Dombrowski called to tell me there was an organization interested in my managing their team.

Maybe I wasn't done after all.

28

Managing Philosophy

If you asked me who I am, you might get a different answer depending on the day. One some days I might tell you I am a baseball man. But on another day I might tell you I am a fisherman. Both are my passions. I also find both somewhat similar. Managing is like fishing in that whether you catch a fish is ultimately up to the fish. You prepare and make the effort. But after all the preparations and effort, you still might find yourself holding an empty hook.

So how do I prepare? Where do I begin?

I have so many thoughts. I often tell people I've been in baseball for 120 seasons—60 in America and 60 in Latin America. I've managed or played in tens of thousands of baseball games. So, yes, where do I begin?

My belief is you begin with the players. You must have the players. The difference between a good manager and a bad manager is this: a good manager wins with a good team, and a bad manager loses with a good team. Either way, you must have a good team. It's that simple. A good manager is not going to win with a bad team, much less a bad manager with a bad team. In Montreal I won with good Expos teams and lost with bad Expos teams. And it always seemed as though I had one or the other—never in between.

When I joined the Milwaukee Braves in 1964, our captain was third baseman Eddie Mathews. Before we broke camp on the last day of spring training, Mathews called a team meeting. "Guys," he said, "the manager has done his job, the coaches have done their job, the trainers have done their job—all to get us ready to start the season. Now it is up to us to perform." I had never experienced anything like that, and Eddie did that every spring. His message stuck with me. It always comes down to players performing.

I'm often asked who the best performers were, the best I saw with my own eyes. I've seen a lot of baseball, witnessed a lot of incredible talent. It's not easy to whittle down to the one best at each position, which leaves you open to second-guessing. But being a former manager, I'm used to being second-guessed. So here goes:

CATCHER: Johnny Bench. Outstanding receiver who could handle a pitching staff with intelligence and authority. Great leader. Unlike many catchers, Bench wasn't afraid to block the plate. Durable. Cannon arm. As a hitter he always seemed to come through in the clutch.

FIRST BASE: Albert Pujols. Power. Strength. Clutch. Ability to take a team on his back and carry it for a season. Underestimated as a first baseman. In his prime Pujols could pick it. The kind of player who gives your team a presence, who brings fear to the opposition.

SECOND BASE: Joe Morgan. Leadership. Intelligence. Great defender. Power for a second baseman. Speed and smart on the base paths. Although he played twenty-two years, until he was forty-one, Morgan averaged forty-two stolen bases a season.

THIRD BASE: Adrián Beltré. Defensively, Brooks Robinson was the best I ever saw. But for an all-around third baseman it has to be Beltré, who I used to hold in my arms when he was a baby in the Dominican Republic. Great defense. Strong arm. Range. Clutch hitter with power. Team leader. Should be a first-ballot Hall of Famer.

SHORTSTOP: Derek Jeter. Leadership. Clutch. A winner. High baseball IQ. Not a power hitter, but he had a knack of getting you that home run when you needed it. He always seemed to do something, with some aspect of his game, to get his team a win.

LEFT FIELD: Barry Bonds. Another guy I held when he was a baby. Bonds had all the tools. Eight Gold Gloves. Not the strongest arm, but accurate with a quick release and always to the right base. One of the best base runners I ever saw. Extremely intelligent hitter. Great instincts. Probably the best eyes at the plate I ever witnessed. Few people refused to hit bad pitches as well as he did. Bonds had the mind-set that he needed only one swing to get it done. And when he got his pitch, he wasn't going to miss it.

RIGHT FIELD: Hank Aaron. Roberto Clemente was the best I saw defensively. But Aaron is underestimated as a defensive right fielder, as was Frank Robinson. Hank had a great arm, accurate. Exceptional base runner. Power. But because of his home runs, people forget what an all-around offensive talent Aaron was. Hank was the complete package.

CENTER FIELD: Willie Mays. Defensively, Curt Flood was the best I saw. His range was incredible. You couldn't hit the ball over Flood's head. Willie was great at all five tools. So graceful in outfield. He played the position beautifully. Great at charging the ball and throwing people out. He had speed on the base paths with outstanding instincts. And then there's Willie's offensive numbers, which speak for themselves.

RIGHT-HANDED PITCHER: Greg Maddux. Probably the best command of pitches—plural—I ever saw. Extremely smart. He always seemed to throw the pitch needed to get a hitter out. Great fielder of his position, with eighteen Gold Gloves to go with four Cy Young Awards. I once saw Maddux in winter ball in Venezuela and asked what he was doing. He said, "I want to get better command of my fastball." He did. Maddux painted the black like few ever have.

LEFT-HANDED PITCHER: Warren Spahn. It might be Clayton Kershaw by the time his career ends, but right now it's Spahn and his 363 career victories. Great all-around athlete who superbly fielded his position. Hit 35 home runs. Fierce competitor. Best move to first base of any lefty I ever saw. He finished with 382 complete games and 63 shutouts and even had 28 saves.

CLOSER: Mariano Rivera. His natural cutter—the cut fastball—was almost like a slider, and it was unhittable. Rivera brought it every day. He had the three C's. Consistency. Clutch. And incredible command. He never seemed to sweat. Performed with ice in his veins. Outstanding athlete who also fielded his position. Durable. He's the standard you measure everyone else against.

MANAGER: Bruce Bochy. If I was a team owner and I had to pick one guy to win a pennant, it would be Billy Martin . . . and then I'd release him. As an everyday and every-year manager, Bochy with his four World Series appearances and three championships is the best. Bruce can see the unseen. His level of anticipation is unlike anything I've witnessed. He sees plays well before they happen. He's probably the best at blending today's sabermetrics and analytics with the human element.

I ended my assessment on Bruce Bochy talking about sabermetrics and analytics because it's become a fixture, and I often get asked about them. Statistics have always been around, and managers have always used them as a guide, as a reference point. But you still have to manage a game with your eyes, and you never want to overlook that baseball has a heartbeat. Numbers serve a purpose, but they're there to do just that—serve. Not dictate. Besides, nowadays everybody has the same analytics. So if everyone has the same information, what's the difference? Answer: the human element.

I do fear that sabermetrics is encroaching too much into the game. I fear that before long they're going to have analytics on how a player hits on a cloudy day with the wind blowing from east to west between five and ten miles per hour just after he got a haircut. I say that jokingly, but at some point it can get ridiculous.

I especially think it can get ridiculous with Minor League players, where I believe data is accumulated and implemented too quickly. Players need time to develop, to learn the game, to adjust. A player at eighteen might be completely different than he is at twenty. Young players should develop under a manager's care instead of by an edict from a spreadsheet. You should also give every Minor League player a fair opportunity to perform. Your prospects will get that opportunity. But the second-tier guy deserves that opportunity, too.

Speaking of prospects, probably because of my years with the Expos, where we always needed to make smart trades for prospects, I constantly preached that nobody should know our Minor League talent better than we do. That might sound like a simple edict, but it isn't always. You should not only know your Minor League talent better than anyone else, but also strive to know the Minor League talent of other organizations better than they do. It's key to surviving as a small-market franchise. It's how we got Pedro Martínez from the Los Angeles Dodgers. Conversely, we almost lost Andrés Galarraga the same way.

When I was with the Expos on the last day of spring training in 1981, we were having an organizational meeting in Daytona Beach, finalizing rosters from the Major League club to the lowest level in the Minors. I was slated to manage the Class Triple-A Denver Bears. With my roster set I was reading a newspaper and half paying attention when the discussion turned to the Class A rosters. I heard someone mention that Galarraga should be released.

"You've got to be kidding me!" I said, punctuating my incredulity by throwing my newspaper down.

"He can't hit the breaking ball," someone said.

"He's nineteen!" I shot back. "How many guys at nineteen hit the breaking ball?"

I reminded them of Tim Wallach, who couldn't hit the breaking ball early in the Minor Leagues but later became a great Expos player. I finally managed to convince the organization to keep Galarraga, who was sent to Class A West Palm Beach.

The next day I heard from Marty Martínez, a former Atlanta Braves teammate who was working with the Seattle Mariners. "Felipe, did you guys release Galarraga?" Marty asked.

"Why?"

"Because I heard you guys were going to release him. And if they release that kid, we're going to sign him."

Andrés Galarraga almost became a Seattle Mariner because of underevaluating our talent and not allowing that talent to develop. It took Galarraga four more years to develop to where he made the big leagues in 1985, en route to a nineteen-year career where he hit 399 home runs while recording a .288 batting average.

Players need that time to develop—in the Minor Leagues and even in the Major Leagues.

The 1998 Expos team I managed was very young, especially our pitching staff. That season was also the year of the home run chase between Sammy Sosa and Mark McGwire. I've known Sosa, a fellow Dominican, since he was fifteen, when he was shining shoes and playing baseball, trying to help his family. Sammy was a good kid, small but put together, kind of naive. I managed him in winter ball and could see his talent, that he had all five tools and big-league potential. I tried hard to get Montreal to sign him, but the asking price was $4,000—too much for the Expos. Omar Minaya, who was a Texas Rangers scout, eventually signed a seventeen-year-old Sosa for $3,500.

In 1998 we were scheduled to play against McGwire and the St. Louis Cardinals in the final four games of the season, when we were about forty games out of first place. In my heart I was rooting for Sosa to win the home run title. I also knew there would be pressure from the Dominican Republic, and especially from the media there, to pitch around McGwire and thus give Sosa a better chance to win. That wasn't going to happen, though.

Number one, you respect the game. I expect Major League behavior from the umpires, the media, the players, and from me, too. I'm demanding that way. You respect the game.

Number two, in 1998 I had a young pitching staff. Asking them to pitch around McGwire wasn't going to help them develop. I had been instructing them all season to be aggressive. So now, for the last four games, I'm going to ask them to be cowards? That wasn't going to happen.

I called the pitchers together before the series. "We came here to play baseball," I said. "I want you guys to be aggressive. You've got to pitch, and we're going to pitch to McGwire. We're going to go after him."

In the first game, against 22-year-old starter Javier Vázquez and a young bullpen, McGwire didn't hit a homer. In the second game he connected off reliever Shayne Bennett, 26, for his 66th homer. In the third game he hit home runs 67 and 68 off starter Dustin Hermanson, 25, and reliever Kirk Bullinger, 28. And in the final game he hit home runs 69 and 70 off starter Mike Thurman, 25, and reliever Carl Pavano, 22.

I regret that McGwire hit 5 homers in four games against us, finishing with 70, 4 more than Sosa, who couldn't keep pace with him. But I don't regret respecting the game. We didn't pitch around McGwire, and he still had to hit those pitches we threw.

After the game, while still in our dugout, I heard someone shout, "Hey, Felipe!" I turned, and it was McGwire coming across the field toward me. He had his batting gloves and a Sharpie in his hands. He signed each glove with the words:

To Felipe, Home Runs 66, 67, 68, 69, 70. Mark McGwire.

He handed me the gloves, shook my hand, and said, "You're a real gentleman. You could've told your guys not to pitch to me." It was brief, but it was impactful. And it was Mark McGwire's classy way of acknowledging I respected him and the game.

Maybe a younger me might have approached those four games differently. But by 1998 I felt confident in my managerial skin because I had paid my dues. And I'm a believer in managers paying their dues in the Minor Leagues, because it's such an excellent place to develop. It's the best school for any baseball man. The more seasoning you get in the Minor Leagues, the better you'll be as a field manager. You learn the bad. You learn there are many ways to lose a baseball game. You learn how to anticipate an approaching catastrophe and how to avoid that catastrophe. You see things in the Minor Leagues you don't see anywhere else.

I prided myself on my observation. The difference between winning and losing is so fragile that you have to observe everything, assimilate quickly, and make a decision. Your mind is always working, which is why many managers don't like doing those mid-inning interviews for TV. You have so many other things on your mind that you're thinking through. I'm always anticipating. I like to act rather than react. People used to accuse me of lifting my pitchers too soon. But I'd rather act and lift a pitcher on my terms rather than react and be forced to take a pitcher out.

Some events—catastrophes—you can't avoid. I've never asked my son Moisés about the play in Game Six of the 2003 National League Championship Series—known as the Bartman Incident. I've never asked Moisés because I've been around him when people have asked him, and he doesn't like it. He tenses. He doesn't talk about it.

Moisés was playing left field for the Chicago Cubs, who were five outs away from defeating the Florida Marlins and heading to the franchise's first World Series since 1945. Luis Castillo hit a lazy fly ball into foul territory along the Wrigley Field wall. Moisés jogged over, jumped to catch it, only to come away empty-handed because Cubs fan Steve Bartman got his hands on the ball first. Moisés was livid then, and I believe he's still seething today.

As a manager, when I saw that on TV, I knew things were going to unravel for the Cubs. And they did. When an opposing batter gets an extra pitch, or a team gets an extra out, it has a deflating effect on everybody, and it often leads to catastrophe. I could immediately see that happening to the Cubs, and I don't believe I was the only person who saw that coming.

Even now, if I go see a ballgame, I go to *see* a ballgame—every pitch, every swing, every action that occurs. I evaluate what I *see*, not what somebody *tells* me. It takes constant concentration. We didn't have sabermetrics and analytics when I was coming up. The information you had was the information in your head, having a good memory. Remembering the last swing, the last pitch, the last at-bat—and sometimes that swing, pitch, and at-bat was last year.

Pedro Martínez remembers times when I would bring in a right-handed pitcher to throw to the left-handed Tony Gwynn. Why? Because of something I saw. Maybe it was something I saw in Gwynn's swing plane, and I knew a certain right-hander with his delivery would give him problems. In those instances I would go with my eyes and against the book and the computer.

It is, after all, the manager and not the book or computer who is the boss. I played for Dick Williams in Oakland and coached under him in Montreal, and I learned from Williams that the manager has to be the boss—the boss of the coaches, the players, and the game. Dick was tough, and you absolutely knew he was the boss. Once the game starts the manager is the biggest authority. He has the most influence. He's in charge of the game and the players.

In connection with that, a good manager must stay on top of his coaching staff. Maybe it's because of my years managing in the Minor Leagues, but I believe a manager should coach his coaches. He should teach and correct his coaches. This is critical, because one man cannot manage a team. He's going to need the input of his coaching staff, as well as the input from his medical people and the head trainer.

The manager should know something about everything—pitching, hitting, base running, fielding, all of it. He should know the game inside out. But while he should have an excellent working knowledge of pitching, his pitching coach should be the expert, and he's going to need to rely on that man. Joe Kerrigan, when he was my pitching coach in Montreal, was a good example of that. Kerrigan was intense, and sometimes his interpersonal skills weren't the best, but he had a knack for finding weaknesses in hitters and knowing how to expose them. He helped me win a lot of games. Another guy I had in Montreal, Perry Hill, is, I believe, the game's best infield instructor. You rely on guys like that, but at the same time, as a manager you need to know your stuff, too. It always comes back to the manager, and I do mean *always*. He's the authority.

When a player comes up from the Minor Leagues he is in the hands of the manager. When he proves that if he doesn't play every day the manager is criticized or fired, that's when he's free. A player free from the manager doesn't have to worry about the lineup. He knows he's in it. Until then he is at my disposal, under my control. Very few players come into the big leagues and are right away free from the manager. Cody Bellinger and Aaron Judge did it in their rookie years. But they are the exception rather than the rule.

Older players, when their numbers and their range and their speed start to decrease, return to the hands of the manager. The manager controls them again. The player might find himself being platooned or not in a day game after a night game. If it's the American League, he might find himself in the designated-hitter role more and more—perhaps exclusively.

I'm a proponent of the DH. It's time for Major League Baseball to institute it in the National League, which I believe is the only league in the world that doesn't use the DH. Traditionalists talk about the strategy in the NL. What strategy? The number-eight hitter doesn't get much to hit because the pitcher comes up next. If someone is on base and the pitcher is up, everybody in the stadium knows he's going to bunt. And he's not going to bunt very well, because pitchers don't practice much of anything anymore other than pitching. They don't practice base running, base stealing, breaking up double plays, hit and runs, none of that. I would argue that the DH creates *more* strategy, because those are all strategies you can employ if you have a real hitter and a real base runner in the game. Instead, we have a wasted at-bat to the point where I believe it's criminal to charge fans money to see pitchers hit.

Anyway, whether it's a rookie or a veteran or all those players in between, a manager should thoroughly know the talent and ability of his players and not ask them to do more than they're capable of doing. When you know what your players can and can't do, you're better equipped to put them in situations where they can perform and succeed. You should mostly find that out in spring training. That's when you teach the fundamentals—base running, hitting, defense, catching. Once the season starts you don't have much time to practice. I remember doing pitching drills one spring. We were going over pickoff moves to second base. When my nephew Mel Rojas tried to spin and throw to second, he fell. He simply couldn't spin and throw to second. So I knew never to ask him to do that.

What you want, though, is effort. You want players to hustle. If a player is not hustling, he should be benched. I don't care who it is. When the other guys who are busting it see a teammate not hustling, they expect the manager to do something. If you don't discipline a player, you might lose the team. And believe me, when you bench a player it gets their attention. It looks bad for them, their family, for everybody connected with them. It affects a lot of people. Benching a player is more effective than taking money out of his pocket.

Years ago, when I was managing the Escogido Lions in the Dominican Winter League, our best player was Pedro Guerrero—a superstar with the Los Angeles Dodgers at the time. We were vying for the playoffs, and Guerrero was our center fielder. We were playing our rival, the Licey Tigers, and at the plate was José González, who I knew was a gap hitter. I kept waving for Pedro, who was playing González to pull, to move to right-center, but he wasn't paying attention. Our second baseman, Nelson Liriano, saw me and turned and yelled to Guerrero. "Hey, Felipe wants you to move over," he said.

Guerrero didn't want to move. He was copping a Mr. Big Leaguer attitude.

Finally, he moved to where I wanted him. Sure enough, the batter hit a fly ball right where Guerrero had been standing. He went back over and easily caught the ball. No problem. Except that after he caught it, Guerrero made an exaggerated waving of his arms to show me up, as if he were saying, *See, you were wrong and I was right.* I tried to ignore him, but when I went to the third base coaching box between innings, I saw a baseball roll past me. Several seconds later a glove the color of Dodger blue tumbled to a stop near me.

I was kind of confused until Teddy Martinez, a player for Licey, shouted to me from the Tigers' dugout: "That was Pedro who threw the ball and glove."

I lost my head. I yelled to Amado Dinzey, a guy who hit fungoes for us. "Amado, go coach third base!" I shouted.

"Me?" he said, stunned.

"Yeah, you! Go coach third base!"

When I got to the dugout I took a swing at Guerrero, but he dodged my punch. Suddenly, my brother Jesús, a player on the team, was in the middle of everything.

"Hey, hey, what are you doing!?" he yelled at me. "There's a game going on!"

I stared at Jesús, and with my authoritative finger pointing at him, I barked, "You're suspended!"

Then I turned to Guerrero and pointed. "You're suspended, too!"

It was an ugly incident, caught on TV. When I went into the manager's office after the game, the team owner was waiting for me. "What happened?" he asked.

"This guy threw a ball and glove at me, and he didn't want to move in the outfield."

"And you're suspending him?"

"Yes," I replied. "Guerrero and Jesús Alou, too."

"If we make the playoffs, do you think we're going to win without Pedro Guerrero?" he asked.

"I don't know."

Deep down, though, I knew we could not win the playoffs without Guerrero. But we did start winning regular-season games—ten straight.

But over those ten days, I started getting pressure. My father came by my house, begging me to let Jesús back on the team. I refused. Then the heavy artillery came—my mother. She also begged me to take Jesús back. Once again I refused.

We made the playoffs, and the owner came to my house before the first game. "Listen," he said, "we're not going to win the playoffs without Pedro. I don't think we have a chance."

I agreed that if Guerrero apologized to me and the team, he could return. The owner pulled out one of those old Cellular One phones that was about as big as a shoe. I didn't want to talk to Pedro, and Pedro didn't want to talk to me, so the owner mediated.

After talking to Guerrero for a couple of minutes, he cupped his hand over the phone's mouthpiece. "Pedro wants to come back and help the team," he said.

"Tell him he has to apologize to the team and me in the clubhouse," I said.

After a few more moments on the phone, the owner covered the mouthpiece again and said, "Pedro said no. He doesn't believe he needs to apologize."

"Then he's not playing," I said.

And that was that.

The next day Pedro changed his mind and came to the clubhouse and apologized. He didn't say much, but it was an apology. He rejoined the team, and with him we won the Winter League championship. Today, we're great friends.

The rift between Jesús and me didn't mend as quickly, and for that I'll forever feel terrible, because he was right and I was wrong. Jesús is a mediator, a peacemaker, and he was only trying to defuse the situation. But in my anger I misinterpreted his intentions, and in my stubbornness I refused to admit that.

Jesús, who lives next door to me in the Dominican, is such a sweet man, very humble, generous, and well loved. If you talk to Pedro Martínez, he'll tell you he would like to spend every day with Jesús, which is quite a compliment. Jim Bouton, the former pitcher famous for the book *Ball Four*, was my brother's teammate with the Houston Astros in 1969 and 1970. In his second book, *I'm Glad You Didn't Take It Personally*, Bouton described Jesús this way: "We called him J. or Jesus, never hay-soos. . . . J. is one of the most delicate, sensitive, nicest men I have ever met. He'd walk a mile out of his way to drop a coin in some beggar's cup." I couldn't agree more. That's my brother.

Not only that, but Jesús is also a very intelligent and astute baseball man. In the 2002 offseason, after the Minnesota Twins released David "Big Papi" Ortiz, Jesús begged the Red Sox to sign Papi. At the time my brother was the director of Boston's Dominican academy. Finally, more than a month after the Twins released him, the Red Sox signed Ortiz, and I believe they are glad they did.

In addition to being an astute baseball man, especially with pitchers, Jesús is the best fisherman along the Dominican Republic's South Coast. I don't know about the North Coast, because I don't know the fishermen there. But on the South Coast, Jesús is the best.

That Jesús is such a wise baseball man and fisherman is no coincidence. Again, I think the two are connected. With fishing you can prepare and put in the effort, yet whether you catch a fish is still ultimately up to the fish. It's the same way with baseball. After you've done all the preparation and put in all the effort, it still comes down to the players.

Ellis Valentine comes to mind when I think of this. Ellis was basically a good guy who struggled with drugs during his career, straightened himself out, and has since worked as a drug and church counselor. Ellis had a ton of talent when he was with the Expos. He had all the tools, and he could really run. His talent was similar to an outfielder I later managed—Vladimir Guerrero. The problem with Ellis was that he was so good, he didn't want to work hard, especially if it was extra work.

My first year coaching in the big leagues, in 1979, I was the Expos' third base and outfield coach. Our manager, Dick Williams, already frustrated with Ellis, wanted me to make him my special spring training project. I took it not only as an edict, but also as a challenge.

My first day working with the outfielders, I was hitting them fungoes, and Ellis begged off, complaining of a sore calf. I told Williams, who went to the head trainer, who told Williams he was unaware of any calf issues with Ellis. The next day I was hitting lazy fly balls to the outfielders, and Ellis took a few before stopping, complaining about his lower back. The next day we were working on throwing to bases, and Ellis, who had a gun for an arm, opted out, citing a sore shoulder. On and on it went until, by the end of the week, he had run through every body part. That was Ellis.

Soon Williams was in my ear again about Ellis, and he wasn't happy. Ellis was a gifted runner, fast, and he had the green light to steal. But that was the problem. If it was up to him, Ellis wasn't going to put in any extra effort. Williams instructed me as the third base coach to give Ellis the steal sign and make him run. But every time I gave him the steal sign, Ellis wouldn't run, claiming he couldn't understand the sign.

"Have a special sign just for him," Williams barked, "and make it simple."

We had a team meeting to go over the signs. When I was done I turned to Ellis and told him we had a special sign just for him. I grabbed my crotch. "When I grab my balls, you're running," I said. The guys started laughing. But I wasn't laughing. And neither was Williams.

The first time he got on base Williams gave me a sign from the dugout for Ellis to steal. Right away I looked at Ellis and grabbed my crotch. I could see players in the dugout covering their faces, laughing. But I was serious. I waited for him to steal second, already anticipating Williams's smile of approval, but Ellis stayed put at first. Williams was fuming. When the inning ended I hustled to our dugout, and before Ellis could jog to right field I confronted him.

"How come you didn't run?" I demanded. "I grabbed my balls!"

Ellis looked at me and said, "Felipe, I thought the sign was when you had *both* hands on your balls."

I couldn't believe it. When I told Williams what Ellis said, everybody in the dugout started laughing again. Everybody except Williams and me. It taught me a lesson. When you're managing players, you can prepare and put in all the effort, but in the end sometimes you're just a guy standing there holding his crotch.

29

You Can Go Home Again

When Dave Dombrowski phoned me during the 2002 offseason, I wasn't prepared for what he would tell me. "The Giants called," he said. "They've asked permission to talk to you about being their next manager. If you're interested, they'd like you to fly out for an interview."

I was interested. The San Francisco Giants were not only the organization I started my career with, but also a team that had just gone to the World Series, losing in the seventh game to the Anaheim Angels. So, yes, I was definitely interested. But I wasn't interested in a six-and-a-half-hour flight from my home in South Florida. Not to interview. I believed that at this stage of my life and career, I had earned the courtesy of not having to do that.

"Tell them I'm interested," I told Dombrowski, "but I'm not interested in flying out there to interview."

I had a fishing trip planned the next day, and when I returned home my wife, Lucie, greeted me at the door. "The Giants are here," she said.

"What do you mean?"

"They've been calling. They're at the Ritz Carlton in Lantana. They want you to come and talk to them."

The only other time I was offered a Major League managing job, with the Montreal Expos, I had also been fishing that day, and I went straight from the lake to the general manager's office without cleaning up. This time I decided to shower and dress nicely.

Brian Sabean, the Giants' general manager, had flown from San Francisco the night before, and he was at the Ritz Carlton with Ron

Perranoski, who lived up the coast in Vero Beach and worked in player development for the organization. I got to Sabean's hotel suite, and we chatted for a while, small talk. I really didn't know Sabean, but I knew Perranoski, who was a contemporary as a player and a coach.

"How do you feel about managing the Giants?" Sabean suddenly asked.

"I'd love to manage the Giants," I replied.

"Great," Sabean replied. "Let me take you guys out to dinner."

Over dinner Sabean matter-of-factly told me I was the manager, and the next day we agreed on a two-year contract with an option for a third year. Before I knew it I was happily on a six-and-a-half-hour flight to San Francisco for an introductory news conference. Afterward, I went into my new office, and on the desk was a handwritten letter from Dusty Baker, the manager who preceded me. Dusty told me what a classy organization the Giants were, how there were good people running it, and that he was happy it was me who got the job, and he wished me success. That's Dusty. A real gentleman and a solid baseball man.

A letter also arrived via fax:

> Dear Felipe,
>
> As an old time player for us I remember you fondly. I always appreciated what a great job you did.
>
> You're a fine leader and you're great for baseball.
>
> Congratulations!
>
> Best Regards,
> George M. Steinbrenner

It felt good. Good to be back to the beginning. Good to be back in the city where I got my first base hit, my first home run, where I learned to drive, where I first met Roberto Clemente, where I was a teammate with players like Willie Mays, Willie McCovey, Juan Marichal, and Orlando Cepeda. It felt comfortable, like slipping your hand back into your favorite well-worn baseball glove.

I was sixty-seven, the oldest man hired to manage a team since

1962, when Casey Stengel came out of retirement at seventy-one to manage the expansion New York Mets. I've always had energy, but I felt especially energized, ready to go. I knew this was going to be my last stop, and Sabean already had plans for me to be his special assistant after I was done managing.

Peter Magowan, the Giants' managing general partner, had two early requests for me:

Call Jeff Kent, who had become a free agent, and try to convince him to re-sign with the organization.

Talk to Barry Bonds and try to get him to play in the annual spring training exhibition game against the Giants' Minor League team in Fresno, California, which Barry always begged out of.

Kent, an outstanding second baseman who I think should be in the Hall of Fame, had been with the Giants since 1997 and won the National League MVP two seasons earlier. It was no secret that he and Bonds did not get along, especially since they had gotten into a well-publicized dugout skirmish during the 2002 season. Kent was polite when we talked, and thankful that I called, but he wasn't interested in returning. Instead, he signed with the Houston Astros.

That spring training Bonds was on a tear. I recall he had ten home runs, and one day we were talking and he said, "They keep accusing me of steroids, so I'm not going to hit any more home runs this spring." And he didn't. Instead, he rocketed line drives all over the place. Incredible.

I talked to Barry about playing in the annual game against the organization's Class Triple-A affiliate in Fresno. "Old man, I'll do it for you," he said, smiling. Because of knowing his father, Bobby, I had known Barry since he was a baby. He always calls me either boss or old man, and in both cases he does so with respect. Leading up to the game, which was at the end of spring training, Bonds assured me he would be there, which made ownership happy because it meant a good gate and goodwill with the Minor League team, which was promoting the heck out of Barry Bonds being there.

But the day before the game Barry flew to San Francisco, saying he had family matters to attend to and that he wouldn't be able to go to Fresno. That's Barry. That's what you learn to deal with, and even accept, when you have a superstar player. It wasn't that big of a deal, and it certainly was not the worst time I had been stiffed by a superstar. That came six years later, when I managed the Dominican Republic team in the World Baseball Classic.

After playing for the United States in the 2006 World Baseball Classic, Alex Rodriguez said he wanted to return to his roots and play third base for the Dominican Republic team in 2009. Needless to say I was thrilled to have him. The other Dominican third basemen—guys like Adrián Beltré, Aramis Ramírez, Edwin Encarnación, and Ronnie Belliard—acquiesced, opting not to play in order to pave the way for A-Rod.

We played three tune-up games during spring training, and the night before we were to leave for Puerto Rico to start the Classic, A-Rod rented a house in Palm Beach and threw a party for the team. It was first-class, with top-notch food, drink, wine, champagne—the works. It was A-Rod at his best.

The next morning Lucie awakened me. "Did you hear?" she asked. "Alex Rodriguez is flying to Colorado to have surgery."

"You've got to be kidding me," I said.

I called our team's media relations man. "Have you heard anything about Alex Rodriguez flying to Colorado today for surgery?" I asked.

"I haven't heard anything," he said. "Let me see what's going on, and I'll call you right back."

Five minutes later he called. "Yeah, it's true," he said.

Now we were flying to Puerto Rico to start the World Baseball Classic without our best player and third baseman, who obviously knew he had hip surgery scheduled and didn't say anything. Boarding the flight that day were a lot of ticked-off players. At the Classic we didn't make it out of the first round, losing two of the three games we played.

Seven years later, at the Latino Hall of Fame induction ceremonies at the Altos de Chavón in La Romana, Dominican Republic,

A-Rod received an award for hitting his 600th home run. He was there with his girlfriend at the time, actress Cameron Diaz. Since I'm on the Hall of Fame committee, I was also there. As Alex accepted his award he made a little speech where he said, "I feel so honored that I got to play for Felipe Alou." It was an unbelievable statement to make, given that he really didn't play for me. As he said it I heard faint rumbling sounds of oohs from the audience that almost sounded like boos. But that was Alex.

Though I never really managed Alex Rodriguez, I did manage Barry Bonds for four seasons, and he was something to behold. Managing Barry Bonds was one of the highlights of my career. I used to fear Barry as an opposing manager—not as a hitter, but as a baseball player. He could beat you with his bat, his glove, his arm, his legs—he was a complete player in every respect. Barry had one of the best swings I ever saw and maybe the best eye for the strike zone of anyone since Ted Williams. I'm not an expert on drugs, but I do believe I know baseball, and I can't imagine there is any drug that can help you see the ball the way Barry saw it, or have the swing he had, or give you instincts on the base paths, or the incredible intellect he brought to the plate, or help you win eight Gold Glove Awards.

To me it's sad that the focus is on steroids and the home runs because Barry was a rare athlete. And it's even sadder to me that an athlete like that could lose his place in history. He was one of the best to ever play the game.

The first two years I had Barry, he hit 45 homers each season and won his third- and fourth-consecutive National League MVP Awards. We won one hundred and then ninety-one games those two seasons, which was the most wins a Giants manager ever recorded in his first two seasons managing the team, even going back to the New York years. The last two years, with Barry hobbled by injuries and with considerably less talent around him, we only won seventy-five and seventy-six games.

By then Barry was calling his own shots. He was always one of the first two guys in the clubhouse, and if I didn't hear from him, I knew he was good to go and he was in the lineup. But sometimes he would stop by my office and make a slashing motion at his throat, saying, "Hey, boss, I can't help you today." A lot of times on those days, he would sleep in the clubhouse. Late in the game I would have somebody wake him to pinch-hit. More often than not Barry would come to the plate and hit a home run or draw a walk, and I would pinch-run for him. He was incredible that way.

People ask me about steroids and the Hall of Fame and what should happen. All I know is that people are in limbo right now. There needs to be a decision, an edict. Fair or not, guilty or innocent, players are being punished by being put in limbo. Those in power need to make a statement. Either put them in or publicly say they'll never go in. One way or another, there should be a decision.

As sad as I am about the Steroid Era in baseball, I feel even sadder at how it infected my country, given the staggering amount of players from the Dominican who have tested positive for steroids. But before people judge, I would invite them to come to the Dominican Republic with me. I'll show them poverty, desperation, despair. I'll show them children with little or no food to eat. Baseball is where the money is, and where there is money there is temptation, there is corruption. Understand, too, that in the Dominican Republic you can buy drugs over the counter that you need a prescription for in the United States. It is a recipe for abuse.

Baseball is the golden ticket, and everybody in the Dominican Republic knows that. I have parents come to me and tell me their son is going to be a great baseball player, that he has great talent, destined for superstardom. I ask them how old the boy is, and they'll say, "Eight." *Eight?* Eight years old, and they *know* for sure he is going to be a superstar Major Leaguer! I try not to shake my head in front of them.

I have a friend in the Dominican Republic we call Negrito who years ago was telling me that his baby boy I used to hold in my arms was going to be a great baseball player. Negrito was an expert at training cockfighting roosters, but his other passion was baseball, and he was a huge fan of the Escogido team. When I managed the Caracas Lions in the Venezuelan Winter League, the general manager there once asked me to bring him a good rooster the next year. I went straight to Negrito, who gave me a beautiful rooster I carried with me onboard the airplane.

As for Negrito's boy who was going to be a great baseball player—he grew up to become Adrián Beltré, who in 2017 recorded his 3,000th hit in Major League Baseball, making him not only a guaranteed first-ballot Hall of Famer but quite possibly the game's greatest third baseman ever. No doubt, Adrián Beltré is the exception, not the rule.

That kind of talent, as with Barry Bonds, is rare. And that kind of talent also demands big money. It was no secret that Barry's salary strained the Giants' payroll, and our best chance to capitalize on his talent coincided with my first year managing the club in 2003. We went 100-61 and won the NL West. In the National League Division Series, we went against the Florida Marlins, who were now owned by the man who had fired me from the Montreal Expos—Jeffrey Loria. The first two games were at San Francisco's Pacific Bell Park, and before Game One my old friend Jack McKeon, who managed the Marlins, ambled over to me on the field, and we shook hands.

"I'm going to tell you this right now," he said. "I'm not pitching to Barry Bonds. I'm going to walk him even if the bases are loaded. I'm sorry."

Here is how the series broke down:

In that first game Marlins pitchers Josh Beckett and Chad Fox walked Bonds three times, twice intentionally, but we still won 2–0, thanks to our ace Jason Schmidt's masterful three-hit shutout.

In Game Two we lost a slugfest, 9–5, with Bonds walking twice, once intentionally, and getting an RBI double.

We lost Game Three, 4–3, in eleven innings, with Bonds again walking twice, both intentionally.

We lost Game Four and the series in a heartbreaker, when Marlins left fielder Jeff Conine threw out J. T. Snow at home plate in the ninth inning to end the game. It was a bang-bang play, causing a big collision with Marlins catcher Iván "Pudge" Rodríguez. Pudge held onto the ball, and we lost 7–6, with Bonds going 0 for 3 with an intentional walk.

In the four games Bonds walked 8 times, 6 of them intentional. When they did pitch to him, not too many of those pitches touched the strike zone. In addition to those 8 walks, Bonds went 3 for 9 with 2 singles, 1 double, 3 runs scored, and 2 RBI. But we lost, and the Marlins went on to beat the New York Yankees in the World Series.

After the game I was in my office talking with some lingering media members when, of all people, Jeffrey Loria showed up. He gave me a hug, and I saw tears in his eyes. "Congratulations on a great season," he said. "I just want you to know I didn't want to fire you in Montreal. I was given bad information." He never told me what the bad information was, and I never asked.

Although we won ninety-one games the following season, in 2004, we finished two games behind the Los Angeles Dodgers in the NL West and one game behind the Houston Astros for the lone wild-card berth. This was a Dodgers team led by Adrián Beltré and his 48 home runs and 121 RBI. They were also managed by Jim Tracy, one of my former bench coaches from the Expos.

I was at that stage of my career where a handful of my former coaches, or what some people might call disciples, were getting Major League managerial jobs. In addition to Tracy, six other former coaches managed in the Major Leagues—Jerry Manuel, Kevin Kennedy, Joe Kerrigan, Pete Mackanin, Luis Pujols, Mike Quade, and Tim Johnson. You're happy for that, but you're not happy about losing to one of them for a playoff spot.

In fact, there wasn't much happiness my last two years managing. I don't care how many years you've been in baseball, you never get used to losing, and we lost a lot in 2005 and 2006. Bonds averaged a tad more than $20 million those two seasons, and it hamstrung our payroll while he battled through injuries. One of the bright spots for those two seasons was reuniting with my son Moisés, who came to us as a free agent, becoming the fourth Alou to play for the Giants' franchise. Both those two seasons also had a couple of off-the-field distractions—one of which was particular disheartening.

Early in August 2005 I was sitting at my desk when our media relations man, Blake Rhodes, came into my office and plopped down a transcript of what a radio guy named Larry Krueger said on the air with our flagship station, KNBR. "Look at what this guy said," Rhodes told me. The words jumped off the page. I could feel my rage rising inside me. Krueger had gone on a rant over our 45-61 record, choosing only to attack me and our Latino players, saying, "I just cannot watch this brand of baseball any longer. A truly awful, pathetic, old team that only promises to be worse two years from now. It's just awful. It really is bad to watch. Brain-dead Caribbean hitters hacking at slop nightly. . . . You have a manager in Felipe whose mind has turned to Cream of Wheat."

His comments not only exploded in a city like San Francisco, which is known for its diversity, but also in the clubhouse of a franchise known for pioneering Latinos into Major League Baseball. For me Krueger's comments brought back all the bigoted stereotypes that never seem to go away. With just a few sentences and seconds, he condemned me, my son who batted .321 for us that season, all of my Latino players, and all of Latin America. I heard that some of the Latino players wanted to retaliate in a physical way, and I could not allow that. I called them all into my office.

"Let me handle this," I told them. "Don't get yourselves in trouble."

When the media came to me, I unloaded. I had a voice now. When I came to the United States in 1956 and they wouldn't let me play in Louisiana because of my skin color, or eat at restaurants or stay in hotels, I didn't have a voice. But now I did and I was going to use it, and I was going to get the message out throughout the world. On ESPN's *Outside the Lines* I called Krueger "a messenger of Satan" and added that "I believe there is no forgiveness for Satan."

Krueger tried to save face and his job by apologizing, showing up at my office door. But I did not believe I was authorized to accept his apology. It wasn't just me he insulted. It was all Latino players as well as all of Latin America. I told him he would have to go to each Latino player in our clubhouse and apologize to them individually, which he didn't do. I later told the media: "He came to apologize to me? You have to be kidding me. There's no way to apologize for such a sin. All of these people have been offended by this idiot. I can't speak for hundreds of millions of people. This guy offended hundreds of millions of people."

KNBR fired Krueger, who within a month landed another Bay Area radio job. Ten years later he returned to KNBR. I see him from time to time, but we've never talked. All these years later, I do forgive him. Even back then I didn't want him to lose his job, especially after I heard he had children. That bothered me. So even though what he said still hurts me today, I forgive him. But what I don't forgive is the system, the mind-set that still fosters the type of bigotry that came out of his mouth.

The following 2006 season was not as tumultuous, but the steroid saga was moving front and center in Major League Baseball, with Commissioner Bud Selig tapping into former senator George Mitchell to conduct an independent investigation. It created a lot of obvious distractions for our team, since it was apparent that one of the largest dots on the radar was Barry Bonds—if not *the* largest dot.

I was ordered that summer to testify before Mitchell's team. They grilled me from 7:30 a.m. to 5 p.m., and I had a game to manage that night. They resurrected my old quote, where I said "players will do anything to get an edge." I didn't mean it to imply steroids, because the worse thing I ever saw in a clubhouse were amphetamines to give players energy, pills to relax, and Wild Turkey bourbon whiskey to keep guys warm on cold days. But they kept coming back to that quote. What they didn't do is ask me about any players specifically. They never mentioned one player's name. Not even Barry Bonds.

As the season wound down, I knew it was going to be it for me. I was at the end of my contract, and I was seventy-one, with a full career behind me. We were losing too much, thirteen of our last fifteen games, and it wasn't fun for me. The last game of the season was a 4–3 loss to the Dodgers in San Francisco, leaving us with a 76-85 record.

I sat in my office, still in my uniform, waiting for the front office to announce that I wouldn't be returning. Blake Rhodes came in.

"What's going on?" I asked. "Who's going to tell me I'm not going to be managing this team anymore?"

"Everybody's sad," he said. "Nobody wants to be the one to tell you."

"Well, somebody better do it," I said. "I have a flight home tonight at 10. I'm ready to go."

Rhodes left, and soon our managing general partner, Peter Magowan, came in. He told me they were going to let me go as the manager, but they would like me to stay on in another capacity with the organization.

He left, and Brian Sabean came to my office. "I want you to be my special assistant," he said. "The assistant to the GM."

I accepted.

The media were hovering outside, and I invited them into my office to tell them what transpired. Henry Schulman, a sportswriter for the *San Francisco Chronicle*, spoke up. "Felipe, all of us here want to thank you for the way you treated us," he said. "Thank you for respecting us and for always being honest with us."

That night I sat on a six-and-a-half-hour red-eye flight home to Florida. I ordered a glass of wine. As the hours and the miles passed, I felt an enormous sense of relief. I wasn't going to be battling the road, losing streaks, opposing teams, or umpires anymore, dealing with the daily pressure, the second-guessing, the grind. I looked out the window and saw the twinkling lights of Dallas, and I knew there was no turning back.

I thought about how I would never manage a Major League team or wear a Major League uniform again, and I was at peace with that. I took a sip of wine, smiled, and leaned back in my seat. I thought about how my baseball career had come full circle, how I had been blessed to return to San Francisco, where it all started. I had gone home to my baseball family, and for that I was happy.

And now, as the airplane continued east in the night sky, farther and farther away from San Francisco, I knew I was going home to my real family, and for that I also was happy.

Epilogue

My eighty-two-year-old eyes scan a baseball field. Not the hard-scrabble one of my youth, where I led a battalion of boys in chopping down a coconut tree that obstructed our ability to play. This one is meticulously manicured, and it is in Boca Chica, about thirty miles east from where I grew up along the southern coast of the Dominican Republic.

People approach me, smiling, shaking my hand, slapping me on my back, congratulating me. It is August 23, 2016, a balmy, breezy summer day, and with a dedication ceremony set to begin, I'm still trying to comprehend what is in front of my eyes. I read the words on the wall of the complex, and I cannot believe them. I blink, and the words are still there:

FELIPE ALOU BASEBALL ACADEMY.

It has not just one but three baseball fields, each of them resplendent in their emerald-green and clay-red colors. The fields are only a half hour away from the field my friends, brothers, and I played on. But it may as well be light-years away.

When we were innocent boys, we played for the pure joy of baseball. Our mitts were often our bare hands. Our ball was often a small piece of fruit. And our bat came from my carpenter father, who would fashion something rudimentary out of a piece of wood.

But these gorgeous new fields I'm looking at are big business, part of a state-of-the-art facility with batting tunnels, pitchers' mounds, a weight room, a gymnasium, a dining hall, classrooms, a computer laboratory, conference rooms, training rooms, offices, and a residence hall for coaches, staff, and up to seventy-three players. The academy will serve as the San Francisco Giants' headquarters for their Latin American operations, while also providing vocational and educational training for international prospects.

I tour the complex. Every hallway I walk down and room I enter have that same new-house smell to it. New paint, carpet, cement, glass, furniture and, of course, the best scent of all when I walk outside—the smell of a freshly mowed baseball field.

I try to soak it in, try to comprehend it all, but like most everything else that has happened in my life, I could never have dreamed of this. *Me?* A boy from Kilometer 12, who grew up in a fifteen-by-fifteen shack with his parents and five siblings, in a home my father built with his own strong hands in 1934, the year before I was born? No, I could never have dreamed of a state-of-the-art complex like this bearing my name.

My chest swells with pride, yet my heart bows with humility. I feel so many emotions. Even sadness. Of all the things I see, it's what I don't see that my mind's eye focuses on. I don't see my parents, José and Virginia Rojas. I don't see my firstborn son, Felipe. I don't see my brother Matty. How can I not feel a tinge of sadness?

My father died on August 3, 1994, when I was managing the Montreal Expos and we had Major League Baseball's best record. He was eighty-nine. Nine days later MLB's players went on a strike that eventually led to that season's cancellation. My mother died fourteen years later, on January 1, 2008. She was ninety-three. They lived long lives, good lives, prosperous lives. My firstborn son, Felipe, wasn't as fortunate. He died on March 26, 1976, his neck broken in a horrible swimming pool accident. He was only sixteen.

And then there is my brother Matty, the third of six siblings. The smallest one, but also the toughest one. Matty suffered a couple of devastating strokes that debilitated him, robbing him of much of his body and mind. When Matty was in and out of the University of Miami Hospital, Juan Marichal opened up his Florida home in nearby Doral for Matty and his wife, Teresa, to stay. We eventually returned Matty to the Dominican Republic, where Jesús and I visited him almost daily. I would talk to Matty about our childhood, playing ball, fishing—the memories. On November 3, 2011, he suffered another stroke, and this one killed him. He was seventy-two.

At his funeral, just before we were to lower his casket and return him to the earth, I was asked to say a few words. I told the throng of people that I never envied my brothers for anything. I always wanted the best for them. When Matty and I were battling for the National League batting title in 1966, I wanted Matty to win and felt so proud and happy for him when he did. But I did envy one thing Matty had—his friends. I always envied that Matty had so many friends.

One day, hopefully not anytime soon, Jesús will be laid to rest next to Matty. I've chosen another cemetery for my final resting spot, the one where my parents are and where my son is.

Life goes on. Life and death. From that small shack at Kilometer 12 have come generations bearing the names Rojas and Alou. Both the names are important. I thought about that when the Giants told me they wanted to name this baseball academy after me. They told me the academy would have three baseball fields, and they were planning to name one after Juan Marichal, another after Ozzie Virgil Sr., and the third for the Alou family.

I thought about that and how when baseball came for me, it took me out of the Dominican Republic and it took my real last name—Rojas. I didn't know how to correct that error then, so when I went to Major League Baseball and made a name for myself and for my family, that name was Alou.

Now, with baseball bringing me back my country, I wanted my name brought with it. The Giants agreed. And so, at the Felipe Alou Baseball Academy, the third field bears two names.

Alou.

And Rojas.

ACKNOWLEDGMENTS

Thank you to all those who encouraged me to tell my story, which is really the story of a family—a poor family that has been richly blessed by Jehovah God. If my wife, Lucie, and my children had not encouraged me to take on this project, I never would have considered it. Because of them, I did. Even then I was stubborn. It was only after the urging of my friend Bruce Bochy, who enthusiastically endorsed both the book and my coauthor, that I finally followed through. I'm glad I did.

How do I thank baseball, the profession I've given my life to yet has given me so much more in return? This beautiful game has provided me a second family and scores of relationships I cherish. Thank you to Horacio "Rabbit" Martínez, who believed that a young man from the Dominican Republic could blaze a trail for our country. Thank you to Dan Duquette for giving me my first opportunity to manage in the Major Leagues. Thank you to Peter Magowan and Brian Sabean for bringing me home to San Francisco and to Bill Neukom, Larry Baer, and Bobby Evans for keeping me here with the Giants.

Thank you to Pedro Martínez for the eloquent foreword he wrote and to Tony La Russa, Joe Torre, Buck Showalter, Reggie Jackson, Bob Costas, and Tom Verducci for publicly and passionately endorsing this book.

Thank you to my father and mother, José and Virginia Rojas. My brothers and sisters and I could not have asked for better parents.

Thank you to my coauthor and friend, Peter Kerasotis, for his persistence in believing my story needed to be told, for his patience with my travel schedule, and for his professionalism. There is no doubt in my mind that Jehovah brought us together. Thank you to his wife, Shelley, for sacrificing time with her husband and for tirelessly reading, editing, and fact-checking everything Peter and I wrote together.

And finally, thank you to my God Jehovah for his love and for the gift of sending his son, Jesus Christ, to die for our sins. I am aware of Jehovah's blessings every day, and I know that without him I am nothing.

Felipe Alou

I first met Felipe Alou at a spring training game. He was managing the Montreal Expos, and I was a local newspaper columnist. Before the game I approached him behind the batting cage at Space Coast Stadium in Viera, Florida. I asked Felipe if he remembered starting his professional playing career as a Minor Leaguer several miles away in Cocoa.

Remember? Felipe rewound his mind forty-four years and remembered everything—his batting average, how many home runs he hit, how many bases he stole, the street he lived on, the family he stayed with, and even the fishing holes he dropped his line in.

We talked . . . and talked and talked and talked. He told me stories of what it was like to be a skinny kid from the Dominican Republic with the wrong skin color for 1956 America, about how being black *and* Latino put him in an automatic 0-2 hole. He was thoughtful and philosophical, telling me stories rich in detail and insight. I didn't want the conversation to end, but Felipe needed to manage his Expos against the Florida Marlins and I had a deadline to meet.

Fast-forward eleven years from that March afternoon in 2000 to August 12, 2011. I'd been laid off the day before and was sitting in the visiting manager's office at Miami's Sun Life Stadium, talking to my friend Bruce Bochy, the San Francisco Giants' manager. Bruce was upset for me and for what our hometown paper had done. I told him it was okay, that I was going to be okay.

"What are you going to do?" he asked.

"I have ideas," I said. "You know, I've always had it in my mind that I'd like to write Felipe Alou's autobiography. He has all the ingredients a writer looks for in a great book."

Bruce stared at me for a few seconds. "You know he's here," he said.

"Here?"

"Yeah, he's here. Felipe works for the Giants, and he lives in South Florida. He's here at the game. You want me to talk to him?"

"Sure."

As I was sitting in the stands, about fifteen minutes before the game was to start, I got a ping notifying me of a text message. It was Bruce.

I talked to Felipe. He's interested.

And so began four years of back-and-forth. Felipe was going to do the book. Then he decided against doing the book. There were letters and phone calls. Hope and despair. The yes and no went back and forth so many times that I wrote two books in the interim and eventually gave up on doing a book with Felipe.

After the 2015 baseball season ended Bochy and I were chatting on the phone, and he casually asked me how things were going with Felipe.

"I've given up on that," I said.

"What?" he exclaimed, surprised.

"Bruce, he tells he'll do it, and then he changes his mind. I've given up."

"Let me talk to him," he said. "Don't give up just yet."

A few days later my phone rang. It was Felipe. "I'm going to do the book," he said. "I know I've told you that many times before, but I promise you this time I won't change my mind."

I drove to Felipe's home in Boynton Beach, Florida, and we spent the afternoon just talking . . . and talking and talking and talking. I didn't pull out a recorder. I didn't take any notes. We just talked. Shortly after, I wrote a book proposal and contacted my agent, tasking him with the job of finding a publisher. What you have in your hands is the result.

So when I think about people to thank, top of the list is Felipe Alou. I know this project worried him, and I know why. He is a man used to being in control, in charge. Putting his words and thoughts and life into the hands of another man was not easy for him. So thank you, Felipe, for entrusting me with your incredible story. And thank you for the friendship we forged that extends beyond the book. I enjoyed all the stimulating conversations. It was fascinating to see how Felipe's mind unraveled complicated subjects. You need not be around him too long to know he's always thinking, and thinking deeply. And when he talks, you don't want to miss a word he says. As the great relief pitcher John Wetteland aptly told *Sports Illustrated* about Felipe, "He speaks in parables."

Many nights Felipe and I stayed up late, talking about Jehovah God, the Bible, religion, world events, politics, philosophy, baseball, family, relationships. And I could tell Felipe enjoyed our dialogue and even our debates as much as I did, because oftentimes he would signal in his own way that we were done working and now it was time for conversing. Or sometimes, before we even began working, we would have a conversation that before we realized it stretched into an hour or two. That's something only close friends do, and I don't use those words loosely.

I was sitting with Felipe when he called Reggie Jackson and asked him to provide an endorsement blurb for the book. Felipe introduced me to Reggie by saying, "My friend here is writing my book..." Hearing him introduce me that way, with the words "my friend," meant a lot. So did the words of his daughter Maria, Moisés's big sister, who one day told me I've bonded with her dad in ways few people do. I treasure that.

After Felipe, a thank-you goes to my agent, Robert Wilson, for believing in this book from day one and for tirelessly working on getting a publisher to believe in it, too. Which leads me to another person I need to thank—my editor Rob Taylor. Thank you, Rob, for your faith in me and this book and for your patience with the manuscript. I knew when I handed it off to you that it was in more than capable hands. Thank you also to others whose hands touched this manuscript through the process of getting it published—Courtney Ochsner, Sara Springsteen, and Annette Wenda.

Special thanks to Felipe's wife, Lucie Alou, and his children, who encouraged him to write this book. And to Bruce Bochy, who gave Felipe that final push over the finish line, telling him not only that he needed to do a book, but that I was the writer he needed to do it with. If not for the family's encouragement and Bruce's endorsement, this project never would have happened.

Thank you, too, to Lucie and Felipe Alou Jr.—a.k.a. Felipito—for the great food and strong coffee that sustained Felipe and me through long working days and nights.

Thank you Maria Rojas and Alvino Jimenez, the spiritual sister and brother I didn't know I had. Maria, I appreciated your hospitality, the insights on your father, and your prayers.

Thank you Teresa Rojas, Matty Alou's daughter, who helped find family photos, and for the tireless efforts of Moisés Alou's wife, Austria. A special thank-you to Suzanna Mitchell with the San Francisco Giants for her invaluable help with getting photos and also to Matt Chisholm, the Giants' director of baseball information. Another special thank-you to Gilles Corbeil for coming through with photos from the Montreal Expos years. You were a lifesaver. Thank you in a big way to Sami Mized for scanning and digitizing photos and getting them just right.

Thank you Tony La Russa for eagerly reading an unedited and unfinished manuscript and then providing a jolt of positive and enthusiastic feedback. Writing is such an insecure profession, and that type of response from someone who knows his way around words told me I was headed in the right direction.

One day Felipe got a phone call from Moisés, telling him that he's been hearing about the book and that it's going to be great.

"Where have you been hearing that from?" Felipe asked.

"Tony La Russa has been telling everybody," Moisés replied.

So thank you again, Tony, and thank you for your official endorsement blurb for the back of the book. And also to Joe Torre, Buck Showalter, Reggie Jackson, Bob Costas, and Tom Verducci, the best baseball writer of my generation and any other generation, for that matter.

Thank you Pedro Martínez for writing such an insightful and moving foreword. It perfectly set the tone for the book. And thank you also to your lovely wife, Carolina, for facilitating everything.

Thank you to colleagues Gordon Edes, Gerry Fraley, and Peter Schmuck for helping connect me with people I needed to connect with when I was hitting a dead end on my own. Also, a special thank you to Bill Madden, who enthusiastically connected me with his agent, who is now my agent too.

Thank you Ernie Rosseau for your friendship and feedback on the manuscript. Your energy is always infectious.

Thank you to Erik and Nathalie Bailey, Randy and Cindy Sturdevant, and Ben and Jen Woodruff for providing me a home away from home all those times when I needed one.

Thank you to my mother, Helene Kerasotis, who kept insisting I take her credit card and fill my car with gas or get a hotel room for a night or two when I needed to be where Felipe was to continue moving the project forward. Mom, your love and support never waver. They're always there, yet I never take them for granted.

And finally, thank you to my beautiful wife, Shelley, for her love, for all the sacrifices she made, and for her own hard work on this book. Projects like this are a team effort, and Shelley's frontline editing, fact-checking, and feedback were invaluable. Shelley, all I can pay you with is my love.

Peter Kerasotis

CHRONOLOGY

Player

1955 Signed with New York Giants in December.

1956 Lake Charles (Louisiana) Giants in Class C Evangeline League and Cocoa (Florida) Indians in Class D Florida State League.

1957 Minneapolis (Minnesota) Millers in Class Triple-A American Association and Springfield (Massachusetts) Giants in Class A Eastern League.

1958 Phoenix (Arizona) Giants in Class Triple-A Pacific Coast League and San Francisco Giants.

1959 San Francisco Giants.

1960 San Francisco Giants.

1961 San Francisco Giants.

1962 San Francisco Giants.

1963 San Francisco Giants.

1964 Milwaukee Braves.

1965 Milwaukee Braves.

1966 Atlanta Braves.

1967 Atlanta Braves.

1968 Atlanta Braves.

1969 Atlanta Braves.

1970 Oakland A's.

1971 Oakland A's and New York Yankees.

1972 New York Yankees.

1973 New York Yankees and Montreal Expos.

1974 Milwaukee Brewers.

Coach and Manager

1976   Special instructor for Montreal Expos.

1977   Managed West Palm Beach Expos in Class A Florida State League.

1978   Managed Memphis Chicks in Class Double-A Southern League.

1979   Montreal Expos third base coach for Dick Williams.

1980   Montreal Expos first base coach for Dick Williams.

1981   Managed Denver Bears in Class Triple-A American Association.

1982   Managed Wichita Aeros in Class Triple-A American Association.

1983   Managed Wichita Aeros in Class Triple-A American Association.

1984   Montreal Expos first base coach for Bill Virdon.

1985   Managed Indianapolis Indians in Class Triple-A American Association.

1986   Managed West Palm Beach Expos in Class A Florida State League.

1987   Managed West Palm Beach Expos in Class A Florida State League.

1988   Managed West Palm Beach Expos in Class A Florida State League.

1989   Managed West Palm Beach Expos in Class A Florida State League.

1990   Managed West Palm Beach Expos in Class A Florida State League.

1991   Managed West Palm Beach Expos in Class A Florida State League.

1992   Bench coach then manager of Montreal Expos, replacing Tom Runnells.

1993   Montreal Expos manager.

1994   Montreal Expos manager.

1995   Montreal Expos manager.

1996   Montreal Expos manager.

1997   Montreal Expos manager.

1998   Montreal Expos manager.

1999   Montreal Expos manager.

2000   Montreal Expos manager.

2001   Montreal Expos manager.

2002   Detroit Tigers bench coach for Luis Pujols.

2003   San Francisco Giants manager.

2004   San Francisco Giants manager.

2005   San Francisco Giants manager.

2006   San Francisco Giants manager.

2007   San Francisco Giants special assistant to Brian Sabean.

2008   San Francisco Giants special assistant to Brian Sabean.

2009   San Francisco Giants special assistant to Brian Sabean; managed the Dominican Republic in the World Baseball Classic.

2010   San Francisco Giants special assistant to Brian Sabean.

2011   San Francisco Giants special assistant to Brian Sabean.

2012   San Francisco Giants special assistant to Brian Sabean.

2013   San Francisco Giants special Assistant to Brian Sabean.

2014   San Francisco Giants special assistant to Brian Sabean.

2015   San Francisco Giants special assistant to Brian Sabean.

2016   San Francisco Giants special assistant to Bobby Evans.

2017   San Francisco Giants special assistant to Bobby Evans.

2018   San Francisco Giants special assistant to Bobby Evans.